The European Court of Human Rights in the Post-Cold War Era

The European Court of Human Rights in the Post-Cold War Era: Universality in Transition examines transitional justice from the perspective of its impact on the universality of human rights, taking the jurisprudence of the European Court of Human Rights as its detailed case study. The problem is twofold: there are questions about differences in human rights standards between transitional and non-transitional situations, and about differences between transitions.

The European Court has been a vital part of European democratic consolidation and integration for over half a century, setting meaningful standards and offering legal remedies to the individually repressed, the politically vulnerable, and the socially excluded. After their emancipation from Soviet influence in the 1990s, and with membership of the European Union in mind for many, the new democracies of Central and Eastern Europe flocked to the Convention system. The voluminous jurisprudence of the European Court of Human Rights can now give us some clear information about how an international human rights law regime can interact with transitional justice. The jurisprudence is divided between those cases concerning the human rights implications of explicitly transitional policies (such as lustration), and those that involve impacts upon specific democratic rights during the transition. The book presents a close examination of claims by states that transitional policies and priorities require a level of deference from the Strasbourg institutions. The book proposes that states' claims for leeway from international human rights supervisory mechanisms during times of transition can be characterised not as arguments for *cultural* relativism, but for 'transitional relativism'.

James A. Sweeney is a Senior Lecturer in Law at Durham University, UK. He is Deputy Director of Durham Global Security Institute.

Routledge Research in Human Rights Law

Available titles in this series include:

The Right to Development in International Law
The Case of Pakistan
Khurshid Iqbal

Global Health and Human Rights
Legal and Philosophical Perspectives
John Harrington and Maria Stuttaford

The Right to Religious Freedom in International Law
Between group rights and individual rights
Anat Scolnicov

Emerging Areas of Human Rights in the 21st Century
The role of the Universal Declaration of Human Rights
Marco Odello and Sofia Cavandoli

The Human Right to Water and its Application in the Occupied Palestinian Territories
Amanda Cahill

International Human Rights Law and Domestic Violence
The effectiveness of international human rights law
Ronagh McQuigg

Human Rights in the Asia-Pacific Region
Towards Institution Building
Hitoshi Nasu and Ben Saul

Human Rights Monitoring Mechanisms of the Council of Europe
Gauthier de Beco

The Positive Obligations of the State under the European Convention of Human Rights
Dimitris Xenos

Vindicating Socio-Economic Rights
International Standards and Comparative Experiences
Paul O'Connell

The EU as a 'Global Player' in Human Rights?
Jan Wetzel

Regulating Corporate Human Rights Violations
Humanizing Business
Surya Deva

The UN Committee on Economic, Social and Cultural Rights
The Law, Process and Practice
Marco Odello and Francesco Seatzu

State Security Regimes and the Right to Freedom of Religion and Belief
Changes in Europe Since 2001
Karen Murphy

The European Court of Human Rights in the Post-Cold War Era
Universality in transition
James A. Sweeney

Forthcoming titles in this series include:

Children and International Human Rights Law
The Right of the Child to be Heard
Aisling Parkes

Jurisdiction, Immunity and Transnational Human Rights Litigation
Xiaodong Yang

The European Court of Human Rights in the Post-Cold War Era

Universality in Transition

James A. Sweeney

Routledge
Taylor & Francis Group
LONDON AND NEW YORK

First published 2013
by Routledge
2 Park Square, Milton Park, Abingdon, Oxon OX14 4RN

Simultaneously published in the USA and Canada
by Routledge
711 Third Avenue, New York, NY 10017

Routledge is an imprint of the Taylor & Francis Group, an informa business

British Library Cataloguing in Publication Data
A catalogue record for this book is available from the British Library

Library of Congress Cataloguing in Publication Data
A catalog record for this book has been requested

ISBN: 978-0-415-54433-7 (hbk)
ISBN: 978-0-203-07928-7 (ebk)

Typeset in Garamond
by RefineCatch Limited, Bungay, Suffolk

MIX
Paper from responsible sources
FSC www.fsc.org FSC® C004839

Printed and bound by CPI Group (UK) Ltd, Croydon, CR0 4YY

To Sarah, Grace and Isla

During the writing of this book I have been fortunate enough to become a dad twice, and so with much love I dedicate it to my wife, Sarah, and my daughters, Grace Frances and Isla Ruth.

I dedicated my PhD to my late sister Ruth, who had only recently died. That was nearly 10 years ago but she is, as Jeff Buckley put it, 'the tear that hangs inside my soul forever' and I love my brother John now more than ever.

Mum, Pops, Dad, Jane – thanks for everything.

Dominus vobiscum

JAS May 2012

Contents

Acknowledgements

Scattered throughout this book elements of the following previous publications are reproduced, with kind permission:

> J.A. Sweeney, 'Restorative justice and transitional justice at the ECHR' (2012) 12(3) *International Criminal Law Review* 313; J.A. Sweeney, 'Human rights and transitional justice: successor trials in Europe and their implications for the universality of human rights' (2012) *Baltic Yearbook of International Law*; J.A. Sweeney, 'Freedom of religion and democratic transition', in M. Hamilton and A. Buyse (eds), *Transitional Jurisprudence and the ECHR: justice, politics, and rights* (Cambridge: CUP 2011); J.A. Sweeney, 'A "margin of appreciation" in the internal market: lessons from the European Court of Human Rights' (2007) 34 *Legal Issues of Economic Integration* 27; J.A. Sweeney, 'Divergence and diversity in post-communist European human rights cases' (2005) 21 *Connecticut Journal of International Law* 1; J.A. Sweeney, 'Margins of appreciation: cultural relativity and the European Court of Human Rights', (2005) 54 *International and Comparative Law Quarterly* 459.

[*International Criminal Law Review* and *Baltic Yearbook of International Law* are published by Brill/Martinus Nijhoff Publishers. *Legal Issues of Economic Integration* is published by Kluwer Law International. *Connecticut Journal of International Law* is published by University of Connecticut. *International and Comparative Law Quarterly* is published by Cambridge University Press.]

Many thanks indeed to Michael Hamilton and Antoine Buyse, with whom I had the privilege of discussing my ideas at their excellent symposium at the Transitional Justice Institute, University of Ulster, in April 2010, and subsequently during the preparation of my chapter for their book. Fortunately, we remain in violent agreement about most things.

Thanks also to Judge Inete Ziemele, who chaired my panel at a European Society of International Law Research Forum in Tallin, May 2011. She very kindly gave me feedback on the issue of successor trials (in the form of feedback on my submission to *Baltic Yearbook of International Law*).

I have had the great honour to work as an expert advisor to the Council of Europe from time to time, predominantly on freedom of assembly projects.

The first of these was in Armenia and was run by Oscar Alarcon. It was a great experience – thanks again Oscar.

Thanks to everyone at Durham Law School and Durham Global Security Institute, Durham University, for their support while I was writing this. Thanks, in particular, to my PhD student, Alice M. Panepinto, for her proof-reading work on the first draft of this book.

Finally, thanks to everyone at Routledge for letting me get these ideas out of my system and onto paper.

Table of cases

European Commission of Human Rights

European Court of Human Rights

Human Rights Chamber for Bosnia and Herzegovina

Human Rights Committee of the ICCPR

Inter-American Commission on Human Rights

Inter-American Court of Human Rights

International Criminal Tribunal for Rwanda

International Criminal Tribunal for the former Yugoslavia

Table of legislation

National Legislation

Introduction

> What is exceptional in a transitional period? [. . .] If the Court is going to accept that there may be reasons for the State to disregard human rights (whether it calls them exceptional or whatever), who then will protect the individual against interferences with these rights?
>
> Judge Ress, Dissenting Opinion in *Jahn v Germany* (Grand Chamber)[1]

> The variety of different attitudes towards the complex problem of 'coping with the past' allows only one conclusion – there cannot be a uniform approach.
>
> Judge Levits, Dissenting Opinion in *Ždanoka v Latvia* (Chamber)[2]

The phrase 'universality in transition' is something of a play on words. It is designed to indicate that, in the course of this book, we will be examining transitional justice from the perspective of its impact on the universality of human rights. But, in case it is not readily apparent, the title also implies that the idea of universality itself has come under some pressures in the post-Cold War operation of the European Court of Human Rights. The quotations that open this introduction highlight the twofold problem: there are questions about differences in human rights standards between transitional and non-transitional situations and about differences between transitions.

The European Court is in a terrifically difficult situation. It is at a crossroads in at least two senses: the geographical one between West and East and the existential one concerning its intention, capacity or authority to deliver 'individual' or 'constitutional' justice.[3] The European Court has been a vital part of European democratic consolidation and integration for over half a century, setting meaningful standards and offering legal remedies to the individually repressed, the politically vulnerable, and the socially excluded. On the 50th anniversary of the European Court in 2009, the President of the Court, Judge Costa observed that:

1 *Jahn v Germany* [2006] 42 EHRR 49.

2 *Ždanoka v Latvia* (Chamber) [2004] ECHR 268.

3 See the discussion in Chapter 1.

> [W]hen the Court was set up, no one, [he thought], could have imagined that it would one day fill the European judicial space to the extent that it does today. Its current influence in Europe, and even beyond, could hardly have been predicted.[4]

According to another judge, 'the Court has almost unlimited powers when it comes to granting remedies to established violations of Convention-acknowledged human rights.'[5]

After their emancipation from Soviet influence in the 1990s, and with membership of the European Union in mind for many, the new democracies of central and eastern Europe flocked to the Convention system. They brought with them some needs, priorities, and experiences with which the European Court was not necessarily familiar and therefore also a need to reconsider some of its substantive jurisprudence in the light of these developments and the institutional pressures under which it was put as a result.

Already prolific, the approach of the Strasbourg institutions to the momentous events signalling the end of the Cold War has gained renewed significance in the light of the events of the 'Arab Spring' of 2011 (and, at the time of writing, well into 2012 – which reveals the notion of 'spring' as a somewhat malleable concept). Rumours of the 'end' of history were perhaps greatly exaggerated: we are yet again presented with democratic transition on a regional scale, albeit with all the fragilities and inherent differences that any 'regional' movement might possess.

Just as the states presently involved in the Arab Spring are, more or less, considering how to move on; how to look back; how to punish; and how to forgive, so too did the states of central and eastern Europe that began their moves away from communist totalitarianism in 1989. These difficult questions can be characterised as dilemmas of transitional justice.[6] Crucially, for the purposes of the present enquiry, however, we now have some clear information about how *an international human rights regime* can interact with transitional justice. This is significant because not only does it pertain to the notion of 'justice' revealed by the actions of states in transition, and the extent to which it is compatible with universal human rights norms, but also to the practical legal question of what an international human rights court should do about it.[7]

To give a very brief sense of what this might mean, we can contrast statements made in cases that will be discussed in detail elsewhere in this book. In

4 J Costa, President of the European Court of Human Rights, 'Solemn hearing of the European Court of Human Rights on the occasion of the opening of the judicial year: Speech' 30 January 2009, available at www.echr.coe.int (accessed 21.5.2012), 3.

5 *Sejdić and Finci v Bosnia and Herzegovina* [2009] ECHR 2122, dissenting Opinion of Judge Bonello.

6 See R. Teitel, *Transitional Justice* (New York: OUP 2000).

7 The international dimension is discussed further in Chapter 1.

the 1984 case of *Guincho v Portugal*,[8] the European Court had stated that although it could not, 'overlook that the restoration of democracy as from April 1974 led Portugal to carry out an overhaul of its judicial system in troubled circumstances which were without equivalent in most of the other European countries',[9] it could not allow deviation from Portugal's commitment in Article 1 ECHR to secure to everyone the rights in the Convention, including the right at issue contained in Article 6 ECHR.

Yet many years later, in *Mkrtchyan v Armenia*, the European Court conceded 'that it may take some time for a country to establish its legislative framework in a transition period'.[10] Moreover in the 2006 Grand Chamber judgment in *Ždanoka v Latvia*, the European Court explained in relation to a restriction on the electoral rights of a communist that:

> While such a measure may scarcely be considered acceptable in the context of one political system, *for example in a country which has an established framework of democratic institutions* going back many decades or centuries, it may nonetheless be considered acceptable in Latvia in view of the historico-political context which led to its adoption and given the threat to the new democratic order posed by the resurgence of ideas which, if allowed to gain ground, might appear capable of restoring the former regime.[11]

This reasoning, which is based not just on self-defending but self-*consolidating* democracy,[12] has at least as much of an impact on the universality of human rights as the common starting point for discussion of the margin of appreciation and cultural relativity: the observation in paragraph 48 of *Handyside v UK* that, 'it is not possible to find in the domestic law of the various Contracting States a uniform European conception of morals.'[13]

Claims for leeway from international human rights supervisory mechanisms during times of transition can be characterised not as arguments for *cultural* relativism, but for 'transitional relativism'.

In course of this book, we shall examine the jurisprudence of the European Court (and former Commission)[14] in order to determine the extent to which the European Court has been receptive to arguments for transitional relativism. The conclusion gauges the impact of the European Court's approach

8 *Guincho v Portugal* (1985) 7 EHRR 223.
9 Ibid., [38].
10 *Mkrtchyan v Armenia* (2009) 49 EHRR 16 [43].
11 *Ždanoka v Latvia* (GC) [2006] ECHR 231, [133].
12 These concepts are discussed in detail in Chapters 6, 7, 8 and 9.
13 *Handyside v UK* (1976) 1 EHRR 737.
14 Note the discussion of the Protocol 11 ECHR reforms, which dissolved the Commission, in Chapter 1.

upon the universality of human rights and suggests that, but for the notion of self-consolidating democracy, there is evidence that the European Court has been able to accommodate not only differences between transitions, but also some of the special needs of transitional justice, without fatally undermining the universality of human rights.

The book is divided into three parts: Part 1 'Concepts', Part 2 'Cases' and, finally, Part 3 'Conclusions'. It is part of the argument of the book that it is necessary to examine not only the European Court's interactions with explicitly transitional policies (such as successor trials, historical accounting, restitution and lustration), but also with cases raising complex issues of democratic rights adjudication. After all, the transition envisaged in transitional justice is a transition to democracy. Thus the section on cases is divided between four chapters on explicitly transitional policies, and three chapters on democratic rights. One of the problems identified in the conclusion is that there is very little cross-fertilisation between the reasoning in these two categories of case. We first look at the concepts that underpin the analysis to follow.

Part I

Concepts

The aim of the first part of the book is to introduce the concepts, and indeed organisations and institutions, which it is necessary to understand before approaching the jurisprudence discussed in the rest of it. We shall examine the Council of Europe; the concept of transitional justice; and the concept of the universality of human rights. The relationship between the latter two is crucial to the conclusions reached in Chapter 9, since it implies the existence of – but does not necessarily justify – the existence of a form of 'transitional relativism.'

1 The Council of Europe, transitional justice and the universality of human rights

1.1 The Council of Europe

In order to understand the issues facing the Court today, it is important first to examine the background to the formation of the Council of Europe and the drafting of the European Convention on Human Rights, and then the process by which the Council of Europe has admitted new member states. The creation of the European Court was a response to the events of World War II and the following discussion shows that key events prior to the formation of the Council of Europe will impact on the cases discussed in Chapters 2 to 8 of this book.

Perhaps needless to say, World War II changed the continent of Europe irrevocably.[1] Europe's borders had moved and its allegiances, both internally and externally, were in a state of flux. World War I had already seen an end to the multinational empires that previously dominated the continent, leaving in its wake a collection of 'new' states carved out of the collapsed empires. This was particularly evident in central and eastern Europe, with the emergence of, for example, Czechoslovakia from the Austro-Hungarian Empire and Poland from parts of Germany, Russia and Austro-Hungary. The 1919 Treaty of Versailles legitimated these new states and other international treaties attempted to protect the national minorities that they inevitably created.[2] In Chapters 7 and 8 we shall see that the issue of national minorities is still very much felt in relation to the exercise of free assembly and association by them.

The reparations imposed on Germany after World War I were proving impossible to maintain and in eastern Europe totalitarian regimes rapidly consolidated. Indeed, the apparent weakness of the Weimar Republic to protect itself from the anti-democratic forces of Nazism is now seen as having

1 On the political history of Europe, see e.g. R. Rose, *What is Europe? A dynamic perspective* (New York: HarperCollins 1996); P. den Boer *et al.* (eds), *The History of the Idea of Europe* (Abingdon: Routledge 1995).

2 For an introduction, see H. Steiner and P. Alston, *International Human Rights in Context*, 2nd edn (Oxford: OUP 2000), 93 *et seq*.

given rise to post-war German jurisprudence on 'self-defending' or 'militant' democracy. In relation to lustration in Chapter 5 and democratic rights in Chapters 6, 7 and 8 we shall see how the deployment of this principle has given rise to significant European human rights jurisprudence.[3] While the Weimar Republic was heading for disaster, in northwestern Europe, democracy was actually expanding towards universal suffrage. Even without taking into account ancient history, interwar Europe was a continent far from homogenous.[4]

In post-1945 Europe even the order established after the 1919 Treaty of Versailles was in tatters. The Spanish Civil War of 1936–1939, in which General Franco established fascist control of Spain that lasted well into the 1970s, crystallised military allegiances that would become significant in World War II.

The descent towards World War II itself began when Nazi Germany annexed Sudetenland from the German-speaking part of Czechoslovakia and it continued with the invasion of Poland. In Chapter 4, we shall see that the exclusion of post-war confiscations of Sudenten German property from the restitution scheme has resulted in difficult human rights cases brought against the Czech Republic. At the same time as the invasion of Poland, and ultimately resulting in their eventual opposition, Hitler permitted Stalin's invasion of the Baltic states with the 'Molotov-Ribbentrop Pact' of 'non-aggression pact' between the USSR and Nazi Germany.[5] The ensuing war between European states became global. To this day the status of the 'Molotov-Ribbentrop' pact is deeply contested and is discussed in Chapter 3.

The physical losses of Europe both through war and genocide and the devastation of land war waged with new destructive technologies required that Europe rebuild itself. Notably, the allegiances that had combined to secure the Nazi's defeat quickly crumbled. Northwestern Europe allied itself with the USA in a 'North Atlantic Europe', while the eastern states fell under the influence of communist Russia, in the so-called Eastern Bloc.[6] These

3 P. Macklem, 'Militant democracy, legal pluralism, and the paradox of self-setermination' (2006) 4(3) *International Journal of Constitutional Law* 488, 491; P. Harvey, 'Militant democracy and the European Convention on Human Rights' (2004) 29(3) *European Law Review* 407, 408; R. Teitel, 'Militating democracy: comparative constitutional perspectives' (2007) 29 *Michigan Journal of International Law* 49, 62.

4 See I. Pogany 'A new constitutional (dis)order for Eastern Europe', in *Human Rights in Eastern Europe* (Aldershot: Edward Elgar 1995), 222–230.

5 See the documents reproduced by Yale Law School's 'Avalon Project', including the treaty of non-aggression itself, signed on 23 August 1939, http://avalon.law.yale.edu/subject_menus/nazsov.asp (accessed 21.5.2012).

6 See Rose, *op. cit. supra* n 1, 38–42.

separate groups of states were aligned on military lines, with North Atlantic Europe engaged in collective defence through the North Atlantic Treaty Organization (NATO)[7] and the eastern states through the Treaty of Friendship, Cooperation and Mutual Assistance – more commonly known as the Warsaw Pact. The first response of the western European states to self-defence had been to prevent a revival of Germany's aggression, in the form of the Brussels Treaty Organisation.[8] However, it was against the Eastern Bloc that defence was now required. Only with the aid of the USA was this possible, hence North American involvement in NATO.

1.1.1 The Council of Europe, human rights and democracy

The idea of a European human rights charter pre-dates the formation of the Council of Europe in 1949.[9] Movements for the unification of Europe proliferated post-1945, but many of them came together for the first time in the form of the 'International Committee of the Movements for European Unity'.[10] The Committee held the 'Hague Congress of Europe' in May 1948 and, among other stated objectives, called for a charter of human rights. The Congress, at which there were high-level delegates from 16 states (and observers from more), was designed to demonstrate the need and support for European unity. At the end of the Congress its conclusions, which suggested the need for some form of pan-European governance, were submitted to the Brussels Treaty Organisation. After some reluctance from the British, it was agreed that a European assembly should be created. This led to the formulation of the Statute of the Council of Europe, which was signed in May 1949.[11]

Unlike NATO, the Council of Europe was not designed to facilitate the *military* defence of western Europe. It was criticised at the time of its formation for not providing for closer European integration – but this role was eventually to be taken on by what became the European Union (a name that

7 Established with the signing of the North Atlantic Treaty on 4 April 1949. See generally Sands and Klein, *Bowett's Law of International Institutions*, 5th edn (London: Sweet & Maxwell 2001), 91–196.

8 The Brussels Treaty Organisation, which comprised the UK, France, Belgium, the Netherlands and Luxembourg, was set up on 17 March 1948, under Article 51 of the UN Charter.

9 A.H. Robertson, 'The political background and historical development of the European Convention on Human Rights', in *European Convention on Human Rights* (London: British Institute for International and Comparative Law 1965), 24. A shorter but updated version of this paper is contained in J.G. Merrills and Robertson, *Human Rights in Europe*, 4th edn (Manchester: Manchester University Press 2001), 1–15.

10 R. Beddard, *Human Rights and Europe*, 3rd edn (Cambridge: Grotius Publications 1993), 19.

11 Statute of the Council of Europe, *European Treaty Series*, No. 001.

France and Italy had actually suggested for the Council of Europe, indicating their early support for further integration).[12]

The Statute of the Council of Europe from the outset is committed to the principles that 'form the basis of all genuine democracy'.[13] Article 3 of the Statute states that every member:

> must accept the principles of the rule of law and of the enjoyment by all persons within its jurisdiction of human rights and fundamental freedoms and collaborate sincerely and effectively in the realisation of the aim of the Council [as set out in the Statute].

According to Article 4, only European states that are 'able and willing' to fulfil the provisions of Article 3 may be invited to join the Council of Europe (the development of more detailed accession criteria is outlined later). Thus democracy, the rule of law, and human rights were always central to the Council of Europe. This is reaffirmed in Article 8 of the Statute, which provides sanctions for member states 'seriously violating' Article 3, including expulsion and suspension of membership. We shall discuss the precise meaning of 'democracy' in the European jurisprudence, and its relationship to transitional justice, in the introduction to the discussion of democratic rights in the transnational context, in chapters 6, 7, and 8.

Robertson suggested there were two reasons for the Council of Europe's stance on democracy. First, as suggested earlier, the ideological conflict of eastern and western Europe was at that time becoming ever more serious. Between the end of the Hague Congress and the Statute being signed communists had taken power in Czechoslovakia, the Greek civil war had begun and the Berlin Blockade[14] had taken place. The need to demonstrate opposition to communism and dictatorship was very clear. The second reason offered by Robertson was that many of the people involved in drafting the Statute had been in resistance movements or suffered at the hands of oppressive regimes before and during World War II (or both). They were acutely aware that the first steps towards dictatorship involved the suppression of individual liberties and that once this process began it was difficult to stop.[15] The Council of Europe would be a means of preventing the descent to tyranny. The Statute was signed on 5 May 1949 by Belgium, Denmark,

12 B. Simpson, *Human Rights and the End of Empire: Britain and the genesis of the European Convention* (Oxford: OUP 2001), 642.

13 Preamble, Statute of the Council of Europe, *op. cit. supra* n 11.

14 Between 24 June 1948 and 12 May 1949 Soviet forces prohibited any land access to Berlin, which was in the Russian zone of Germany. See C. Pennacchio, 'The East German communists and the origins of the Berlin blockade crisis,' (1995) 29(3) *East European Quarterly* 294.

15 Robertson, *op. cit. supra* n 9, 27.

France, Ireland, Italy, Luxembourg, the Netherlands, Norway, Sweden and the UK. After seven ratifications, the Statute came into effect on 3 August 1949.

The main institutions of the Council of Europe are its Committee of Ministers and Parliamentary Assembly (originally referred to as the 'Consultative Assembly', and now known as PACE: the Parliamentary Assembly of the Council of Europe).[16] The Committee of Ministers is comprised of the foreign ministers of the Member States or their alternative.[17] The Committee of Ministers has a special role within the European Convention system, which is detailed shortly. While the Committee of Ministers is more of an executive body, PACE is the deliberative organ of the Council.[18] It has been suggested that, in relation to democracy, lawyers have for too long focused their attention exclusively on the European Convention and its enforcement rather than on the wider activities of the Council of Europe.[19] Heeding this advice to some extent, we shall see that in the light of the enlargement of the Council of Europe PACE has issued detailed guidance on decommunisation.[20]

1.1.2 The Genesis of the European Convention on Human Rights

The creation of the ECHR itself was spurred on by the activities of the United Nations, which was founded in 1945. The Universal Declaration of Human Rights, from which the European Convention took much of its inspiration, was signed in 1948.[21]

The European Convention was created both in response to the atrocities committed in World War II and once again as a reaction to the powerful communist Eastern Bloc. The Convention was to be built on the democratic values that informed the Statute of the Council of Europe and were considered common to the states that first signed it, evidencing their common heritage and shared cultural values.[22] It is therefore notable that the newer Contracting Parties to the ECHR are now participants in a mechanism that was specifically designed to symbolise the difference between them and the system's early members.

16 Article 10 Statute of the Council of Europe, *op. cit. supra* n 11.
17 Article 14 Statute of the Council of Europe, *op. cit. supra* n 11.
18 Article 22 Statute of the Council of Europe, *op. cit. supra* n 11.
19 C. Gearty, 'Democracy and human rights in the European Court of Human Rights: a critical appraisal' (2000) 51 *Northern Ireland Legal Quarterly* 381, 396.
20 PACE Resolution 1096 (1996).
21 UN General Assembly Resolution 217A (III) UN Doc. A/810, at 71 (1948).
22 D. Seymour, 'The extension of the European Convention on Human Rights to Central and Eastern Europe: prospects and risks', (1993) 8 *Connecticut Journal of International Law* 243, 244.

The symbolic nature of the European Convention and, in particular, the European Court of Human Rights raises interesting questions in relation to the evolution of transitional justice itself. Ruti Teitel's genealogy of transitional justice identifies the first phase of its evolution as being the internationalisation of judicial responses to World War II, most evidently typified by the International Military Tribunal at Nuremberg.[23] It could be argued that post-war moves towards the creation of a European human rights court are part of the same process. A European human rights court could represent a symbolic break with the past and a sign of greater things to come.[24]

For the Soviet forces involved in rebuilding Germany, 'democracy' could be imposed from without by utterly controlling its political and economic system in order to support anti-fascist policies. The western powers, also aiming to promote a concept of democracy, chose to do so via free elections and human rights.[25] The incompatibility of these approaches to governance in post-war Europe is clear and runs deeper than the simple opposition of liberalism and communism.

Creating an institutional mechanism for protecting human rights was one of the first matters on the agenda of the new Council of Europe, with its limited membership. The Council of Europe could have hesitated at this point, out of concerns that it would simply duplicate the ongoing efforts of the UN to formulate mechanisms for the international protection of the values enshrined in the UDHR. As Beddard has noted, it is fortunate this position was not taken, since it took another 17 years for the UN to secure agreement on the international covenants on civil and political rights and economic, social and cultural rights.[26]

Given the difficulties faced by the UN, the time it took to draft the ECHR was not especially long: a period lasting just over one year.[27] Throughout the year there were, however, some matters on which states disagreed with some consistency. Primarily, these were the precise details of the enforcement mechanisms and certain of the suggested rights.[28] Indeed from the first suggestions that there might be a charter of human rights, the British government opposed the creation of a court. The erosion of sovereignty necessitated by submission to an international court was novel and it was also suspected that the proposed mechanisms might be too heavily politicised to be effective.

23 R. Teitel, 'Transitional justice genealogy' (2003) 16 *Harvard Human Rights Journal* 69, 70.

24 See T. Allen, 'Restitution and transitional justice in the European Court of Human Rights' (2007) 13(1) *Columbia Journal of European Law* 1, 6 (although Allen would not agree that this is the case).

25 G. Sandford, *From Hitler to Ulbricht* (Princeton: Princeton University Press 1983).

26 Beddard, *op. cit. supra* n 10, 22.

27 Discussion of the actual process by which the Convention was adopted is outside the scope of this book. For a detailed examination of the Convention's drafting, see Beddard, ibid.; Simpson, *op. cit. supra* n 12; J.G. Merrills and Robertson, *op. cit. supra* n 9. See also M. Janis, R. Kay and A. Bradley, *European Human Rights Law*, 2nd edn (Oxford: OUP 2000), 16–22.

28 Beddard, *op. cit. supra* n 10, 22.

Moreover, the idea that an individual might be able to petition the court directly was seen by many as either superfluous or another impermissible challenge to the sovereignty of states. As we shall discuss later in this book, these sovereignty-based concerns were to resurface in the jurisprudence of the European Commission and Court of Human Rights in discussions of the existence and width of Respondent States' 'margin of appreciation'.

As to the rights themselves, the Council of Europe found difficulty in finalising the list of rights and separating 'core' rights from other desirable objectives. Particularly problematic were the right to peaceful enjoyment of one's possessions; the right of parents to have their children educated in accordance with their own religious and philosophical convictions; and the right to free and fair elections.

The final version of the Convention was opened for signature on 4 November 1950 and opted for a compromise between the various competing positions. The problematic rights were consigned to an additional protocol. The jurisdiction of the Court itself was to be optional[29] and the right of individual petition would also be subject to an optional declaration by the states parties before it could be invoked.[30]

1.1.3 Enlargement of the Council of Europe

We have already seen that the end of World War II was the catalyst for the creation of the Council of Europe. The initial signatories of the European Convention had only recently been at war with each other, twice, and so even the early operation of the Council of Europe had a post-conflict or transitional element to it.

Spain, Portugal and Greece all had difficult phases of totalitarian rule extending well into the 1970s. Greece re-ratified the European Convention in 1974, Portugal ratified in 1978 and Spain in 1979. We shall examine cases from these states that have raised issues of transitional justice in Part Two, but, since by far the most significant enlargement of the Council of Europe took place after the end of the Cold War, it is the cases from this period that are more numerous.

Membership of the Council of Europe is by invitation only. If the Committee of Ministers deems a European state 'able and willing' to comply with the conditions of Article 3 of the Statute of Council of Europe (noted earlier), then it may be invited to join the Council.[31]

29 Old Article 46 ECHR.

30 Old Article 25 ECHR.

31 Article 4 Statute of the Council of Europe, *op. cit. supra* n 11; see A. Duxbury, 'Bigger or better? The role of human rights and democracy in determining membership of the European institutions' (2004) 73 *Nordic Journal of International Law* 421; H. Winkler, 'Democracy and human rights in Europe: a survey of the admission practice of the Council of Europe' (1995) 47 *Austrian Journal of Public and International Law* 148.

Duxbury's comparative analysis of admission to NATO, the EU and Council of Europe argued that the Council of Europe had been more concerned with rights and democracy than the others from the outset.[32] However, she also argued that at least pre-1990, and specifically in relation to the admission of Spain and Portugal, PACE did not make a detailed examination of candidate states' human rights and democratic records. After 1990 the Council of Europe applied 'seemingly more rigorous' standards.[33] The Council established an 'elaborate procedure' involving expert reports and visiting missions, as well as more robust and detailed supervision by PACE.[34] Although the Council of Europe's investigations became increasingly detailed, at the same time, the term 'able and willing' to comply with Article 3 of the Statute came more to mean, 'able in the future',[35] prompting Duxbury to observe that:

> in the eyes of the Council of Europe the borders of Europe were determined by a State's ability and willingness to adhere to such standards in the future, indicating a movement to a policy of qualified heterogeneity.[36]

It is the profound implications that this approach has had on the types of case coming before the European Court of Human Rights that this book seeks to examine.

1.1.4 Implications of enlargement

The enlargement of the Council of Europe in the early 1990s, to include the emergent democracies of central and eastern Europe, has led to a change in the role of the Council in relation to democracy and, by extension, a change in the role of the European Court of Human Rights. No longer can the European Court claim solely to be engaged in the defence of existing democratic guarantees: it must assist in the building and consolidation of democracy. This is a radical change in the way that the Court operates, and has not been met with universal approval.

Peter Leuprecht was elected as Deputy Secretary General of the Council of Europe in 1993, after working for the Council in increasingly senior roles since 1961. He resigned his post in 1997 because of disagreement with the perceived dilution of Council of Europe standards and values since its period of enlargement, and his reasons for so doing are well documented. Leuprecht was particularly concerned about the admission of Russia into the Council of

32 Duxbury, ibid., 439.
33 Ibid., 441.
34 Ibid., 442.
35 Duxbury, ibid., cited former Council of Europe Deputy Secretary General Peter Leuprecht as the source for this observation. Leuprecht's comments are discussed shortly.
36 Duxbury, *op. cit. supra* n 31, 444.

Europe.[37] Mark Janis has since argued that Russia's ratification of the European Convention, in circumstances in which it clearly does not uphold fully the rights it enshrines, goes so far as to undermine the very legality of Strasbourg law. Elizabeth Evenson has echoed Janis's concerns about potential non-compliance of newer Contracting Parties.[38]

At the time enlargement began, there were very serious practical questions about how the European Court would cope with its new role. Some of these were addressed by the adoption of Protocol 11 to the ECHR, which came into effect in 1998. The principal changes introduced by Protocol 11 were the abolition of the European Commission of Human Rights (so that both the admissibility and the merits of cases are decided by the European Court, albeit in different compositions),[39] the institution of a permanent European Court of Human Rights and the removal of the quasi-judicial role initially played by the Committee of Ministers. The Committee of Ministers still plays a very important role in the enforcement of European Court decisions, under Article 46 ECHR, and has been instrumental in encouraging the Court to issue 'pilot judgments' in systemic cases (discussed in Chapter 4).

Other significant changes from Protocol 11 included requiring the compulsory acceptance of both the jurisdiction of the European Court of Human Rights and the right of individual petition. Several important practical issues remain: the Council recognises that the Court's workload is 'excessive' and that the geographical and gender balance of the Court's various incarnations could be improved. Some of these issues may be addressed by Protocol 14, which finally came into effect in 2010 after being adopted by the Committee of Ministers in 2004. It is notable, in this context, that it was Russia that for several years prevented Protocol 14's entering into force by refusing to ratify it (although it had signed it in 2006).[40] In the meantime so-called 'Protocol 14*bis*' was agreed in view of the 'urgent need to introduce certain additional procedures to the Convention in order to maintain and improve the efficiency

37 P. Leuprecht, 'Innovations in the European system of human rights protection: is enlargement compatible with reinforcement?' (1998) 8 *Transnational Law and Contemporary Problems* 313.

38 E. Evenson, 'Reforms ahead: enlargement of the Council of Europe and the future of the Strasbourg system' (2001) 1 *Human Rights Law Review* 219 (2001), 224–225.

39 See Articles 26–29 ECHR.

40 http://conventions.coe.int/Treaty/Commun/ChercheSig.asp?NT=194&CM=7&DF=&CL=ENG (accessed 21.5.2012); see also P. Leach, 'Strasbourg's oversight of Russia – an increasingly strained relationship' (2007) *Public Law* 640, at 640 noting that at the time of writing 'the Russian stance alone [was] preventing the far-reaching reforms set out in the Protocol from being brought into effect'; see also J. Costa, President of the European Court of Human Rights, 'Solemn hearing of the European Court of Human Rights on the occasion of the opening of the judicial year: Speech', 30 January 2009, available at www.echr.coe.int (accessed 21.5.2012), 7 noting that 'Protocol No. 14 has still not entered into force, and I regret it. The causes of this blockage are well known.'

of its control system'[41] and which required only three states to express their consent to be bound by it.[42]

When Protocol 14 entered into force Protocol 14*bis* ceased to have effect. The full Protocol 14 made some significant changes to the way in which the European Court operates.[43] There were changes to the composition of the Court, the terms of judicial office, the admissibility process and the enforcement of judgments. It also paved the way for the European Union to accede to the European Convention on Human Rights, a development that is difficult because it will require constitutional changes from the Union before it can be realised. In spite of all these changes, then President of the European Court Luzius Wildhaber observed pessimistically in 2004 that the Court would still face an 'excessive workload'.[44]

The changes to the admissibility criteria are the most significant because they raise an essentially existential question about the role and future of the European Court itself. Under Article 35 ECHR, as amended by Protocol 14, an individual application may now be declared inadmissible where the applicant has not suffered a 'significant disadvantage.' Shortly after Protocol 14 was concluded Marie-Aude Beernaert argued that this change would go so far as to undermine the fundamental right of individual petition.[45]

Beernaert's criticism can be seen as part of an ongoing debate about the future role of the European Court. In essence, the question is whether it should focus on 'individual' or 'constitutional' justice.[46] Showing a clear preference for constitutional justice, Greer has explained that the pursuit of 'individual justice' is not a question of whether to continue receiving individual applications, but whether the European Court should attempt to:

> ensure every genuine victim of a violation receives a judgment in their favour from the Court however slight the injury, whatever the bureaucratic cost, whether or not compensation is awarded, and whatever the likely impact of the judgment on the conduct or practice in question.[47]

By contrast the pursuit of 'constitutional justice' is the attempt to:

> ensure that cases are both selected and adjudicated by the Court in a manner which contributes most effectively to the identification,

41 Preamble, Protocol 14*bis*, *European Treaty Series*, No. 204.

42 Article 6(1) Protocol 14*bis*.

43 S. Greer, *The European Convention on Human Rights* (Cambridge: CUP 2006), 159 *et seq*.

44 Cited in ibid., 136.

45 Marie-Aude Beernaert, 'Protocol 14 and new Strasbourg Procedures: towards greater efficiency? And at what price' (2004) 5 EHRLR 544, 553 and 556.

46 See Greer *op. cit. supra* n 43, 165 *et seq*.

47 Ibid., 166.

> condemnation, and resolution of violations which are serious for the applicant, for the Respondent State [. . .] or for Europe as a whole.[48]

Sadurski has observed that the massive expansion of the Council of Europe presented a chance to move away from 'individualised justice' and:

> a possibility to liberate oneself from the fiction that the European Court of Human Rights does not scrutinise the objectionable *laws* of CoE Member States but merely corrects bad individual *decisions*.[49]

Others, such as Cali, dodge the issue completely by arguing that the European Court is a *sui generis* institution in the light of which these questions cease to be fundamental.[50] The classification of the justice to be delivered, from this perspective, is less important than the very real issue of the Court's caseload problems.

However, the 'constitutional justice' approach as part of the solution to the Court's troubles is gaining ground. In 2002 Greer was able to cite the then President, Luzius Wildhaber, former President Rolv Ryssdall and former Registrar as having advanced the case for constitutional justice in their personal capacities.[51] Likewise, there have been a series of Council of Europe conferences about reform of the Convention system since Protocol 14: in Interlaken in 2010, in Izmir in 2011, and in Brighton in 2012. While in the 'Brighton Declaration', the states' parties reaffirmed their 'attachment' to the right of individual application,[52] the conference also stated that:

> In response to more effective implementation at the national level, the Court should be in a position to focus its efforts on serious or widespread violations, systemic and structural problems, and important questions of interpretation and application of the Convention, and hence would need to remedy fewer violations itself and consequently deliver fewer judgments.[53]

It might be possible to identify in advance those individual applications that give rise to serious and widespread violations, or derive from systemic and

48 Ibid.

49 W. Sadurski, 'Partnering with Strasbourg: constitutionalism of the European Court of Human Rights, the accession of Central and East European states to the Council of Europe, and the idea of pilot judgments' (2009) 9(3) *Human Rights Law Review* 397, 451.

50 B. Cali, 'The purposes of the European Human Rights system: one or many?' (2008) 3 *European Human Rights Law Review* 299, 206.

51 Greer *op. cit. supra* n 43, 169.

52 Declaration of the High Level Conference meeting at Brighton on 19 and 20 April 2012 at the initiative of the United Kingdom Chairmanship of the Committee of Ministers of the Council of Europe, http://www.coe.int/en/2012419-brighton-declaration/ (accessed 21.5.2012), [2].

53 Ibid., [33].

structural problems, but Greer's definition of constitutional justice was wider than this. Recall that the distinctively constitutional element comes from the cases that have a particular impact on the Respondent State or Europe as a whole. This would seem to be reflected in the Brighton Declaration's reference to 'important questions of interpretation and application of the Convention'. The problem with *this* constitutional element is that until the European judges have deliberated on a case, it is virtually impossible to gauge how profound, or constitutional, their reasoning will be. Indeed, even within a single case, some judges may identify much wider issues than others: perfect examples would be the dissenting opinions of Judges Ress and Levits, quoted at the opening of this book.[54]

To the extent that reforming the handling of cases is a question of administration, it behoves experts in management to contribute to the discussion: human rights lawyers and academics alone are no more qualified to improve the flow of documents between two people than anyone else. There are other recommendations, such as for the greater use of advisory opinions[55] or the creation of a European Fair Trials Commission,[56] but these do not get to the essence of the normative challenges that the European Court has faced as a result of its jurisdiction over the new Contracting Parties to the European Convention. For that we need to examine the related advice of the Council of Europe on dismantling communism and the concept of transitional justice.

1.2 Transitional justice

In this chapter, the Council of Europe's political guidance on 'dismantling communism' is placed in the context of the concept of transitional justice. The relationship between transitional justice and international human rights supervision is shown to be extremely complex because, at first glance, many transitional policies seem to be in conflict with international human rights law. In this chapter, we shall set out the relationship. Further into this chapter, the claim for special treatment by international human rights enforcement mechanisms during transitional periods is characterised as a claim of what can be termed 'transitional relativism'.

1.2.1 The Council of Europe and dismantling communism

In 1996 the Parliamentary Assembly of the Council of Europe (PACE) issued Resolution 1096 (1996) on 'measures to dismantle the heritage of former communist totalitarian systems'.

54 Judge Ress, Dissenting Opinion in *Jahn v Germany* (GC) [2006] 42 EHRR 49; Judge Levits, Dissenting Opinion in *Ždanoka v Latvia* (Chamber) [2004] ECHR 268.

55 Brighton Declaration, *op. cit. supra* n 52, [12(d)].

56 Greer *op. cit. supra* n 43, 282.

Resolution 1096 was a political statement of how the Council understood the heritage of the former communist states, the goals of the transitional process and the dangers of its failure. It was based on text proposed in a report by the Council of Europe Committee on Legal Affairs and Human Rights, with former Romanian foreign minister and present Member of the European Parliament (MEP) Adrian Severin acting as rapporteur. The Resolution has been cited relatively rarely in its jurisprudence of the European Court of Human Rights. Despite its apparent lack of explicit impact on the jurisprudence of the Court, the issues identified in the Resolution provide a very coherent route into exploring the relationship between human rights and transitional justice in the Council of Europe.

In Resolution 1096, PACE observed that the former communist states were, at the institutional level, characterised by (over)centralisation, the militarisation of civilian institutions, bureaucratisation, monopolisation and overregulation.[57] At the societal level, their heritage 'reaches from collectivism and conformism to blind obedience and other totalitarian thought patterns'.[58] The goal of the transitional process was, therefore, to create pluralist democracies, based on the rule of law and respect for human rights and diversity.[59]

The risks of the process were that the transition would be incomplete, that oligarchy would flourish instead of democracy and that the new states would be riven by corruption and organised crime.[60] At worst, PACE observed, this could lead to the peaceful or violent restoration of the former regime.[61] PACE also noted that weaker states could be at risk from the influence of larger less democratic regimes.[62]

Most importantly for the current enquiry, Resolution 1096 also spelled out some aspects of the difficult relationship between facing the past and governing the present. In stark terms, PACE recognised that: 'The key to peaceful coexistence and a successful transition process lies in striking the delicate balance of providing justice without seeking revenge.'[63]

The orientation of the Resolution and Report to the content of the transitional process is interesting from two perspectives. First, they noted the thematic link between the post-Cold War measures and the successful dismantling of the heritage of totalitarian states 'of the fascist persuasion' during the twentieth century, notably in Germany, Italy and Spain.[64] This suggests that

57 Resolution 1096 (1996), [1].
58 Ibid.
59 Ibid, [2].
60 Ibid, [3].
61 Ibid.
62 Ibid.
63 Ibid., [3]
64 Thus the report states that it is based on discussion papers submitted not only by experts from Romania and the Czech Republic, but also by an expert on Germany's dismantling of the past: Report, [2].

in dealing with human rights cases arising from central and eastern Europe, the European Court of Human Rights may be able to draw on principles formulated in response to these earlier experiences. Thus, it might be an overstatement to presume that the circumstances presented by the new Contracting Parties are inherently different to those who founded the Council of Europe in the post-World War II era or those encountered after the southern European transitions. Certainly the scale of the changes is vast and this has raised institutional issues about the ability of the Court system to handle the sheer number of potential applicants, as discussed earlier. The actual substantive legal principles to be litigated, however, may have parallels in existing cases.

Second, the Resolution and Report both identified that the process of dismantling the totalitarian heritage of the Council's members may itself impact on human rights. We shall see that this, rather than the actions of the former regime, has been the foundation of much of the Court's work: indeed, this is the catalyst for recognising transitional relativism. Resolution 1096 was quite clear that interferences with human rights can and should be avoided during the transitional process:

> [A] democratic state based on the rule of law must, in dismantling the heritage of former communist totalitarian systems, apply the procedural means of such a state. It cannot apply any other means, since it would then be no better than the totalitarian regime which is to be dismantled. A democratic state based on the rule of law has sufficient means at its disposal to ensure that the cause of justice is served and the guilty are punished [. . .] A state based on the rule of law can also defend itself against a resurgence of the communist totalitarian threat, since it has ample means at its disposal which do not conflict with human rights and the rule of law.

Resolution 1096 went on to identify four principles that should guide the transition process: demilitarisation, decentralisation, demonopolisation and debureaucratisation.[65] These, it argued, should be accompanied by a 'transformation of mentalities', aimed at fostering democratic values such as tolerance, respect for diversity, subsidiarity and accountability for one's actions.[66]

In Resolution 1096, these general principles were accompanied by some more specific recommendations, which, it will be seen, reflect the issues arising in many of the cases brought before the European Court of Human Rights. The detail of these recommendations is introduced in the corresponding sections of Part Two, but here their broad scope is outlined in order

65 PACE Resolution 1096 (1996), [5].
66 Ibid., [6].

to show the types of human rights issue arising from the new Contracting Parties.

The first recommendation related to ensuring individual criminal responsibility for acts of the previous regime. PACE recommended that 'criminal acts committed by individuals during the communist totalitarian regime be prosecuted and punished under the standard criminal code'. (The cases arising from such prosecutions are discussed in Chapter 2.) The second PACE recommendation was that the prosecution of individual crimes must take place alongside the rehabilitation of those who were convicted of spurious crimes under the previous regime and that compensation available to such people must not be (much) lower than that available to anyone else unjustly sentenced from crimes under the standard criminal code. Third, PACE recommended that persons should be able to access any files kept on them by the secret service of the outgoing regime. (This is discussed in Chapter 3.) Fourth, PACE advised that unlawfully expropriated property should be restituted (or compensation be provided, discussed in Chapter 4). The Resolution also gave relatively detailed guidance on the conduct of 'lustration' or vetting procedures. (These are discussed in Chapter 5.)

Resolution 1096 was a political statement. This is consistent with the constitutional function of PACE within the Council of Europe. Like all political organs, it does not necessarily speak with one voice and neither does its view remain consistent. PACE Resolution 1481 (2006) took an even firmer view of the totalitarian past of the new Contracting Parties and called for international condemnation of crimes of past and existing totalitarian regimes. Also in 2006 PACE adopted Recommendation 1736 (2006), 'On the need for international condemnation of the Franco regime', showing that it was not only the experiences of the former communist states that were occupying the Council of Europe.

1.2.2 Transitional justice

PACE Resolution 1096 and its programme for 'dismantling communism' dealt both with elements of what political scientists would recognise as democratic transition and what lawyers would recognise as transitional justice. The broad theme of democratic transition is outside the scope of this book, suffice it to reiterate the introductory comments outlining that there is abundant literature on the 'waves' of democratic transition that have taken place throughout history[67] and competing explanations as to the relationship between internal and external factors in successful transitions. Indeed, the orthodoxy for much of the twentieth century was that internal factors, rather than external factors such as pressure from organisations such as the Council

67 In particular, S. Huntington, *The Third Wave: democratisation in the late twentieth century* (Norman: University of Oklahoma Press 1991).

of Europe, were the most significant.[68] It is, therefore, worth remembering that, as only one element of the Council of Europe, itself an external factor in each state's transitional process, the impact of the European Court of Human Rights' jurisprudence on the ultimate success or otherwise of the Contracting Parties' transition should be kept in perspective.

In addition to being part of the process of democratisation, the more specific recommendations of Resolution 1096 can be viewed within the paradigm of 'transitional justice'. The notion of transitional justice can be understood in two main ways: as an umbrella term for 'the full range of processes and mechanisms associated with a society's attempts to come to terms with a legacy of large-scale past abuses, in order to ensure accountability, serve justice and achieve reconciliation'[69] or, more theoretically, as the modified notion of justice inherent in these policies. The first view was expressed in a report by the UN Secretary General, the second by the prolific writer in this field, Ruti Teitel.[70] Under this second view, transitional justice is the 'conception of justice associated with periods of political change, characterized by legal responses to confront the wrongdoings of repressive predecessor regimes':[71]

> In contexts of political upheaval, transitional jurisprudence comprises a partial and nonideal conception of justice: provisional and limited forms of constitutions, sanctions, reparations, purges, and histories.[72]

Teitel's reference to a non-ideal conception of justice is crucial to understanding the dilemma faced by international human rights bodies when they are compelled to adjudicate over the compliance of transitional policies with international human rights law. Others, such as Posner and Vermeule have supported the processes contained within the umbrella term 'transitional justice' as used by the UN, but have argued that they can be placed along a spectrum that would see them merely as notable elements of 'ordinary justice'.[73] This approach would evaporate their 'non-idealism'.

One way to determine whether 'transitional justice' is merely a series of policies encountered in transition, or something more interesting, is to

68 P. Schmitter, 'An introduction to southern European transitions from authoritarian rule: Italy, Greece, Portugal, Spain, and Turkey', in G. O'Donnell *et al.* (eds), *Transitions from Authoritarian Rule: southern Europe* (Baltimore: Johns Hopkins University Press 1986), 5; J.C. Pevehouse, *Democracy from above: regional organisations and democratization* (Cambridge: CUP 2005), 2.

69 United Nations Security Council, *Report of the Secretary General: the rule of law and transitional justice in conflict and post-conflict societies*, UN Doc S/2004/616, 4.

70 R. Teitel, 'Transitional justice genealogy', 16 *Harvard Human Rights Law Review* (2003) 69, 69.

71 Ibid., 69.

72 R. Teitel, *Transitional justice* (New York: Oxford University Press 2000), 215.

73 E. Posner and A. Vermeule, 'Transitional justice as ordinary justice' (2004) 117 *Harvard Law Review* 761.

examine its history. Ruti Teitel did this by presenting a 'genealogy' of transitional justice.[74] According to Teitel, the first sign of a truly 'transitional' justice was the internationalisation of criminal justice at Nuremburg, coupled with the assertion of individual criminality for 'state' wrongs. For Teitel, this marked the start of the first 'phase' of transitional justice, the post-war phase.[75] A second phase, Teitel argued, began in the post-Cold War era and was characterised by a return to national, rather than international, initiatives, but which by being more restorative in their orientation juxtaposed truth to justice and traded normal notions of justice for peace. The South African Truth and Reconciliation Commission is emblematic of this phase. Teitel's genealogy of transitional justice stretches to a third phase, however. No longer merely identifying distinctive responses that were apparent in transition, Teitel has been critical of the co-option of some of the assumptions of (or growing popular recognition of the idea of) transitional justice in the war on terror.

Teitel's genealogical analysis and criticism demonstrates that transitional justice is not merely a collection of techniques or simply a clear moral agenda to be promoted with evangelical zeal, but a collection of values that can be *observed* in legal responses to transitional dilemmas. Teitel's description of transitional jurisprudence as a non-ideal conception of justice indicates that observing the existence of 'transitional' justice is not the same as unequivocally advocating it.[76]

In her extremely useful historical account of how key individuals led to the 'field' of transitional justice, Paige Arthur has argued, by contrast, that the 'field' of transitional justice does, in fact, have the normative aim of facilitating the transition to democracy.[77] However, the introduction to Teitel's 2000 book only ever aimed to *describe* 'a distinctive conception of law and justice in the context of political transformation'.[78] Outside that context, in stable democracies, broadly comparable *policies* (such as enhanced scrutiny of the public servants' loyalty) may well be interesting but are not, and could never be, evidence for the existence of *transitional* justice.

Arthur has argued that scholars such as Teitel:

> still fall into the trap of imputing ideas about 'transitional justice' to actors who, presumably, were unlikely to have held them, particularly in their discussions of the immediate post-World War II era.[79]

74 Teitel, *op. cit. supra* n 70.
75 Ibid.
76 Teitel, *op. cit. supra* n 72, 215.
77 P. Arthur, 'How "transitions" reshaped human rights: a conceptual history of transitional justice' (2009) 31 *Human Rights Quarterly* 321, 358,
78 Teitel, *op. cit. supra* n 72, 4.
79 Arthur, *op. cit. supra* n 77, 28.

For the view of transitional justice adopted in this book, which, it is fair to say, is influenced by Teitel, Arthur's argument does not undermine the identification and description of distinct types of 'justice' emanating from the first two phases of Teitel's genealogy. From the perspective of an observer, it does not *necessarily* matter whether the observed have the same perspective about what they are doing.

Teitel's crucial observation was that legal responses play an extraordinary and constitutive role in periods of transition.[80] That is not to say an extraordinarily *good* role, but one that law, lawyers and legal theorists are not used to playing or are even necessarily capable of recognising that they *are* playing.

1.2.3 Transitional justice in the Council of Europe

An overview of the approach of the Council of Europe to the states from central and eastern Europe would suggest that, although the Council has advocated states taking certain transitional measures, it has not itself sought to capitalise on the constructive or constitutive role that the identification of transitional justice implies law can play.

A study of the Council of Europe documents shows that the term appeared for the first time only in 2008, in a draft recommendation of the Committee of Ministers put forward by the Steering Group for Equality between Men and Women (CDEG) on the role of women and men in conflict prevention and resolution and in peace building.[81] Indeed, this is the *only* time that the concept has been defined and applied in the political activity of the Council of Europe.[82]

Domestic and regional programmes of transitional justice have been 'welcomed' by the Council, for example in the Secretary General's Seventh and Ninth Reports on Serbia and Montenegro's 'compliance with obligations and commitments and implementation of the post-accession co-operation programme'.[83]

In relation to the Balkans generally,[84] and Serbia in particular,[85] the Council of Europe's Commissioner for Human Rights, Thomas Hammarberg, has observed that there is a shortage of successful transitional justice processes, 'such as formal truth-seeking efforts, reparations to victims, and the vetting of officials who may be implicated in past crimes', with the focus instead being almost

80 Teitel, *op. cit. supra* n 72, 4.

81 Council of Minister doc. CM (2008)36, 25 February 2008; see also the Explanatory Memorandum CM (2008)36 add 25 February 2008.

82 The draft declaration was eventually adopted at the 1036th meeting of the Ministers' Deputies: CM/Notes/1036/4.2 12 September 20081.

83 SG/Inf (2005)5 final 14 March 2005; SG/Inf (2005)16 final 11 October 2005.

84 Contribution of the Commissioner for Human Rights to the work of the Committee of Experts on impunity, CommDH (2009)32, 27 August 2009.

85 Report by the Commissioner for Human Rights, Thomas Hammarberg, on his visit to Serbia (13–17 October 2008), CommDH (2009)8.

exclusively on criminal prosecutions of war crimes.[86] At a roundtable on the situation of human rights defenders in the Council of Europe, the Commissioner also noted that some such people in post-conflict or crisis situations were at risk of being identified with the political opposition.[87] In his 2009 Annual Activity Report, he noted that this was a particular problem in Serbia.[88]

This is in stark contrast to the United Nations, which seems to have adopted the practices commonly associated with the emergence of 'transitional' justice.[89] The Secretary General's report to the UN Security Council, 'The rule of law and transitional justice in conflict and post-conflict societies', has been noted already. In 2010 the UN Secretary General issued a 'Guidance Note' entitled 'United Nations Approach to Transitional Justice'. There is a wealth of research and practitioner-focused material available online via the UN Rule of Law Coordination and Resource Group, established in 2006.[90] Moreover, if international criminal justice is an embodiment of transitional justice, then the various tribunals and, now, the International Criminal Court, that the UN has created or helped to create corroborate the conclusion that the UN is supportive of transitional justice. Likewise the UN's 2005 'Basic Principles and Guidelines on the Right to a Remedy and Reparation for Victims of Gross Violations of International Human Rights Law and Serious Violations of International Humanitarian Law'[91] do much to support the validity of policies commonly associated with transitional justice.

Despite the Council of Europe's limited engagement with the language of transitional justice, the European Court of Human Rights has had to deal with some extremely difficult issues arising from some perhaps not initially obvious incongruities between the aims of policies commonly associated with, on the one hand, transitional justice and the standards of European human rights law, on the other.

1.2.4 Transitional justice and human rights: the odd couple

Often when we think of the relationship between human rights and transitional justice we are concerned with looking at attempts to deal with the

86 Contribution of the Commissioner for Human Rights to the work of the Committee of Experts on impunity, CommDH (2009)32, 27 August 2009, [3].

87 Report of the roundtable on the situation of Human Rights Defenders in the member states of the Council of Europe, organised by the Office of the Commissioner for Human Rights (Strasbourg, 3–4 November 2008), CommDH (2009)15.

88 Thomas Hammarberg, Commissioner for Human Rights of the Council of Europe, 'Annual Activity Report 2009', CommDH (2010)8, 14 April 2010, [3.2].

89 UN, *op. cit. supra* n 69.

90 http://www.unrol.org/ (accessed 21.5.2012).

91 UN, 'Basic principles and guidelines on the right to a remedy and reparation for victims of gross violations of international human rights law and serious violations of international humanitarian law' adopted by General Assembly Resolution 60/147 of 16 December 2005 (UN Doc. A/RES/60/147).

human rights violations of the previous regime. For example, Teitel notes that, 'the most vigorous enforcement of human rights law occurs in transitional periods', citing the creation of ad hoc tribunals to prosecute human rights abusers from the Rwandan and Bosnian conflicts.[92] Likewise, David Little's work on dealing with human rights violations in transitional societies concentrates on the relationship between the opposing impulses of retribution and reconciliation in dealing with human rights offenders of the former regime.[93]

Arthur has observed that early participants in the formation of a 'field' of transitional justice saw it as a new area of human rights practice.[94] She noted that up until the mid-1980s human rights organisations were focused on 'shaming' repressive governments. When the Latin American transitions started to happen, it opened up the possibility of pursuing the distinctly transitional objective of ending impunity for members of the former regime.[95] Indeed, Arthur argued that without changing its approach, the human rights movement was in danger of losing its central *raison d'être*.[96]

The concept of human rights provides us with a motive for seeking to understand and to address the actions of repressive regimes. However, there is no 'right' to transitional justice as such. We shall see in Chapter 2 that there have been convincing arguments about the existence of an international duty to punish human rights abuses by members of prior regimes.[97] However, Chapters 3 and 4 on human rights-based claims for access to historical information and the restitution of property, respectively, maintain that attempts to gain justice for victims have been fraught with difficulty.

In this book, we shall see that the principal interaction between human rights law and transitional justice has not concerned the actions of the former regime, but of the current one. Transitional measures taken by the new Contracting Parties to the European Convention have, themselves, impacted on human rights. Thus the principal enquiry here is into allegations that transitional justice policies violate human rights, either substantively or procedurally. Recall (again) that Teitel described transitional jurisprudence as a 'nonideal conception of justice'.[98] From this perspective, it is unsurprising, therefore, that the policies giving rise to the observation of transitional justice might come into conflict with human rights law.

92 Teitel, *op. cit. supra* n 72, 228.

93 D. Little, 'A different kind of justice: dealing with human rights violations in transitional societies' (1999) 13 *Ethics and International Affairs* 65.

94 Arthur, *op. cit. supra* n 77, 324, citing José Zalaquett, a future commissioner of the Chilean National Commission on Truth and Reconciliation.

95 Ibid., 334.

96 Ibid., 335.

97 See D. Orentlicher, 'Settling accounts: the duty to prosecute human rights violations of a prior regime' (1991) 100(8) 2537.

98 Teitel, *op. cit. supra* n 72, 215.

In the course of Posner and Vermeule's argument that 'transitional' justice could be subsumed within 'ordinary' justice, they identified several 'rule of law dilemmas'.[99] The point of Posner and Vermeule's argument was not to eschew these dilemmas but to show that their existence had been overstated and thus to demonstrate that the 'transitional' policies were not presumptively suspect. The problem for international and judicial bodies such as the European Court of Human Rights is that any rule of law 'dilemma' may, in fact, give rise to an admissible complaint that a human right has been violated.

The international and judicial dimensions are important institutional factors. In addition to factors such as the separation of powers that affect *all* courts considering transitional justice, the international institutional context of European Convention law thus adds another dimension.[100]

To take just a few of the policies discussed by Teitel or included in PACE Resolution 1096, successor trials may engage the principle of non-retroactivity in criminal law guaranteed by Article 7 ECHR; restitution may engage the present occupiers' rights to peaceful enjoyment of possessions guaranteed by Article 1, Protocol 1; lustration, and the consequent loss of livelihood, may engage the right to home, family and private life in Article 8 ECHR. Outside the specific recommendations of PACE Resolution 1096, attempts to limit the political activity of people whose political views even begin to resemble those of the previous regime or threaten the territorial integrity of the new one will engage *inter alia* Articles 9, 10, 11 and 17 ECHR as well as Article 3, Protocol 1.[101]

There were early signs that the jurisprudence of the European Court would simply ignore arguments based on transition. In *Guincho v Portugal*,[102] the European Court bluntly declined to take the difficult transitional context of Portugal at the time into account when assessing the reasonableness of the length of proceedings in a civil action for damages sought in relation to a road traffic accident. The European Court stressed that, in Article 1 ECHR, Portugal had guaranteed to secure to everyone the rights in the Convention, including Article 6, and that there was an unavoidable obligation to organise its legal system in compliance with the Convention.[103]

99 Posner and Vermeule, *op. cit. supra* n 73.

100 E. Brems 'The margin of appreciation doctrine in the case-law of the European Court of Human Rights' (1996) 56 *Zeitschrift für Ausländisches öffentliches Recht und Völkerrecht* 240, 293; see also A. Buyse and M. Hamilton, 'Conclusions', in *Transitional Jurisprudence and the ECHR* (Cambridge: CUP 2011), 287; E. Brems, 'Transitional justice in the case law of the European Court of Human Rights' (2010) 5 *International Journal of Transitional Justice* 282, 285.

101 This selection of articles is more fully explained at the start of Part 2.

102 *Guincho v Portugal* (1985) 7 EHRR 223.

103 Ibid.

In this regard it is worth noting the argument that, since the European Court has already recognised that the Convention is a 'living instrument', it has a 'mandate' to reorient European human rights law to reflect the idea of transition.[104] However, evolutive interpretation of the Convention has tended in the past to result in standards being raised, rather than in the approval of context-specific rights limitations. A clear example would be the evolving standards in relation to Article 3 ECHR, where in *Selmouni v France*, the Court explained that:

> having regard to the fact that the Convention is a 'living instrument which must be interpreted in the light of present-day conditions' [. . .] the Court considers that certain acts which were classified in the past as 'inhuman and degrading treatment' as opposed to 'torture' could be classified differently in future. It takes the view that the increasingly high standard being required in the area of the protection of human rights and fundamental liberties correspondingly and inevitably requires greater firmness in assessing breaches of the fundamental values of democratic societies.[105]

Thus there is no clear basis within the Court's existing jurisprudence on the Convention as a living instrument to introduce a different, lower standard of review for states emerging from periods of democratic transition. Likewise, the margin of appreciation doctrine, which we shall see shortly has been singled out as a potential vehicle for transitional justice in Convention law, has always gone 'hand in hand' with a European supervision and, in any event, interferences with qualified Convention rights must always be necessary in a *democratic*, not a transitional, society.

There were signs that not only would the European Court be disinclined to accept transitional arguments, but also that it would be particularly strict towards the new states. For example, in his separate concurring opinion to the 1993 Plenary[106] judgment in *Brannigan and McBride v the United Kingdom*,[107] Judge Martens expressed caution about the majority's treatment of older cases on the margin of appreciation because they had been based on the assumption that the states to which the Convention applied had been democracies for a

104 M. Varju, 'Transition as a concept of European human rights law' (2009) *European Human Rights Law Review* 170, 172.

105 *Selmouni v France* (2000) 29 EHRR 403, [101].

106 Before Protocol 11, the largest formation of the European Court was known as the 'Plenary', to which under ex-Rule 51 of the Rules of Court a Chamber could, and in this case did, relinquish jurisdiction. Current Rule 72 of the Rules of Court allows a Chamber to relinquish jurisdiction to the Grand Chamber in much the same way.

107 *Brannigan and McBride v UK* (1994) 17 EHRR 539.

long time. He continued: 'Since the accession of eastern and central European States that assumption has lost its pertinence.'[108]

In the same case, the dissenting opinion of Judge Makarczyk was critical that the discretion left to the UK by the majority under Article 15 would give the wrong signals to the new Contracting Parties:

> what is considered by the old democracies as a natural state of affairs is seen as a privilege by the newcomers, which is not to be disposed of lightly. A derogation made by a new Contracting Party from Eastern and Central Europe would call into question this new legitimacy and is, in my opinion, quite improbable. Any decision of the Court concerning Article 15 should encourage and confirm this philosophy.[109]

This opinion reiterates that, at this point in time, the European Court seemed like it would be very strict indeed towards the new Contracting Parties. It is also worth noting that, improbable as it might have seemed at the time to Judge Makarczyk, two of the new Contracting Parties, Georgia and Armenia have, in fact, now attempted to make use of Article 15 ECHR. (This is discussed further in Chapter 7.)

Judge Gölcüklü dissented from the 1996 Grand Chamber majority judgment in *Loizidou v Turkey*. He explained that the Loizidou case, concerning property rights in northern Cyprus had:

> another political dimension for our Court. Its judgment will certainly have consequences for future cases – whose origins go back to the Second World War – against new members of the Council of Europe, such as the countries in central or eastern Europe previously governed by communist regimes.[110]

Again we can see some nervousness about the new Contracting Parties. This perspective is strengthened by examining another case against the UK, in which the European Court found the UK in violation of Article 10 ECHR in relation to certain restrictions on spending to promote electoral candidates. The partly dissenting opinion of Judge Valticos in *Bowman v UK* stated that there was 'something slightly ridiculous in seeking to give the British

108 Note, *inter alia*, F. Ni Aolain, 'Transitional emergency jurisprudence: derogation and transition', in A. Buyse and M. Hamilton, *Transitional Jurisprudence and the ECHR* (Cambridge: CUP 2011), 33; W. Sadurski, 'Partnering with Strasbourg: constitutionalism of the European Court of Human Rights, the accession of Central and East European states to the Council of Europe, and the idea of pilot judgments' (2009) 9(3) HRLR 397, 430 – both also point to this quotation.

109 *Brannigan and McBride v UK, op. cit. supra* n 107, Dissenting Opinion of Judge Makarczyk, [1].

110 *Loizidou v Turkey* (1997) 23 EHRR 513, Dissenting Opinion of Judge Gölcüklü.

Government lessons in how to hold elections and run a democracy.'[111] Likewise, the partly dissenting opinion of Judge Sir John Freeland, joined by Judge Levits advocated:

> [A] cautious approach to be adopted in adjudicating internationally on rules prescribed by long-established democratic parliaments on matters so intimately involved with their own composition and operation.[112]

These disparate comments combine to present a picture of a European Court that would be particularly unreceptive to argument for deference based on transitional justice. Nevertheless, there *were* concerns about the European Court's ability to uphold the universality of human rights in the enlarged Council of Europe and the next section shows how concerns about a threat of cultural relativism can be recast as concerns about 'transitional relativism'.

1.3 The universality of human rights and transitional relativism

In the immediate aftermath of the end of the Cold War, and as the new states joined the Convention system, concerns about the implications for the universality of human rights far outweighed concerns about impediments to the achievement of transitional justice. Likewise, it was not contemplated that the achievement of transitional justice might be in conflict with human rights norms. Nevertheless, this section shows that the issues of universality and transitional justice are closely connected, such that the incorporation of explicitly transitional exceptions to human rights norms might undermine the universality of human rights via the recognition of a form of 'transitional relativism'.

1.3.1 The universality debate

The universality of human rights is founded on the understanding that if all humans are equal, then the rights that they hold as a result of being human are the same regardless of the culture or democratic credentials of the state into which the individual happens to be born.[113] This is the fundamental justification for the ideals expressed internationally in the work of the United Nations and also regionally by the Council of Europe.

Cultural relativists have argued that the concept of human rights is a western liberal idea and has no (or a different) value outside the western

111 *Bowman v UK* (1998) 26 EHHR 1 Bowman, Partly Dissenting Opinion of Judge Valticos.

112 *Bowman v UK*, Partly Dissenting Opinion of Judge Freeland, joined by Judge Levits, [12].

113 For an introduction to this justification for human rights, and to alternative justifications, see J. Shestack, 'The philosophical foundations of human rights', in J. Symonides (ed.), *Human Rights: concepts and standards* (Aldershot: Ashgate 2000).

context. They contend that universalists fail to understand their own enculturation and the resulting unconscious bias of their position. Any system of social justice grounded in a given culture is a defence of the 'good life' as conceptualised by that system, regardless of its substantive content. The values promoted by the system are *relative* only to the society from which they are derived and are incapable of universality. It is unjustifiable to impose on one society a system of social justice deriving from another. The imposed system would be culturally alien and adherence to it could not be guaranteed.[114]

Even from within a human rights system the extent to which a relativist position is adopted can pose problems for the protection of human rights. The difficulty is that wherever there is a plurality of possible meanings for a given human right, then without the philosophical means to make value judgments about the desirability of different meanings or approaches, the relativist is compelled to tolerate any permutation of the right in question.[115] The relativist is incapable of moral criticism because each differing morality is equally valid. Thus, in the name of respect for local culture, the international observer of human rights abuses is robbed of their critical faculties. However, a careful examination of relativism's theoretical foundations exposes significant logical problems with its arguments.

First, as a prescriptive theory, cultural relativism contradicts itself. As Fernando Teson has written: '[I]f it is true that no universal moral principles exist, then the relativist engages in self-contradiction by stating the universality of the relativist principle.'[116] Similarly, Alison Dundes Renteln argued that relativism[117] is susceptible to the charge of self-refutation because 'it asserts the absolute prescription that all prescriptions are relative.'[118] Moreover, in spite of their purposed opposition to universal values, relativists reserve for themselves at least one universal value – that we should follow, and be defined by, our own culture. The conservative tendencies of such a position notwithstanding, it serves to demonstrate that the relativists have not explained the foundation of their argument.

The second main theoretical problem with relativism can be described as the 'tolerance trap'. If it is conceded that there is no universal meaning to

114 A. An-Na'im, 'Human rights in the Muslim world' (1990) 3 *Harvard Human Rights Journal* 13. This perspective informs An-Na'im's efforts to demonstrate that human rights values are, in fact, not alien to Islam. And vice versa.

115 This type of relativism is what Teson has referred to as 'metaethical relativism': F. Teson, 'International human rights and cultural relativism' (1985) 25 *Virginia Journal of International Law* 869, 886. Note, however, that Alison Renteln has argued that the premise of this type of relativism (labelled by her as 'ethical relativism as descriptive (factual) hypothesis') does not actually imply tolerance. (A. Renteln, *International Human Rights – universalism versus relativism* (New York: Sage Publications 1990).

116 Teson, *op. cit. supra* n 115, 888.

117 By relativism, Renteln was referring to the particular strand she described as 'ethical relativism as prescriptive (value) hypothesis'.

118 Renteln, *op. cit. supra* n 115, 72.

'human rights', the existence in relative harmony of the varying conceptions of 'human rights' necessitates their tolerance. Indeed, this is the core argument of the relativists. Thus we should tolerate and respect the choices made by unfamiliar systems of social justice because they promote what is valued by that particular society. The logical problem here is that relativism seeks to derive an 'ought' from an 'is' in violation of the Humean dichotomy between normative and descriptive propositions.[119] The observation that cultural values vary from society to society, and that therefore what is held worthy of protection also varies, is a description of a factual situation. The 'call for tolerance'[120] is, by way of contrast, a normative judgment about what ought to be. A normative proposition such as 'we ought to tolerate diverse cultures' cannot be inferred from a purely factual statement such as 'there are diverse cultures.'

There are considerable complications to both arguments, but for the purposes of this brief introduction to the universality debate it is sufficient to recognise that the philosophical pedigree of cultural relativism is at least questionable.[121] Of more immediate importance is the way in which, in spite of its logical weaknesses, the rhetoric of cultural relativism has been hijacked by political elites in order to repress their own population.[122] In this way, culture may sometimes be motivated as a state's untouchable 'trump card' reason for failing to comply (fully) with human rights standards. Less controversially, relativism tends to be equated with a conservative view of public international law that affords greater respect to state sovereignty (which is to some extent challenged by international human rights law).

If the European Court of Human Rights were to recognise that transitional states needed more leeway from a human rights perspective, in order to pursue transitional policies, then the people in those states might defensibly complain that the European Court was failing in its commitment to universality or sliding into the quagmire not of *cultural* but, rather, of *transitional* relativism. Indeed, as the next section shows, even before enlargement of the Council of Europe the European Court was already under pressure concerning its commitment to universality.

1.3.2 The universality debate at the ECHR: the margin of appreciation

The European Court allows states a certain discretion to 'do things their own way' from time to time, by recognising that they have a 'margin of

119 E. Hatch, *Culture and Morality* (New York: Columbia University Press 1983) 67.

120 Ibid.

121 J. Tilley, 'Cultural relativism' 22 *Human Rights Quarterly* (2000) 501 contains a particularly incisive critique of cultural relativism.

122 J. Donnelly, *Universal Human Rights in Theory and Practice* (New York: Cornell University Press 1989) 119; R. Higgins, *Problems and Processes in International Law* (Oxford: OUP 1994) 96.

appreciation'.[123] The way that the European Court leaves a 'margin of appreciation' to states has been singled out as the means by which relativism might find its way into the Convention jurisprudence.

This 'margin of appreciation' can be distinguished from the general discretion left by the Convention to states in how to implement detailed human rights protection in their domestic law.[124] The idea of a margin of appreciation is used in the Court's reasoning to measure and monitor states' discretion to interfere with or otherwise limit human rights in specific instances. In essence, it expresses that Contracting Parties have some space in which they can balance for themselves conflicting public goods. It is therefore closely connected to the principle of subsidiarity.

The principle of subsidiarity in the European Convention results from the division of power between national and international institutions.[125] Subsidiarity is evidenced by the relationship between four key articles of the Convention.[126] The principal obligation in the European Convention, in Article 1 ECHR, is for the Contracting Parties themselves 'to secure to everyone within their jurisdiction the rights and freedoms in the Convention'. In Article 13, this is coupled with the requirement to provide an effective remedy in domestic law for violations of those rights. Under Article 35, the European Court can only deal with complaints after all domestic remedies have been exhausted. Finally, Article 53 implies that Contracting Parties can protect rights to a higher degree than the Convention (because it states that nothing in the Convention should be construed as limiting human rights already protected in domestic law).

The practice of recognising and respecting states' margin of appreciation is a judicial reflection of subsidiarity: it is derived from the case law of the Court

123 See generally, H. Yourow, *The Margin of Appreciation Doctrine in the Dynamics of European Human Rights Jurisprudence* (The Hague: Kluwer 1996); G. Letsas, *A Theory of Interpretation of the European Court of Human Rights* (Oxford: OUP 2007); Y. Arai-Takahashi, *The Margin of Appreciation Doctrine and the Principle of Proportionality in the Jurisprudence of the ECHR* (Oxford: Intersentia 2002); E. Brems, 'The margin of appreciation doctrine in the case-law of the European Court of Human Rights' (1996) 56 *Zeitschrift für Ausländisches öffentliches Recht und Völkerrecht* 240; M. Hutchinson, 'The margin of appreciation doctrine in the European Court of Human Rights' (1999) 48 *ICLQ* 638; T. Jones, 'The devaluation of human rights under the European Convention' (1995) *Public Law* 430; P. Mahoney, 'Marvellous richness of diversity or invidious cultural relativism' (1998) 19(1) *Human Rights Law Journal* 1; J. Schokkenbroek, 'The basis, nature and application of the margin of appreciation doctrine in the case law of the European Court of Human Rights' (1998) 19(1) *Human Rights Law Journal* 30; J.A. Sweeney, 'A "margin of appreciation" in the internal market: lessons from the European Court of Human Rights' (2007) 34(1) *Legal Issues of Economic Integration* 27.

124 As required by Art. 1 ECHR.

125 See generally, G. Carozza, 'Subsidiarity as a structural principle of international human rights law' (2003) 97 *AJIL* 38; c.f. P. Mahoney, *op. cit. supra* n 123.

126 See H. Petzold, 'The Convention and the principle of subsidiarity', in R. Macdonald, F. Matscher and H. Petzold (eds), *The European System for the Protection of Human Rights* (Dordrecht: Martinus Nijhof 1993), 49–59.

and Commission, not from the text of the Convention itself. Its relevance can be raised by the Court on its own initiative, or by the Contracting Parties themselves, by way of a 'defence' to the allegation that they have violated a Convention right.

The margin of appreciation doctrine's implications for universality can be seen as far back as the well-known 1976 case of *Handyside*.[127] The European Court was called on to discuss to what extent free expression could be limited in order to protect morals. The Court stated that:

> It is not possible to find in the domestic law of the various Contracting States a uniform European conception of morals. The view taken by their respective laws of the requirements of morals *varies from time to time and from place to place* which is characterised by a rapid and far-reaching evolution of opinions on the subject. [. . .] Consequently, Article 10 para. 2 leaves to the Contracting States a margin of appreciation.[128]
>
> [emphasis added]

The Court thus appeared to recognise some form of inter-temporal, European, moral diversity. Such comments have provoked hostile reactions to the continued recognition of a national margin of appreciation. For example, Lord Lester has expressed his deep concern in the following terms:

> The danger of continuing to use the standardless doctrine of the margin of appreciation is that, especially in the enlarged Council of Europe, it will become the source of a pernicious 'variable' geometry of human rights, eroding the acquis of existing jurisprudence and giving undue deference to local conditions, traditions, and practices.[129]

Lord Lester's concerns are not isolated. Eyal Benvenisti has added that:

> The juridical output of the [European Court of Human Rights] and other international bodies carries the promise of setting universal standards for the protection and promotion of human rights. These universal aspirations are, to a large extent, compromised by the doctrine of the margin of appreciation. [. . .] Margin of appreciation, with its principled recognition of moral relativism is at odds with the concept of the universality of human rights.[130]

127 *Handyside v UK* (1976) 1 EHRR 737.

128 Ibid., [48].

129 A. Lester, 'Universality versus subsidiarity: a reply' (1998) 1 *European Human Rights Law Review* 73, 76.

130 E. Benvenisti, 'Margin of appreciation, consensus and universal standards' (1999) 31 *International Law and Politics* 843, 844.

Criticism of the margin of appreciation is not confined to commentators. Judge De Meyer, in his partly dissenting opinion in the case of *Z v Finland*, was particularly critical of the doctrine:

> In the present judgment the Court once again relies on the national authorities' 'margin of appreciation'. I believe that it is high time for the Court to banish that concept from its reasoning. It has already delayed too long in abandoning this hackneyed phrase and recanting the relativism it implies.[131]

Crucially, these concerns have been amplified by the expansion of the Council of Europe. For example, in 1999 Paul Mahoney asked:

> Will the ECHR standards be diluted, not just to accommodate the problems of the fledgling democracies [of central and eastern Europe], but generally, across the board for the whole of the ECHR community? Will the principles painstakingly built up over the years in the jurisprudence of the Commission and Court be left by the wayside?[132]

Likewise Lord Lester's suspicion of the margin of appreciation concept was:

> increased by the fact that the Court's territorial jurisdiction is being rapidly widened to cover the inhabitants of some forty European countries of diverse political cultural backgrounds and traditions.[133]

The concerns about the margin of appreciation doctrine were strengthened by the Council of Europe's enlargement, but were not exclusive to it. The concerns were principally about variation between the existing, apparently democratic, Contracting Parties. This is significant for the discussion that follows, since it would suggest difficulties in recognising differences not only between the old and new Contracting Parties, but between the very different situations of the various new Contracting Parties themselves.

The view of the European Court's Grand Chamber in the 2004 case of *Broniowski v Poland* would seem to confirm the critics' fears about the uses to which the margin of appreciation would be put in the enlarged Council of Europe. The substantive findings in this case are discussed in Chapter 4, but it is the reasoning that is important here. Not for the first time the European

131 *Z v Finland* 25 EHRR 371, Partly Dissenting Opinion of Judge De Meyer. Judge De Meyer made similar comments in the footnote to his separate concurring opinion in *Ahmed & Others v UK* Reports 1998-VI (2000) 29 EHRR 1.

132 P. Mahoney, 'Speculating on the future of the reformed European Court of Human Rights' (1999) 20 *Human Rights Law Journal* 1, 3.

133 Lester, *op. cit. supra* n 129, 74.

Court explained that notion of the 'public interest' as a basis for interfering with the right to peaceful enjoyment of possessions in Article 1, Protocol 1, was, 'necessarily extensive'.[134] The Court found it 'natural' that the margin of appreciation available to domestic legislatures in implementing social and economic policies should be a wide one. It continued:

> This logic applies to such fundamental changes of a country's system as the transition from a totalitarian regime to a democratic form of government and the reform of the State's political, legal and economic structure, phenomena which inevitably involve the enactment of large-scale economic and social legislation.[135]

At this point, the existence of a relationship between transition, universality and the margin of appreciation becomes crystal clear. If the *Handyside* judgment gave rise to concerns about moral or cultural relativism, then surely *Broniowski* does the same for transitional relativism.

1.3.3 Transitional justice and universality

It is notable that prior to and during the enlargement of the Council of Europe commentators and judges alike identified threats to the universality of human rights. The margin of appreciation doctrine was singled out as the most likely factor to lead to the crystallisation of those threats. The quotation from *Broniowski* confirms that, in reality, it was more transitional relativism than cultural relativism that would impact on the universality of human rights.

This conclusion would seem to be supported by the quotation from *Ždanoka v Latvia* given in the Introduction, where it was noted that the European Court held a measure that might be justifiable in Latvia that 'may scarcely be considered acceptable in the context of [another] political system, for example in a country which has an established framework of democratic institutions going back many decades or centuries'.[136] This would seem to be an admission both of transitional relativism and that the European Court was content to dispense 'nonideal' justice, in the sense of how Teitel described transitional jurisprudence.[137]

Indeed, if we think about the various transitional policies recommended, for example, in PACE Resolution 1096, it becomes clear that it is not only in relation to rights in which a margin of appreciation is commonly recognised that the European Court might be asked to show some lenience to transitional states. There have been several admissible cases on the application of Article 7 ECHR,

134 *Broniowski v Poland*, (2006) 43 EHRR 1, [149].
135 Ibid., [149].
136 *Ždanoka v Latvia* (GC) [2006] ECHR 231, [133].
137 That is, in the sense that Teitel used this phrase *op. cit. supra* n 72, 215.

on retroactive criminal law, to successor trials. On the one hand, if the European Court were radically to alter its findings or reasoning in transitional cases, it would undoubtedly impact on the universality of human rights. If, on the other hand, it did not, it could be accused, at best, of being out of touch with current thinking on transitional justice or, at worst, of ignoring the 'perverse situations in which the enforcement of human rights could be the trigger for war rather than the conveyor of peace'.[138] The Court is in a double bind.

It important to concede at this point that the presentation of cultural relativism above was a little one-sided. In fact, many people, this author included, have argued that it is not only possible but, indeed, desirable to reconcile the legal protection of international human rights with more local values.[139] A parallel argument can be made in relation to transitional justice: that a way can be found to reconcile the pursuit of transitional justice with adherence to universal human rights norms.

There is a small (but growing) literature on transitional justice and universality. Lieselotte Viaene and Eva Brems have drawn lessons from the universality debate to discuss resistance to transitional justice policies on cultural grounds, particularly in the light of the arguable emergence of an international law of transitional justice.[140] The importance of this research is corroborated by Barbara Oomen's advocacy of a local perspective in transitional justice activities.[141]

This is potentially problematic because the comments critical of the margin of appreciation doctrine (noted earlier) demonstrate that many see human rights as having universalising tendencies, whereas it seems that transitional justice is most successful when it tends towards the particular.[142] This observation suggests not only that the European Court may face difficult decisions about distinguishing between democratic and transitional states, but also between different transitions.

In what follows, it is argued that some of the critical thinking employed to understand the perceived threat to the universality of human rights from cultural relativism (which we saw *was* identified as an issue during enlargement

138 Dissenting Opinion of Judge Bonello in *Sejdi and Finci v Bosnia and Herzegovina* [2009] ECHR 2122. This case is discussed in detail in Chapter 8.

139 J.A. Sweeney, 'Margins of appreciation: cultural relativity and the European Court of Human Rights' (2005) 54 *International and Comparative Law Quarterly* 459; see also the discussion in Brems *op. cit. supra* n 100, 204.

140 L. Viaene and E. Brems, 'Transitional justice and cultural contexts: learning from the universality debate' (2010) 28(2) *Netherlands Quarterly of Human Rights* 199.

141 B. Oomen, 'Transitional justice and its legitimacy: the case for a local perspective' (2007) 25(1) *Netherlands Quarterly of Human Rights* 141.

142 Oomen, ibid.; J. Ramji-Nogales, 'Designing bespoke transitional justice: a pluralist process approach' (2010) 32 *Michigan Journal of International Law* 1; L. Viaene and E. Brems, 'Transitional justice and cultural contexts: learning from the universality debate' (2011) 28(2) *Netherlands Quarterly of Human Rights* 199, 220 *et seq.*; note also the comments of the UN Secretary General *op. cit. supra* n 69, 4.

of the Council of Europe) is an untapped source that can help to understand the approach of the European Court of Human Rights to the questions of transitional justice that have arisen before it. While Viaene and Brems drew on this literature to understand cultural opposition to transitional justice, this book draws on it to examine human rights-based opposition to transitional justice.

1.4 Conclusion

In Chapter 1, we have examined the creation and enlargement of the Council of Europe, noting the institutional pressures under which it has been put. We saw that, although the Council of Europe has had little explicit engagement with the notion of transitional justice, it is certainly involved in activities commonly associated with it. Most importantly, we have seen that where the European Court of Human Rights is compelled to engage with states' transitional policies or priorities there are potential implications for the universality of human rights. In particular, the European Court is subject to two competing impulses: maintaining the universality of human rights or facilitating transition by conceding a level of transitional relativism. There is growing recognition of the need to examine how the European Court has coped with all this.[143]

The next stage is to establish exactly what an enquiry into transitional justice in the jurisprudence of the European Court might resemble. First and foremost, it is obviously necessary to examine the European Court's interactions with key transitional justice policies. Thus, following the typology presented by PACE Resolution 1096, in Chapters 2, 3, 4 and 5, we shall examine cases about successor trials (and other forms of transitional criminal justice), openness, restitution and lustration respectively. These map on to Ruti Teitel's categories of transitional criminal justice, historical justice, reparatory justice and administrative justice (the concepts are discussed in more detail in each chapter).[144]

However, a mere analysis of these cases would fail to capture the *Ždanoka v Latvia* case mentioned earlier and in the Introduction, which concerned restrictions on electoral rights – clearly of great democratic significance. And we noted earlier that membership of the Council of Europe is meant to be predicated on an ability and willingness to uphold democratic values. Likewise, for Ruti Teitel, a key marker of transitional constitutional[145] and administrative justice[146] is the notion of self-defending (or militant) democracy, on which the reasoning in *Ždanoka* and other cases has been based.[147]

143 See, for example, A. Buyse and M. Hamilton, *Transitional Jurisprudence and the ECHR* (Cambridge: CUP 2011), to which this author contributed; Brems, *op. cit. supra* n 100.
144 Teitel, *op. cit. supra* n 72.
145 Ibid., 203.
146 Ibid., 177.
147 See *Ždanoka v Latvia* (GC), *op. cit. supra* n 136, [100].

Thus, in Chapters 6, 7 and 8, we shall move from examining particular transitional justice *policies* to examining particular democratic *rights* in the transitional context, namely the rights to free expression, freedom of peaceful assembly, freedom of association, freedom of thought, conscience and religion and the right to free elections.[148] Each of these chapters is subdivided between an analysis of those cases in which the Respondent State cited the transitional context as a justification for a rights-restrictive measure or action and those in which it is possible to discern systemic democratic problems or 'echoes' of totalitarianism.

It is readily conceded that this latter distinction is not watertight, since it is clear that some of the high-profile cases in which states have put great weight on the transitional context raise deeply troubling systemic concerns. Likewise, judges in particular cases have disagreed as to whether the case concerned defective legislation or the defective application of sound legislation.[149] Thus the subdivision in these chapters is not meant to replicate the debate on 'individual' or 'constitutional' justice.

The goal is therefore to taxonomise, to record and to analyse the European Court's jurisprudence on transitional justice. In doing so, we shall be alert not only to what this tells us about the states' transitional policies, but also about whether the European Court itself has delivered a form of 'transitional' justice: whether and to what extent it has conceded a level of transitional relativism. As suggested already, the latter is particularly significant because of the implications for the universality of human rights.

148 The choice of articles is explained more fully in the introduction to Part 2.

149 See the Concurring Opinion of Judge Malinverni, joined by Judges Vaji and Kovler in *Seyidzade v Azerbaijan* [2009] ECHR 1983 (discussed further in Chapter 8).

Part II

Cases

Section A

The ECHR and transitional policies

A.1 Introduction

We shall see that human rights law has interacted with transitional justice policies, such as those explained by PACE Resolution 1096, in two main ways: where applications have been brought by victims of former regimes seeking a measure of justice (for example, through reparation or access to information for the facilitation of historical justice) and where applications have been brought by people who allege that the transitional policy *itself* violates their human rights. The latter situation is the principal focus of this inquiry, since it leads to Respondent States citing the transitional context as a justification for *prima facie* rights restrictive measures. It is the European Court's response to such arguments that will be the focus of most of our attention in what is to follow, since it amounts to a claim of transitional relativism. Nevertheless it is important to note a third category from the outset: cases in which the European Court has supervised (and frequently criticised) the procedural guarantees *within* transitional policies, without necessarily finding that the policy aim as a whole is incompatible with the Convention. Thus in relation to restitution and lustration policies, in particular, we shall examine procedural justice in detail.

2 Transitional criminal justice

Prosecution and amnesty

2.1 Introduction

Choices about criminal justice in transitional periods have the potential both to affect the construction of the new democratic society and to address past wrongs.[1] At its starkest, transitional criminal justice is manifested by one of two distinctive policy approaches, both of which have profound implications for the rule of law and adherence to international human rights standards: using criminal law to punish members of the previous regime through 'successor trials' or, by contrast, granting an amnesty to them in the name of peace.[2] Human rights law both supports and restrains transitional criminal justice policies.

It supports them by providing a motive and even a legal obligation to prosecute those who violated human rights in the prior regime. Orentlicher's classic work argued that there is an international legal duty to prosecute violations of the previous regime.[3] The UN's 'Basic Principles and Guidelines on the Right to a Remedy and Reparation for Victims of Gross Violations of International Human Rights Law and Serious Violations of International Humanitarian Law' recognise, *inter alia*, that states have a duty to investigate and, where there is sufficient evidence, to prosecute people responsible for human rights abuses.[4]

However, international human rights law restrains transitional criminal justice by potentially closing off certain policy choices, such as amnesties, and

1 R. Teitel, *Transitional justice* (New York: OUP 2000), 67.

2 Ibid., 72.

3 D. Orentlicher, 'Settling accounts: the duty to prosecute human rights violations of a prior regime' (1991) 100(8) *Yale Law Journal* 2537; see also D. Orentlicher, '"Settling accounts" revisited: reconciling global norms with local agency' (2007) 1(1) *International Journal of Transitional Justice* 10.

4 UN, 'Basic Principles and Guidelines on the Right to a Remedy and Reparation for Victims of Gross Violations of International Human Rights Law and Serious Violations of International Humanitarian Law' adopted by General Assembly Resolution 60/147 of 16 December 2005 (UN Doc. A/RES/60/147), [4].

by ensuring that prosecutions do not entail the retroactive application of criminal law.

The regional human rights system of the Organisation of American States has explicitly examined the relationship between domestic amnesties and international human rights law.[5] Both the Inter-American Commission and Inter-American Court have made detailed contributions in this regard.[6] Beginning in a series of cases reported together in 1992, *Alicia Consuelo Herrera et al v Argentina*,[7] the Inter-American Commission established that amnesty laws may violate the right to a fair trial, the right to judicial protection and the positive obligations to prevent, investigate and punish violations of the right to life. This reasoning has been followed in case reports involving the amnesty laws of Uruguay, El Salvador and Chile.

The Inter-American Court of Human Rights explicitly reaffirmed the position of the Commission in its 2001 judgment in the *Barrios Altos* case. It stated that:

> all amnesty provisions, provisions on prescription and the establishment of measures designed to eliminate responsibility are inadmissible, because they are intended to prevent the investigation and punishment of those responsible for serious human rights violations such as torture, extrajudicial, summary or arbitrary execution and forced disappearance, all of them prohibited because they violate non-derogable rights recognized by international human rights law.[8]

Like the Commission, it went on to find violations of, *inter alia*, the right to a fair trial, the right to judicial protection and the positive obligations emanating from the right to life.

There are several examples of amnesties in Europe relating to the close of World War II, the southern European transitions of the 1970s and the post-Cold War era,[9] but they have not been examined in detail in the jurisprudence of the European Court of Human Rights.

5 See, generally, J.S. Davidson, *The Inter-American Human Rights System* (Aldershot: Dartmouth Publishing Company Co Ltd 1997); D.J. Harris and S. Livingstone (eds), *The Inter-American System of Human Rights* (Oxford: Clarendon 1998); J.M. Pasqualucci, *The Practice and Procedure of the Inter-American Court of Human Rights* (Cambridge: CUP 2003).

6 See, generally, D. Rodriguez-Pinzon, 'The Inter-American system and transitional processes', in M. Hamilton and A. Buyse (eds), *Transitional Jurisprudence and the ECHR: justice, politics, and rights* (Cambridge: CUP 2010).

7 *Alicia Consuelo Herrera et al. v Argentina*, Report No. 28/29, Cases 10.147, 10.181, 10.240, 10.262, 10.309 and 10.311, Annual Report of the Inter-American Commission 1992–1993.

8 *Chumbipuma Aguirre et al v Peru* (2001) Series C No. 75, [41].

9 See the Amnesty Law Database of the 'Beyond Legalism' project at Queen's University Belfast, available at: http://www.law.qub.ac.uk/schools/SchoolofLaw/Research/InstituteofCriminologyandCriminalJustice/Research/BeyondLegalism/AmnestyLawDatabase/ (accessed 10.8.2010); see also L. Mallinder, *Amnesty, Human Rights and Political Transitions* (Oxford: Hart 2008).

A rare example of a direct challenge to an amnesty law can be seen in the 1991 admissibility decision in *Dujardin v France*, which concerned moves towards self-determination of the southwest Pacific islands of New Caledonia (which were a *sui generis* collectivity of France). In its decision, the European Commission was surprisingly receptive to a French general amnesty law. The applicants were the relatives of four gendarmes killed in 1988, the circumstances of whose deaths were covered by the amnesty. The applicants complained on the basis of Articles 2 and 6 ECHR. The Commission observed that the impugned amnesty law was 'entirely exceptional in character' and 'was adopted in the context of a process designed to resolve conflicts between the various communities of the islands'.[10] It continued:

> It is not for the Commission to assess the advisability of the measures taken by France to that end. The State is justified in adopting, in the context of its criminal policy, any amnesty laws it might consider necessary, with the proviso, however, that a balance is maintained between the legitimate interests of the State and the interests of individual members of the public in having the right to life protected by law.[11]

It found that the balance was, in this case, maintained. This is a rather different approach to that which was being developed contemporaneously within the Inter-American system. It more readily accepts that there might be a defensible level of transitional relativism.

The European Court of Human Rights has more recently allied itself to the Inter-American and developing international orthodoxy in the admissibility decision in *Ould Dah v France*.[12] The applicant, a Mauritanian army officer, complained that his conviction for acts of torture committed in Mauritania violated Article 7 ECHR. He asserted that the French courts should have applied Mauritian law to his case, specifically a 1993 amnesty law, rather than French law. The discussion focused on the conditions in French law for the assertion of universal jurisdiction in relation to torture. The European Court disagreed with the applicant, observing that to allow reliance on the Mauritanian Amnesty Law would have deprived the substance of the universal jurisdiction provided for by the United Nations Torture Convention of 1984. It went on to state that: 'Like the United Nations Human Rights Committee and the ICTY, it considers that amnesties are generally incompatible with the duty of States to investigate such acts.'[13]

Without the benefit of the amnesty, the European Court found that the applicant's actions constituted offences defined with sufficient accessibility and

10 *Dujardin and Others v France* (dec.) App no 16734/90 (ECommHR, 2 September 1991), D.R. No. 72, 236, 244.

11 Ibid.

12 *Ould Dah v France* (dec.) App no 13113/03 (ECtHR, 17 March 2009).

13 Ibid. (author's translation of text).

foreseeability by French law and international law. The applicant could therefore have predicted the risk of being prosecuted and convicted for the acts of torture he committed between 1990 and 1991 and his application to the European Court was manifestly ill founded. Interestingly, the Court added that:

> in general, we cannot exclude the possibility of a conflict between on the one hand, the need to prosecute crimes committed and, secondly, the desire for reconciliation of the social body of a country.

This is a clear recognition that international human rights law may present a barrier to the pursuit of reconciliation via the use of amnesties. The European Court has reiterated this position in *Association 21 December 1989 & Others v Romania*.[14]

With all this in mind, it is perhaps no surprise that we saw in Chapter 1 how the Council of Europe's Commissioner for Human Rights, Thomas Hammarberg, observed in 2009 that transitional measures in central and eastern Europe have focused almost exclusively on criminal prosecutions for war crimes.[15] These prosecutions have generated significant human rights jurisprudence, with the applicants attempting to forestall their prosecution by reference to Article 7 ECHR on the non-retroactivity of criminal law. The remainder of this chapter will focus on such prosecutions – sometimes referred to as successor trials.

2.2 Successor trials and retroactivity

Successor trials have a complex relationship with international human rights law because the conduct of the individual on trial is subjected to a set of standards that is applied with some degree of hindsight and is, therefore, potentially tainted with retroactivity – which runs counter to intuitions founded on the rule of law. Human rights law, including Article 7 ECHR, also generally prohibits retroactive criminal prosecutions and could therefore inhibit the implementation of this transitional policy. The new democratic regime must attempt to sidestep or eliminate the rule of law dilemma that retroactivity presents through the deployment of legal techniques of varying degrees of ingenuity.[16]

Chief among these is the appeal to a higher pre-existing law,[17] such as international humanitarian law, which can 'mediate' the rule of law dilemma.[18] The standards of international law can be presented as settled and thus allow a

14 *Association 21 December 1989 & Others v Romania*, App nos 33810/07 and 18817/08 (ECtHR, 24 May 2011), [144].

15 Contribution of the Commissioner for Human Rights to the work of the Committee of Experts on impunity, CommDH (2009) 32, 27 August 2009, [3].

16 E. Posner and A. Vermeule, 'Transitional justice as ordinary justice' (2004) 117 *Harvard Law Review* 761, 792.

17 Ibid., 793.

18 Teitel, *op. cit. supra* n 1, 21.

prosecution based on them to avoid the charge of retroactivity. Most of the European cases discussed later originated in prosecutions that had taken this approach. Other options include strictly applying the law of prior totalitarian regime under which certain actions carried out by that regime should have been criminal at the time. This was the approach taken in the Berlin Wall cases discussed in the next section. Taking nominal, but formally applicable, domestic law seriously may help to resist the accusation that victors' justice is being imposed.[19] However, critics would argue that in employing this or any of the other legal techniques, successor regimes are merely using subterfuge to disguise the retroactivity of the punitive legislation.[20] In response, Posner and Vermeule have provided examples to show that similar techniques for balancing retroactivity and justice exist in many legal systems and they argue that the accusation of subterfuge mistakenly holds transitional states up to standards that would be unrealistic in well-established democracies.[21]

The Council of Europe is certainly conscious of the potential for retroactivity. In PACE Resolution 1096, the Parliamentary Assembly gave the following advice:

> The Assembly also recommends that criminal acts committed by individuals during the communist totalitarian regime be prosecuted and punished under the standard criminal code. If the criminal code provides for a statute of limitations for some crimes, this can be extended, since it is only a procedural, not a substantive matter. Passing and applying retroactive criminal laws is, however, not permitted. On the other hand, the trial and punishment of any person for any act or omission which at the time when it was committed did not constitute a criminal offence according to national law, but which was considered criminal according to the general principles of law recognised by civilised nations, is permitted. Moreover, where a person clearly acted in violation of human rights, the claim of having acted under orders excludes neither illegality nor individual guilt.

This advice is based on the text of Article 7 ECHR and the jurisprudence emanating from it.[22] The guidance from the Council of Europe is far less

19 G. Bruce, 'East Germany', in L. Stan (ed.), *Transitional Justice in Eastern Europe and the Former Soviet Union* (Abingdon: Routledge 2009), 25.

20 J. Elster, *Closing the Books: transitional justice in historical perspective* (Cambridge: CUP 2004), 83.

21 E. Posner and A. Vermeule, *op. cit. supra* n 16, 797.

22 In the sense that it purported to draw a distinction between procedural and substantive retroactivity. This distinction is not to be found in the Charter of the International Military Tribunal (Nuremberg Tribunal), annexed to the London Agreement of 8 August 1945 (United Nations, Treaty Series, vol. 82) or the UN Convention on the Non-Applicability of Statutory Limitations to War Crimes and Crimes against Humanity (United Nations, Treaty Series, vol. 754).

detailed than the advice on prosecution initiatives provided in 2006 by the Office of the UN High Commissioner for Human Rights as part of its series of 'Rule-of-Law Tools for Post-Conflict States'.[23]

Article 7(1) ECHR itself contains two main principles: first, that, 'no one should be held guilty of any criminal offence on account of any act or omission which did not constitute a criminal offence under national or international law at the time when it was committed'; and, second, that no heavier penalty shall be imposed than the one that was applicable at the time a criminal offence was committed. The omission of the second element of Article 7 from Resolution 1096 is regrettable. Further, Article 7(2) states that the two core principles 'shall not prejudice the trial and punishment of any person for any act or omission which, at the time when it was committed, was criminal according to the general principles of law recognised by civilised nations'.

The potential for Article 7 to impact on successor trials led Portugal to make a reservation when it ratified the European Convention in 1978.[24] The reservation states that Article 7 will be applied subject to Portuguese constitutional law stipulating the penalties applicable to officers, officials and associates of the General Directorate of Security (and its forerunner the International and State Defence Police (PIDE)) and giving military courts jurisdiction in such cases. The PIDE was the Portuguese secret police and was responsible for many instances of repression during the Estado Novo authoritarian regime.[25] The recommendation in PACE Resolution 1096, that successor trials should be conducted under the 'standard criminal code', can be taken as implicit criticism of the use of military courts for successor trials such as in the Portuguese transition.

Both Resolution 1096 and Article 7 ECHR explicitly deny that prosecutions rooted in an appeal to international standards extant at the material time constitute retroactivity. In its transitional jurisprudence on Article 7, the European Court has thus been called on to pronounce on the content and historical development of international law, international humanitarian law and international criminal law. The European Court has a mixed reputation in this regard. For example, its approach to the legal classification of rape as torture in *Aydin v Turkey*[26] has been described as 'progressive'[27] and has led to

23 Office of the UN High Commissioner for Human Rights, *Rule-of-Law Tools for Post-Conflict States: prosecution initiatives* (Geneva: United Nations 2006) (HR/PUB/06/4).

24 List of Declarations with Respect to Treaty No. 005 – Convention for the Protection of Human Rights and Fundamental Freedoms, available at: http://conventions.coe.int/Treaty/Commun/ListeDeclarations.asp?NT=005&CM=8&DF=&CL=ENG&VL=1 (accessed 4.8.2010).

25 T. Gallagher, *Portugal: a twentieth century interpretation* (Manchester: Manchester University Press 1983), 117 *et seq.*

26 *Aydin v Turkey* (1998) 25 EHRR 251.

27 C. McGlynn, 'Rape, torture and the European Convention on Human Rights' (2009) 58(3) *ICLQ*, 565–95.

important developments in the jurisprudence of both the International Criminal Tribunal for Rwanda[28] and the International Criminal Tribunal for the former Yugoslavia.[29] By contrast, the European Court's approach to state responsibility in *Behrami v France*[30] has been subject to more criticism.[31] In *Behrami*, the European Court found that it did not have jurisdiction to hear a case brought against France, one of the states involved in the multinational administration of Kosovo, in a case brought by the family of children killed or maimed by unexploded NATO ordinance. Several of the cases in the following hinge on finely balanced interpretations of the applicable international law.

In addition to presenting legal issues of potential retroactivity, successor trials also play an important role in the establishment of historical justice: in the course of successor trials, domestic courts will make findings of fact about events during the totalitarian era. Teitel has argued that successor trials play a more nuanced role in addition to particular findings of fact. Trials, Teitel argued, 'are traditional ceremonies affording a ritual to publicly contextualize and share past experience of wrongdoing'.[32] Thus the significance of successor trials goes beyond the findings of fact in particular cases and contributes to the establishment of a collective memory or even an official truth. However, there is great potential for politicisation in the use of trials to construct historical knowledge.[33]

The relationship between judicial processes and historical justice is examined in more detail in Chapter 3. For now suffice it to observe that the European Court's findings of fact may amplify or contradict domestically constructed historical narratives, with a consequent impact on the transition itself. Indeed, the judgments of the European Court necessarily become part of the process of historical accounting, whether in cases relating to successor trials or other transitional issues and by not only their legal findings but also by the presentation of historical matter as background material.

2.2.1 Setting the tone: the Berlin Wall cases

The prosecution of East German border guards and their superiors after German reunification has presented some novel and difficult issues. This section focuses on two cases brought before the European Court of Human

28 *Prosecutor v Akayesu* Case no ICTR-96-4-T, 2 September 1998.

29 *Prosecutor v Delalic*, Judgment, IT-96-21-T, 16 November 1998; see para. 487 *et seq*.

30 *Behrami v France (Admissibility)* (71412/01) (2007) 45 EHRR SE10.

31 See, e.g., M. Milanovic and T. Papic, 'As bad as it gets: the European Court of Human Rights' *Behrami* and *Saramati* decision and general international law' (2009) 58(2) *ICLQ* 267; A. Breitegger, 'Sacrificing the effectiveness of the European Convention on Human Rights on the altar of the effective functioning of peace support operations: a critique of *Behrami & Saramati* and *Al Jedda*' (2009) 11(2) *International Community Law Review* 155.

32 Teitel, *op. cit. supra* n 1, 75.

33 Teitel, *op. cit. supra* n 1, 76.

Rights that concerned such prosecutions. The two cases are introduced together since they were decided by an identically constituted Grand Chamber of the European Court of Human Rights; the judgments were issued on the same day (22 March 2001); and large portions of the judgments are verbatim reproductions of one another. It is in the contrast between certain elements of them that the fault lines on the application of transitional justice in the reasoning of different judges become clearer.

The applicants in *Streletz, Kessler and Krenz v Germany*[34] had all occupied senior positions in the government of the German Democratic Republic (the GDR, or East Germany) and Socialist Unity Party.[35] Krenz had briefly served as the leader of East Germany in 1989, but the prosecution against the GDR's leader from 1971 until 1989, Erich Honecker, was discontinued on health grounds and he was permitted to leave the country for Chile.[36]

The regime had attempted to stop the flow of refugees to the Federal Republic of Germany (West Germany) by building the infamous Berlin Wall in 1961. The integrity of the border was supported by anti-personnel mines, automatic-fire systems and armed border guards.[37] The European Court observed that official figures show at least 264 people were killed, although there were reports that it could in reality be up to around 1000 or more.[38] Border guards were told that 'border violators' should in all cases be arrested as adversaries or, if necessary, 'annihilated'.[39] They were instructed to lay landmines 'with a view to halting the movements of "border violators" and . . . bringing about their arrest or annihilation'.[40]

As a result of their actions during time spent as members of the GDR's National Defence Council, Streletz and Kessler were convicted in 1993 of incitement to commit intentional homicide in relation to victims who died after triggering anti-personal mines or being shot by East German border guards as they attempted to cross to West Germany. In 1997 Krenz was convicted of intentional homicide as an indirect principal for his role in relation to two particular decisions of the Political Bureau and two of the National Defence Council, all of which concerned border policing and which caused the deaths of four people who were shot dead by East German border guards. Each applicant had attempted several forms of domestic appeal against their sentence. The applicants had been sentenced to between five and a half and seven and a half years' imprisonment.

The case of *K.-H.W. v Germany*[41] was brought not by a senior official, but by a former border guard. The President of the European Court agreed to the

34 *Streletz, Kessler and Krenz v Germany* (2001) 33 EHRR 31.
35 Ibid., [16].
36 G. Bruce, *op. cit. supra* n 19, 26.
37 *Streletz, Kessler and Krenz v Germany*, *op. cit. supra* n 34, [13].
38 Ibid.
39 *Streletz, Kessler and Krenz v Germany*, *op. cit. supra* n 34, [15].
40 Ibid.
41 *K.-H.W. v Germany* (2003) 36 EHRR 59.

applicant's request that his identity not be disclosed.[42] In 1993 K.-H.W. was convicted of intentional homicide in relation to the death of a 29-year-old man who was shot dead while trying to swim away from East Berlin on the night of 14 to 15 February 1972. At the time of the events, K.-H.W. was aged 20. He was given a suspended sentence of one year and 10 months' juvenile detention. This approach to sentencing was quite common and indeed only two German border guards actually served time for their actions.[43] Teitel has identified the combination of prosecution with minimal punishment as a frequent occurrence within transitional criminal justice and categorised it as a form of transition justice that can be labelled the 'limited criminal sanction'.[44]

All the applicants in these cases subsequently argued before the European Court of Human Rights that their rights under Article 7 ECHR had been violated. They all argued that the acts on account of which they had been prosecuted did not constitute offences at the time when they were committed. None was successful. However, there was a difference of approach in the two cases and while *Streletz, Kessler and Krenz* was decided unanimously, there was some dissent in relation to *K.-H.W.*

The approach to transitional criminal justice taken by the newly reunified Germany was to seek prosecution of crimes perpetrated by the previous regime through a strict application of the criminal law of the GDR that was in existence at the time.[45] Posner and Vermeule would characterise the German courts' technique for addressing the potential retroactivity of successor trials as 'taking nominal law seriously'.[46]

The applicants in both Berlin Wall cases argued that, in light of state practice at the time, the acts for which they were convicted did not constitute offences.[47] The *ex post facto* interpretation of the GDR's criminal law that was necessitated for their conviction to go ahead had been impossible for them to foresee at the time the material events took place.[48] They also alleged that the acts for which they were prosecuted did not constitute offences under international law.[49] In both cases, the government argued that the domestic courts' interpretation of the GDR law was legitimate and that although contrary practice was established at the time it was foreseeable that the killing of unarmed fugitives might give rise to prosecution at some point, particularly

42 Ibid., [1].
43 G. Bruce, *op. cit. supra* n 19, 26.
44 Teitel, *op. cit. supra* n 1, 46 *et seq.*
45 *Streletz, Kessler and Krenz*, *op. cit. supra* n 34, [27]; *K.-H.W.*, *op. cit. supra* n 41, [21].
46 Posner and Vermeule, *op. cit. supra* n 16, 794.
47 *Streletz, Kessler and Krenz*, *op. cit. supra* n 34, [46]; *K.-H.W.*, *op. cit. supra* n 41, [41].
48 *Streletz, Kessler and Krenz*, *op. cit. supra* n 34, [47]; *K.-H.W.*, *op. cit. supra* n 41, [42].
49 Ibid.

after a change of regime.[50] Indeed, if the GDR authorities had applied their own law correctly they would have arrived at the same conclusion.[51]

The consideration of foreseeability raised different issues in the two cases. In *Streletz, Kessler and Krenz*, the European Court observed that the gulf between the written law and the actual practice was 'to a great extent the work of the applicants themselves'.[52] This was obviously not the case for *K -H.W.*, who claimed that he was the last link in the chain of command and had always followed the orders he was given.[53] In dealing with this argument, the majority coupled the application of nominal law with an appeal to international principles. The majority identified that the GDR criminal code explicitly stated that both civilians and members of the armed forces were prohibited from citing orders they had received as justification for violating human rights, public international law or the written criminal law.[54] The Court also drew attention to the fact that the applicant had voluntarily enlisted in the army, which amounted to his giving allegiance to the regime.[55] Moreover, unlike the applicants in *Streletz, Kessler and Krenz*, K.–H. W. was given a suspended sentence precisely because of his having merely followed orders.

The approach of the majority in *K.–H. W* was not without its critics. Indeed, both Judges Baretto and Pellonpää in their partly dissenting opinions described the applicant as a victim of the regime.[56] Even in their concurring opinion, Judges Bratza and Vajić conceded that soldiers in the applicant's position had been 'indoctrinated'.[57]

In its conclusions on foreseeability, the European Court made the same point of principle in both cases. The European Court acknowledged that the more general problem of how to approach the prosecution of members of the former regime had arisen in a number of other states that had gone through a process of democratic transition.[58] It went on to explain that:

50 *Streletz, Kessler and Krenz*, *op. cit. supra* n 34, [48]; *K.-H.W.*, *op. cit. supra* n 41, [43]; note that in other cases the European Court has been at pains to take into account the way that the law was applied at the material time: C. Murphy, 'The principle of legality in criminal law under the European Convention on Human Rights' (2010) *EHRLR* 192, 196, citing *Kafkaris v Cyprus* (2008) 49 EHRR 35, [145].

51 *Streletz, Kessler and Krenz*, *op. cit. supra* n 34, [48]; *K.-H.W.*, *op. cit. supra* n 41, [43].

52 *Streletz, Kessler and Krenz*, *op. cit. supra* n 34, [78].

53 *K.-H.W.*, *op. cit. supra* n 41, [66].

54 *K.-H.W.*, *op. cit. supra* n 41, [77], citing Article 95 of the 1968 GDR Criminal Code; and [78] citing Article 258 of the 1968 GDR Criminal Code.

55 *K.-H.W.*, *op. cit. supra* n 41, [74].

56 *K.-H.W.*, *op. cit. supra* n 41, Partly Dissenting Opinion of Judge Cabral Barreto, [6]; Partly Dissenting Opinion of Judge Pellonpää, joined by Judge Zupančič, first paragraph.

57 *K.-H.W.*, *op. cit. supra* n 41, Concurring Opinion of Judge Sir Nicolas Bratza, Joined By Judge Vaji , second paragraph.

58 *Streletz, Kessler and Krenz*, *op. cit. supra* n 34, [80]; *K.-H.W.*, *op. cit. supra* n 41, [84].

> *it is legitimate* for a State governed by the rule of law to bring criminal proceedings against persons who have committed crimes under a former regime; similarly, the courts of such a State, having taken the place of those which existed previously, *cannot be criticised* for applying and interpreting the legal provisions in force at the material time in the light of the principles governing a State subject to the rule of law.[59]
>
> [emphasis added]

In this passage, the European Court recognised that there is something distinctive in transitional cases in which crimes committed by and under the previous regime are being considered. This is even clearer in the concurring opinion of Judge Levits in *Streletz, Kessler and Krenz*, which demonstrates that the Court was fully aware that the courts of the GDR and the German courts after reunification were completely different in their approach to the interpretation and application of the law.[60] Judge Levits conceded that the interpretation of the same legal texts by them would lead to different results.[61] In his view, however, there was 'no room' for any solution other than to apply the 'old' law according to the approach to interpretation and application of the law that was inherent in the new democratic political order.[62]

The European Court did not hold itself out as dispensing transitional justice or being conscious of a need for transitional relativism: the Court stressed parallels with its non-transitional jurisprudence. In the past the Court has generally recognised that there is inevitable judicial interpretation in the criminal law, allowing for the explanation of doubtful points and adaptation of the law to changing circumstances.[63] In *Streletz, Kessler and Krenz* and *K. –H. W.*, the Court found that the same concept 'remains wholly valid' even in cases like these, where one state had succeeded the other.[64] Taking this into account, the Court found that the acts committed by the applicants were defined with sufficient accessibility and foreseeability in the GDR at the material time and, therefore, that their prosecution was compatible with Article 7(1) ECHR.[65] Nevertheless, we shall see that in relation to several rights-restrictive measures adjudicated on in the transitional period, the European Court has similarly struck a balance between the foreseeability or

59 *Streletz, Kessler and Krenz*, *op. cit. supra* n 34, [80].

60 *Streletz, Kessler and Krenz*, *op. cit. supra* n 34, Concurring Opinion of Judge Levits, [5].

61 *Streletz, Kessler and Krenz*, *op. cit. supra* n 34, Concurring Opinion of Judge Levits, [6].

62 *Streletz, Kessler and Krenz*, *op. cit. supra* n 34, Concurring Opinion of Judge Levits, [8].

63 P. van Dijk *et al.* (eds), *Theory and Practice of the European Convention on Human Rights* (Oxford: Intersentia 2006), 654.

64 *Streletz, Kessler and Krenz*, *op. cit. supra* n 34, 82; *K.-H.W.*, *op. cit. supra* n 41, [85] [emphasis added]; c.f. Murphy, who is not convinced by this reasoning: C. Murphy, 'The principle of legality in criminal law under the European Convention on Human Rights' (2010) 2 *EHRLR* 192, 201.

65 *Streletz, Kessler and Krenz*, *op. cit. supra* n 34, [89]; *K.-H.W.*, *op. cit. supra* n 41, [91].

precision of the measure and the proximity of its introduction or application to major transitional issues.[66]

By fitting the 'taking nominal law seriously' approach within the general human rights jurisprudence on the gradual evolution of criminal law, the European Court allowed Germany to at least downplay the rule of law dilemma presented by the disjuncture between the totalitarian and democratic eras. It found legal continuity between the eras in the text of the positive law. Indeed, in his concurring opinion in *Streletz, Kessler and Krenz*, Judge Zupančič expressly stated that the approach of the FRG courts to the application of GDR criminal law had been 'legally consistent'.[67]

In a much briefer element of its judgments in *Streletz, Kessler and Krenz* and *K.-H.W.*, the European Court also found that the acts constituted offences that were defined with sufficient accessibility and foreseeability in international law at the material time.[68] This contributed to the prosecutions' compliance with Article 7 ECHR. This appeal to international law as a mediating factor was relatively weak, but the European Court certainly validated it as a potentially Convention-compliant approach to successor trials and, in doing so, set the tone for the majority of cases that will be discussed later.

In terms of the element of the crime, the Court held that in *K.-H.W.*, it was not necessary to refer to international humanitarian law. The majority based its findings on domestic law augmented by international human rights law on the right to life and freedom of movement. This is interesting because in the reasoning on international law, the majority did not explicitly identify what provisions of international law made the actions of K.-H.W. criminal. Nevertheless, in his concurring opinion, Judge Loucaides argued cogently that the applicant's actions were also crimes against humanity. This would have been a safer line of reasoning within the majority judgment. Although in their separate opinions, Judges Baretto, Pellonpää and Zupančič all cast doubt on whether the crimes really were defined with enough clarity in international law in 1972, they did not undermine the central proposition that, if they were so defined, the prosecution would not be retroactive. In other words, they did nothing to dispel transitional democracies' appeal to international law as a Convention-compliant means of facing the rule of law dilemma and avoiding an explicit appeal to transitional relativism.

PACE Resolution 1096 had attempted to forestall any problems that statutes of limitation might pose for successor trials. The issue was not litigated

66 Note the discussion in Chapter 9.

67 *Streletz, Kessler and Krenz*, *op. cit. supra* n 34, Concurring Opinion of Judge Zupančič.

68 *Streletz, Kessler and Krenz*, *op. cit. supra* n 34, [105]. The Concurring Opinion of Judge Loucaides expands on the Court's fairly terse reasoning in this regard. Strangely, in his formally *concurring* Judge Zupančič stated that he found it 'difficult to agree' with the finding in paragraph 105. However, in his view, the judgment did not rely on the concept of an 'international offence' anyway.

in *Streletz, Kessler and Krenz*, but it did arise in relation to *K.-H.W.* The majority did not fully consider the compatibility of extending time limits from a European human rights perspective, since they found that the relevant GDR laws excluded the application of limitation periods to crimes against peace, humanity or human rights.[69]

In summary, in these two cases the European Court confirmed that states facing the rule of law dilemma presented by successor trials could resort both to 'taking nominal law seriously' *and* to an appeal to international norms, without violating the European Convention on Human Rights. Thus human rights law did not necessarily impede the transitional aim at stake. By validating *both* approaches, the European Court suggested to other states that they would have some flexibility in choosing transitional criminal justice approaches that aligned with the legal and historical circumstances of their transition. The former approach, taking nominal law seriously, required more justification since the latter was envisaged both in the text of the Convention and in Resolution 1096. Although the transitional context was acknowledged and discussed in relation to the application of existing jurisprudence on the clarification of criminal law via judicial interpretation, and on the notion of international criminality, the judgments were presented as a logical extension of existing ECHR principles rather than as a transitional exception to them. It did not therefore *appear* to modify its own conception of justice to achieve this outcome. In this sense, the European Court did not hold itself out as 'doing' transitional justice – except insofar as it granted anonymity to K.-H.W. This final point is developed further in the conclusion to this chapter.

2.3 Dealing with the communist past

If the reasoning in the German border cases set the tone for how to approach the rule of law dilemma presented by successor trials from a human rights perspective, they did little to restrain dissent in how that approach would be applied. Although a series of cases followed the trend of validating domestic prosecutions via the mediating tool of both extant domestic and international standards, in *Korbely v Hungary*,[70] which dealt with the famous unsuccessful Hungarian uprising of 1956, the Court made a sharp departure. This section will outline the developing orthodoxy and then turn to the *Korbely* case.

2.3.1 The developing orthodoxy

In two admissibility decisions concerning cases brought against Estonia, the European Court confirmed that international law extant at the relevant time could trump any purported domestic authorisation to commit crimes against

69 *K.-H.W.*, *op. cit. supra* n 41, [110].
70 *Korbely v Hungary* [2008] ECHR 847; (2010) 50 EHRR 48.

humanity. The applicants in *Kolk & Kislyiy v Estonia*[71] were convicted of crimes against humanity for their part in the mass deportation of Estonian civilians to remote areas of the USSR in 1949. The applicant in *Penart v Estonia*[72] was convicted of crimes against humanity for his role in the planning and execution of an operation that led to the killing of three civilians in 1953 and 1954. In both decisions, the Court stated clearly that:

> even if the acts committed by the applicant could have been regarded as lawful under the Soviet law at the material time, they were nevertheless found by the Estonian courts to constitute crimes against humanity under international law at the time of their commission. The Court sees no reason to come to a different conclusion.[73]

Thus the complaints of the applicants under Article 7 ECHR were manifestly ill founded.

The trend continued with the Court's judgment in *Kuolelis, Bartoševičius and Burokevičius v Lithuania*.[74] The reasoning in this case is relatively straightforward and it was decided unanimously. Nevertheless, it is worth briefly summarising the facts as presented in the judgment since they intersect with events of real historical significance.[75]

Lithuania was annexed by the USSR in 1940.[76] The applicants in *Kuolelis, Bartoševičius and Burokevičius v Lithuania* opposed attempts to declare Lithuanian independence that began in 1990. These attempts were actually led by the Communist Party of Lithuania itself. In response, the applicants formed an alternative communist party that remained allied to the USSR. The applicants were well-known politicians, and they personally supported and assisted the USSR's attempts to coerce Lithuania to renounce the independence it went on to declare in March 1990. The context is interesting here, since the applicants were actively involved in the 'losing' side of the transition. However, in contrast to the *Kononov* case discussed later, Russia did not intervene on the applicants' behalf.

The USSR's coercion of Lithuania was effected by an economic blockade and, in 1991, military force. The USSR's attempts to maintain control over Lithuania only stopped after the failed coup against USSR President Gorbachev in August 1991. After the failed coup the USSR eventually recognised

71 *Kolk & Kislyiy v Estonia* (dec.) App nos 23052/04 and 24018/04 (ECtHR, 17 January 2006).

72 *Penart v Estonia* (dec.) App no 14685/04 (ECtHR, 24 January 2006).

73 *Kolk & Kislyiy v Estonia*, *op. cit. supra* n 71; *Penart v Estonia*, *op. cit. supra* n 72 – paragraphs not numbered.

74 *Kuolelis, Bartoševičius and Burokevičius v Lithuania* [2008] ECHR 152.

75 Ibid., [7] *et seq.*

76 Ibid., [8]; note the brief discussion of this in Part 1 and that it forms the backdrop to several cases in Chapter 3.

Lithuania as a sovereign independent state as from March 1990 and renounced the annexation of Lithuania that had taken place in 1940.[77]

The applicants in *Kuolelis, Bartoševičius and Burokevičius* were convicted under Articles 68 and 70 of the Lithuanian Criminal Code, as amended in November 1990. They argued that Lithuania had really only become independent after the failed Moscow coup of 1991 and that the amendments to the criminal law made in November 1990 were therefore not effective. Crucially, these changes had replaced various offences of an anti-Soviet nature with offences against the sovereignty of the new Republic of Lithuania.[78] Citing Article 7 ECHR, they argued that they had been convicted for acts that, at the time, could not have been foreseeable as criminal offences under domestic or international law.[79]

Here the Court quite explicitly took into account the transitional context, noting:

> that the historical and political background to the present case is an important element, reflecting as it does a period of tension caused by the transition between two different legal systems after the re-establishment of the independence of the Republic of Lithuania.[80]

The Court found that the political will of the new Lithuanian government was well established and that, as well-known politicians, the applicants should have been well aware of the 'great risks' that they were taking in attempting to overthrow it.[81] The crimes for which the applicants were convicted were therefore deemed to be sufficiently clear and foreseeable as a matter of domestic law.[82] In the light of this, the European Court found that it was not required to examine any arguments in relation to whether the crimes were defined in international law.

Even more so than in the German border cases, the reasoning in *Kuolelis, Bartoševičius and Burokevičius* focused on sufficient clarity in the relevant domestic law. Essentially, the European Court took a stand on the point at which the new independent and democratic Lithuania was in a position to pass 'laws' that were understood as such and were therefore capable of defining offences that were sufficiently clear and foreseeable. The Court's clear reference to the transitional context suggests that an argument based on the uncertainty of domestic criminal law in transitional periods was not formally invalid, but rather that it was not supported by the facts of this case. This at least implies

77 These are the facts as reported in the judgment in *Kuolelis, Bartoševičius and Burokevičius*, *op. cit. supra* n 74.

78 *Kuolelis, Bartoševičius and Burokevičius v Lithuania*, *op. cit. supra* n 74, [77].

79 Ibid., [96].

80 Ibid., [117].

81 Ibid., [120].

82 Ibid., [121].

a transitional margin within which the Court could recognise distinctions between transitions or within different periods of the same transition.

In all the cases discussed thus far, the Court found that the approach of the state to confronting the rule of law dilemma posed by successor trials was valid both in terms of its approach and on the facts of the case (although, in *K.-H.W.*, there was dissent on the latter point). This begins to build a picture of the European Court as an institution that is relatively permissive in terms of the way it has established that these approaches do not challenge the orthodoxy of international human rights law. Without holding itself out as recognising any form of transitional relativism, the Court was able to accommodate the transitional policy of prosecution. In *Korbely v Hungary*,[83] however, a Grand Chamber of the Court[84] found a violation of Article 7 in circumstances that merit some detailed discussion because of its unorthodox approach to the relationship between war crimes and crimes against humanity.

2.3.2 *Korbely v Hungary*

The *Korbely* case was decided in 2008 and concerned the prosecution of a retired military officer for his part in quelling the 1956 Hungarian uprising against Soviet rule. The prosecution related specifically to an event on 26 October 1956, when the applicant led a group of officers in a mission to regain control over the police department building in the town of Tata, which revolutionaries had occupied. During the course of the mission, three people were killed – one of whom was shot and killed by the applicant himself.

After a series of domestic cases and appeals the applicant was convicted of multiple homicide, which, according to the Hungarian courts, constituted a crime against humanity punishable under Article 3(1) of the Geneva Convention. As such, the prosecution was not subject to statutory limitation.

In the formulation of her proposition that international law is a useful mediating concept in periods of political flux, Ruti Teitel used the Hungarian prosecutions for events in 1956 as an example.[85] She noted that the Hungarian Constitutional Court had declared unconstitutional an explicitly retroactive statute that revived certain political offences. The impugned law was discontinuous with the rule of law. However, Teitel stressed that the same court upheld a new statute that authorised prosecutions relating to the 1956 events and which were based on war crimes and crimes against humanity (in fact, it

83 *Korbely v Hungary*, *op. cit. supra* n 70.

84 The case was initially referred to the second section of Court, but the Chamber relinquished jurisdiction in favour of the Grand Chamber in accordance with Article 30 ECHR. Article 30 allows a Chamber to relinquish jurisdiction where a case 'raises a serious question affecting the interpretation of the Convention or the Protocols thereto, or where the resolution of a question before the Chamber might have a result inconsistent with a judgment previously delivered by the Court'. See *Korbely v Hungary*, *op. cit. supra* n 70, [3].

85 Teitel, *op. cit. supra* n 1, 20–21.

was these cases that formed the background to *Korbely v Hungary* and as such they were duly summarised in the ECtHR's judgment).[86] The rule of law required continuity, Teitel argued, and this was precisely what international law provided.[87] Taking this into account, it is all the more striking that the ECtHR found a violation of Article 7 in *Korbely*.

The European Court observed that the prosecution was based wholly on international law and therefore confined itself to checking accessibility and foreseeability of the Geneva Conventions.[88] Hungary had argued that common Article 3 of the Geneva Conventions left it a margin of appreciation regarding its interpretation, within which it had stayed.[89] Hungary fell short, however, of arguing for the existence of a margin of appreciation under Article 7 ECHR.

The European Court quickly found that the Geneva Conventions were accessible to Korbely.[90] The real question was whether his prosecution was foreseeable, in the sense of whether the interpretation of the Geneva Conventions that would permit his prosecution was valid.

The Geneva Conventions apply to armed conflict. Article 3 of each Geneva Convention is identical and, in relation specifically to non-international armed conflict, prohibits *inter alia*, 'violence to life and person, in particular murder of all kinds', in respect of persons taking no active part in the hostilities. Thus it is always important to determine whether particular events amount to an armed conflict and to characterise it as international or non-international.

It should be observed at this stage that the prominence given to interpreting common Article 3 of the Geneva Conventions by both the Hungarian and European courts is slightly surprising. On a normal understanding of the Geneva Conventions, 'grave breaches' of them constitute not *crimes against humanity* but *war crimes*. War crimes and crimes against humanity are not synonymous. War crimes are committed within a conflict, while crimes against humanity may not necessarily be so. War crimes may often be committed against civilians of the opposing side in the conflict. Crimes against humanity are often committed against a state's own population. Initially, the European Court seemed to appreciate this, when it observed that in the materials presented by the Hungarian government there was nothing cited that demonstrated how actions contrary to common Article 3 of the Geneva Conventions could in fact be crimes against humanity.[91]

Erring on the side of caution, the European Court then went on to determine for itself whether Korbely's actions could be classified as crimes against humanity. The European Court of Human Rights rightly observed that

86 *Korbely v Hungary*, *op. cit. supra* n 70, [16] *et seq.*
87 Teitel, *op. cit. supra* n 1, 20.
88 *Korbely v Hungary*, *op. cit. supra* n 70, [74].
89 Ibid., [67].
90 Ibid., [75].
91 Ibid., [80].

although murder is capable of constituting a crime against humanity, other elements are necessary as well. In 1956 the most pertinent of these was that the crime in question should not be an isolated or sporadic act but should instead form part of 'state action or policy'.[92] The European Court found that the Hungarian Supreme Court had not addressed this question and that, therefore, it was 'open to question' whether the constituent elements of a crime against humanity were made out in Korbely's case.[93]

The peculiar part of the judgment is the European Court's discussion of whether the man shot by Korbely was a non-combatant for the purposes of common Article 3 of the Geneva Conventions. If the decisive question was whether it was foreseeable that Korbely's actions would lead to a prosecution for *crimes against humanity*, then the classification of the victim under the Geneva Conventions was superfluous. The essential questions were whether the actions for which the applicant was prosecuted constituted murder; committed against a civilian population; in a systematic or organised manner in the furtherance of a particular policy. This was explained cogently in the dissenting opinion of Judge Loucaides. The applicability or otherwise of common Article 3 of the Geneva Conventions would only have been relevant if Korbely were being prosecuted for war crimes, which he was not.

Regardless of this, the Court's approach to the disputed events was problematic for another reason. It hinged on the interpretation of the actions of both Korbely and his victim. Indeed, it was so finely balanced that the essential question was whether when, on the afternoon of 26 October 1956, the victim reached into his coat and brought out a handgun, he was in the process of surrendering it or attempting to fire on the applicant and his men. The Hungarian Supreme Court had found as a matter of fact that Korbely knew the victim intended to hand over the gun.[94] These are precisely the sort of highly specific and hotly contested events about which domestic successor trials may contribute to the formation of a collective memory and the achievement of historical justice.

The European Court reviewed the findings of fact made by the domestic courts and found that within them there was nothing that could lead to the conclusion that the victim intended to surrender. The victim had 'embarked on an animated quarrel with the applicant, at the end of which he drew his gun with unknown intentions'.[95] In the view of the European Court, it was not clear enough that the victim was taking no active part in the hostilities and so it could not be said that he gained protection under the Geneva Conventions. In response to this, the joint dissent by Judges Lorenzen, Tulkens, Zagrebelsky, Fura-Sandström and Popović stated that the majority

92 Ibid., [82].
93 Ibid., [85].
94 Ibid., [44].
95 Ibid., [91].

had, 'on a flimsy, uncertain basis, quite simply substitute[d] their own findings of fact for those of the Hungarian judicial authorities.'[96]

Instead, the dissent argued that:

> In view of the complexity of the task of reconstructing the facts of the case more than fifty years after they occurred, we see no reason to place more reliance on the conclusions reached by the Court than on those of the domestic courts. On the contrary, we consider that the national courts were in a better position to assess all the available facts and evidence.[97]

The dissenters' reference to the national courts being in a 'better position' is identical to one of the justifications for recognising a margin of appreciation in relation to other articles of the Convention.

The significance of this is that if the European Court of Human Rights seeks to validate reliance on international norms as one means of securing the legal consistency required to avoid the rule of law dilemma presented by successor trials, without conceding any transitional relativism, then its guidance on the content of those international norms is crucial. With both its approach to the applicable international law and its approach to the domestic findings of fact, the European Court missed the opportunity to 'improve' the transitional policy. The implications of this judgment for the delivery of 'historical justice' are developed in Chapter 3.

2.4 Dealing with the pre-communist past: the *Kononov* case and 'historical truth'

Finally in this chapter, we turn to a case brought in the post-Communist era but which deals with events that took place before that era had even begun. The case of *Kononov v Latvia* concerned the killing of a number of villagers during World War II. In this case, a Chamber of the European Court, sitting prior to the judgment in *Korbely*, found a violation of the Convention[98] but a Grand Chamber, sitting afterwards, reversed the Chamber's findings.[99]

In a sense, it could be argued that this case is not a transitional justice case at all or, if it were, that it concerned the transition between war and peace at the end of World War II. To that extent the instant parallels might lay with cases concerning the prosecution of Nazi collaborators, which the European Court has consistently found do not violate Article 7 ECHR, rather than the

96 Ibid., Joint Dissent by Judges Lorenzen, Tulkens, Zagrebelsky, Fura-Sandström and Popović.

97 Ibid.

98 *Kononov v Latvia* (Chamber) [2008] ECHR 695.

99 *Kononov v Latvia* (GC) [2010] ECHR 667.

cases discussed elsewhere in this chapter.[100] However, in its submissions before the Chamber, the Latvian government drew attention to the importance of trials such as this for the restoration of democracy in Latvia, for establishing 'historical truth' and guaranteeing justice for victims of war crimes and crimes against humanity.[101] This is a notably explicit statement that successor trials have a role in the transitional process and shows that, in their attempt to make a break with the past, new governments can face difficult choices about where to draw the baseline: similar issues have arisen in relation to the question of whether reparations ought to be made only to people who suffered under communism or also to those who suffered in the Nazi era.[102]

In *Kononov*, the Russian government intervened before both the Chamber and the Grand Chamber in support of the applicant, stressing, *inter alia*, that it was wrong to classify the USSR as an 'occupying power' in Latvia in 1944.[103] The involvement of Russia in this case, brought in the post-Cold War era, and after Latvian independence in 1991, adds a further dimension to the case since the applicant's allegiances appear to have lain with the former Soviet Union. Indeed, after the war, the applicant was celebrated as a Soviet war hero[104] and received the Order of Lenin, the highest distinction awarded in the USSR, for his activities as a partisan.[105] Until his retirement in 1988, he worked as an officer in the Soviet police force.[106]

According to the domestic courts and the Latvian government, the applicant led a group of communist Red Partisans (wearing German uniforms) in a reprisal attack on a village that was suspected of spying for the Germans and who had been supplied weapons by them. In the attack, six men and three women were killed, one of whom was nine months' pregnant. None was armed at the time. Most of the men were shot dead. One was shot and then burned to death. All the women were burned to death (although one had also been shot first): the pregnant victim, who had not been shot, was pushed through a window into a burning house.[107] The applicant contested that all the victims were collaborators and traitors; that an ad hoc military tribunal had delivered judgment against them; that he had refused to lead the operation, the aim of

100 See, e.g., the 1997 admissibility decision of the European Commission in *Touvier v France* (dec.) App no. 29420/95 (ECommHR, 13 January 1997) and the 2001 admissibility decision in *Papon v France (No. 2)* (dec.) App no. 54210/00 (ECtHR 15 November 2001). In both cases, the elements of the application based on Article 7 ECHR and which related to alleged war crimes and crimes against humanity committed during World War II were declared inadmissible.

101 *Kononov v Latvia* (Chamber), *op. cit. supra* n 98, [92].

102 See the discussion in Chapter 4.

103 *Kononov v Latvia* (GC), *op. cit. supra* n 99, [174].

104 *Kononov v Latvia* (GC), *op. cit. supra* n 99, [158].

105 *Kononov v Latvia* (Chamber), *op. cit. supra* n 98, [30].

106 Ibid.

107 This version of the facts is summarised in *Kononov v Latvia* (Chamber), *op. cit. supra* n 98, [13–21].

which had been not to seek reprisal but to bring the villagers to stand trial; that during the operation he hid behind a bush and did not participate; and that after the events the commanding officer had, in fact, reprimanded the Red Partisans for failing to capture the wanted villagers.[108]

Kononov was charged, prosecuted and found guilty of war crimes for his part in the killing of the villagers. The Latvian statute of limitations did not apply to such crimes. Note that this case, unlike *Korbely*, dealt explicitly with war crimes and not crimes against humanity and, therefore, the law of the Geneva Conventions was undoubtedly relevant. When Kononov alleged that his conviction violated Article 7 ECHR, it fell again to the European Court to determine whether the interpretation of the relevant international law that underpinned his prosecution was sufficiently accessible and foreseeable. If his actions were not war crimes, then the statute of limitations would protect him from prosecution.

The Chamber found no reason to contest the facts as they had been found by the Latvian courts.[109] The Chamber's 4:3 majority finding that there was a violation of Article 7 ECHR was based on the conclusion that under the law applicable at the time the victims were combatants and that therefore their summary execution was not a war crime. This conclusion was supported by a strikingly personal concurring opinion by Judge Myjer, which drew on his upbringing in the Netherlands in the post-war era and went on to explain why he felt that there could be no forgiveness for collaboration with the Nazis. In legal terms, Judge Myjer also argued that it was only after the Nuremburg trials in 1945–1946 that it had become clear that anyone who committed similar crimes could be held personally responsible. Thus Kononov's acts, committed in 1944, could not be classified as war crimes to which the statute of limitations did not apply.

In its submissions the Latvian government had identified that the Nuremburg trials only punished crimes perpetrated by the Nazis, whereas trials such as Kononov's allowed some redress for war crimes and crimes against humanity that were perpetrated by the Allies.[110] It was the fact that this case concerned the trial of someone on the side of the Allies that made the case stand out – but perhaps misleadingly. This point was developed in the joint dissenting opinion of Judges Fura-Sandström, Davíd Thór Björgvinsson and Ziemele, in a passage that also drew attention to the enlargement of the Council of Europe. They pointed out that:

> This case is allegedly different since the applicant belonged to the Allied powers fighting against the Nazis. The legal basis for such an approach is

108 This version of the facts is summarised in *Kononov v Latvia* (Chamber), *op. cit. supra* n 98, [22–24].

109 *Kononov v Latvia* (Chamber), *op. cit. supra* n 98, [111].

110 *Kononov v Latvia* (Chamber), *op. cit. supra* n 98, [92].

> unclear. Why should criminal responsibility depend on which side those guilty of war crimes were fighting on? There is certainly nothing in the Convention itself to limit the application of Article 7 to Nazi crimes alone. On the contrary the Article is drafted broadly and with a specific purpose as the *travaux préparatoires* amply show. True enough, today the Convention covers many more States then at the time of its drafting. However, now that this expansion has taken place, does that mean that more recent States Parties have different rights and obligations under Article 7? Or, in other words, that the Convention should operate with double standards? We do not think so.[111]

They argued that the majority's interpretation of the international law at the time was faulty and that the fact that the Court found the villagers held 'pro-Nazi views' could not deprive them of the protection afforded to civilians in international humanitarian law.[112] They also drew attention to the historical context,[113] which might suggest that collaboration with Nazi Germany against the USSR was essentially a hard choice between totalitarian regimes.[114]

In 2010 the Grand Chamber revisited the Kononov case and, contradicting the Chamber, found by a majority of 14:3 that there was no violation of the Convention. Attempting to put the actions of the villagers in context, the Latvian government drew on the dissent in the Chamber and argued that the Soviet and Nazi occupations of Latvia were 'equally unlawful'.[115] Likewise, the government of Lithuania intervened before the Grand Chamber arguing that the Baltic states suffered aggression from both Nazi Germany *and* the USSR.[116]

The Grand Chamber did not rule on the question of whether the victims were 'civilians who had directly participated in hostilities' or combatants: it simply found that even if they were, they were unarmed at the time and, thus, applying the law as it was understood in 1944, were *hors de combat*.[117]

The Grand Chamber considered the questions of accessibility and foreseeability together. It found that, given his role as a commanding military officer, he could have foreseen in 1944 that his actions would constitute war crimes.[118] The applicant also argued that his prosecution was 'politically unforeseeable'

111 *Kononov v Latvia* (Chamber), *op. cit. supra* n 98, Joint Dissenting Opinion of Judges Fura-Sandström, Davíd Thór Björgvinsson and Ziemele Dissent, [3].

112 Ibid., [12].

113 Ibid., [12]; note, in particular, footnote 14.

114 See also *Kononov v Latvia* (Chamber), *op. cit. supra* n 98, Dissenting Opinion of Judge David Thór Björgvinsson, [2].

115 *Kononov v Latvia* (GC), *op. cit. supra* n 99, [152].

116 Ibid., [179].

117 Ibid., [216].

118 Ibid., [237].

and was, in fact, a political exercise.[119] In this regard, the European Court went on to 'recall' its earlier dicta on foreseeability in the context of changes of regime. The Grand Chamber stated that the successor courts 'cannot be criticised' for applying and interpreting the legal provisions in force at the material time in the light of the principles governing a state subject to the rule of law *and* with regard to the 'core principles on which the Convention system is built'.[120]

This actually extends the approach from *Streletz* and *K.-H.W.* in two ways. First, it grafts appreciation of the change of regime on to the foreseeability of prosecutions based on international law (not just on domestic law). Second, it more explicitly addresses not only transition towards establishing the rule of law, but also transition towards compliance with the core principles of the ECHR.

2.5 Conclusion

In this chapter, we have seen that successor trials have occupied the European Court far more than other transitional criminal justice policies such as amnesties. It has also come under interesting political pressures in cases relating to states from the former USSR.

In its approach to the national successor trials that have come before it, the European Court has, in every case, accepted the broad legitimacy of the Respondent State's attempt to circumvent the rule of law dilemma that they present. This is equally true of the prosecutions based on taking nominal law seriously and those based on international law. With regard to the latter, the jurisprudence shows that factually well-supported prosecutions, based on a legally and historically valid interpretation of war crimes and crimes against humanity, do not amount to retroactive prosecutions. In its early jurisprudence, the Court even validated a national amnesty. Without being particularly explicit in the recognition of transitional relativism, the European Court has not acted as a barrier to transitional criminal justice.

We have also seen that the European Court has great potential to assist in the formulation, implementation and improvement of transitional policies. It is in a position to give valuable advice to states as to how to ensure that their successor trials are compatible with the European Convention. However the Court's track record on confirming whether the interpretation of the relevant law and claimed findings of facts were reasonable is more mixed. Although it claims to recognise that domestic courts have the primary role as fact-finders, its approach to the facts of the case in *Korbely* and the wider circumstances of *Kononov* were a little problematic. The legal guidance given regarding the relevance of common Article 3 of the Geneva Conventions to the prosecution in *Korbely* was also a little unorthodox.

119 Ibid., [234].
120 Ibid., [241].

The final question is to determine the implications for the universality of human rights. The Court's approach has, albeit implicitly, engaged with both senses of transitional relativism: diversity between transitional states was recognised in accordance with the principle of subsidiarity, but diversity between the transitional states and democratic states has been downplayed.

It was clear even from *Streletz, Kessler and Krenz* and *K.-H.W.* that there would be more than one Convention-compliant way of justifying successor trials including those based on taking nominal law seriously and those based on international law. Thus, we have seen cases rooted both in domestic law and international law. In *Kuolelis, Bartoševičius and Burokevičius v Lithuania*, where the validity of the prosecution depended on whether acts of the newly independent state of Lithuania had the force of law, the Court appeared open to the suggestion that in some transitions there would be a point at which it was too soon to pass valid laws – although that was not made out on the facts. In this way, the Court has not undermined the principle of subsidiarity and neither has it imposed a one-size-fits-all solution on all the transitional states. Given the observation in Chapter 1 that transitional justice is most successful when it tends towards the particular,[121] this is to be welcomed.

Diversity between the transitional and non-transitional cases is only opaquely visible in the Article 7 cases on successor trials. There is perhaps one, limited, sense in which the European Court *did* actively participate in the delivery of transitional justice, although the implications for universality are minimal. The applicant in *K.-H.W.* was granted anonymity. Article 35(2)(a) ECHR prohibits the European Court from dealing with anonymous applications. However, where an applicant lodges an application in his own name, he is asked whether he objects to his identity being disclosed. Rule 47(3) of the Rules of Court states that applicants who do not want their identity to be disclosed must submit a statement giving reasons for their request. According to Rule 47(3) the decision is taken by the President of the Chamber, who may also choose to authorise or grant anonymity of his own motion. In many cases involving children, for example, the applicant is referred to only by their initials.[122]

The applicant in *K.-H.W.* was noted as being relatively young and he was sentenced as a juvenile. Nevertheless, he was aged 20 at the time of the events and 49 by the date of the European Court's judgment. The judgment simply records that he asked for the Court not to disclose his identity and that the President granted his request.[123] There would seem to be no compelling reason to grant the applicant anonymity on the grounds of his age. Although the judgments in *K.-H.W.* and *Streletz, Kessler and Krenz* arrived at the same conclusions, it is clear that the Court heard arguments concerning the

121 See Chapter 1.

122 For example, *V & T v UK* (2000) 30 EHRR 121, a case concerning the trial and detention of children named Venables and Thompson who murdered a toddler.

123 *K.-H.W.*, *op. cit. supra* n. 41, [1].

difference in status of the applicants. The decision to grant K.-H.W. anonymity may reflect this difference. In its guidance on prosecution initiatives the Office of the UN High Commissioner for Human Rights has warned that pursuing only low-level perpetrators of crimes may lead to a perception of scapegoating.[124] The approach of the European Court to granting anonymity has had the effect of preventing K.-H.W. becoming precisely such a scapegoat, for example, by having his full name repeated endlessly in the cases and commentary that have followed the judgment – including in this book.

124 Office of the UN High Commissioner for Human Rights, *Rule-of-Law Tools for Post-Conflict States: prosecution initiatives* (Geneva: United Nations 2006) (HR/PUB/06/4), 7; see also Posner and Vermeule, *op. cit. supra* n 16, 800.

3 Openness, secrecy and historical justice

3.1 Introduction

In Chapter 1, we saw that an important element of transitional justice is the attempt to achieve some form of 'historical justice', sometimes via assisting in the formation of collective memories or even the establishment of an official truth. In the first part of this chapter, we shall see that openness and access to previously secret information are crucial to this. In the second part of the chapter, we shall see that the European Court's approach to the facts of particular cases, and the historical context in which they are placed, has a complex but clearly identifiable impact on historical justice.

3.2 The right to truth

Transitional periods are often characterised by moves to gain access to previously held secrets and to forge a more authentic past. Thus, in some states, there have been truth commissions – most notably in South Africa after the apartheid regime. Such moves have not been common in post-Cold War Europe.[1] Indeed, Teitel has argued that experiences during the communist era may have led the people of central and eastern European to be particularly sceptical of any attempt at forging a state-sponsored historical narrative.[2]

Independently of official truth commissions, there is some legal recognition of a 'right to truth' or a 'right to know'.[3] Articles 32 and 33 of the 1977 First Additional Protocol to the Geneva Conventions gives recognition to the rights of relatives of people who go missing during international armed conflict to know their fate and the International Committee of the Red Cross

1 R. Teitel, *Transitional justice* (New York: OUP 2000), 92.

2 Ibid., 93.

3 See, generally, Office of the UN High Commissioner for Human Rights, 'Study on the Right to Truth' E/CN.4/2006/91 (8 February 2006).

has now claimed that the right to know is a customary norm applicable in both international and non-international armed conflict.[4]

Much of the legal and theoretical work on the right to know in circumstances other than international and non-international armed conflict developed in response to the phenomenon of enforced disappearances in the 1970s, but its scope has since broadened.[5] For example, in its discussion of the initial report by Guatemala submitted under Article 40 ICCPR, the UN Human Rights Committee stated that the Guatemalan government should 'allow the victims of human rights violations to find out the truth about those acts, to know who the perpetrators of such acts are and to obtain appropriate compensation'.[6] The UN's Updated Set of Principles for the Protection and Promotion of Human Rights Through Action to Combat Impunity contains principles on both the inalienable right to truth, and victims' right to know. Principle 2 states that:

> Every people has the inalienable right to know the truth about past events concerning the perpetration of heinous crimes and about the circumstances and reasons that led, through massive or systematic violations, to the perpetration of those crimes. Full and effective exercise of the right to the truth provides a vital safeguard against the recurrence of violations.[7]

Within the UN's Updated Set of Principles there are also principles on the preservation of archive material and measures for facilitating access to archives. In contradistinction to PACE Resolution 1096, which is discussed again shortly, the UN Principles do not specifically address the issue of access to secret service files collected under the former regime.

The UN Human Rights Committee's recommendations to Guatemala on the right to truth were not made in contentious proceedings. The Inter-American Court of Human Rights has, however, addressed the construction of a right to truth in an application brought before it. The case of *Chumbipuma Aguirre et al. v Peru*, known as the Barrios Altos case, concerned the 1991 massacre of 15 people by members of the Peruvian Army who were acting for the 'death squadron' known as the Colina Group.[8] The events took place under the presidency of Alberto Fujimori and it is notable that when the case came

4 Ibid., [6–7]; ICRC, *Customary International Humanitarian Law: volume 1: rules* (Cambridge: CUP 2005), Rule 117.

5 UN High Commissioner for Human Rights, 'Study on the Right to Truth', *op. cit. supra* n 3, [8].

6 Concluding Observations of the Human Rights Committee: Guatemala. 03/04/1996. CCPR/C/79/Add.63. (Concluding Observations/Comments), [25].

7 Updated Set of Principles for the Protection and Promotion of Human Rights through Action to Combat Impunity, E/CN.4/2005/102/Add.1.

8 *Chumbipuma Aguirre et al v Peru* (Inter-American Court of Human Rights, 14 March 2001), [2(d)].

before the Inter-American Court the successor Peruvian government acquiesced completely to the findings of the Inter-American Court.[9]

In addition to finding that a purported amnesty law relating to these events violated the Inter-American Convention, the Court found that the events of 1991 disclosed violations of the right to life, the right to humane treatment, the right to a fair trial and the right to judicial protection.[10] In relation to the right to truth, the Inter-American Commission had argued that it could be founded on the right to a fair trial and the right to judicial protection and had its roots in the right to seek and receive information.[11] The Court did not make a separate finding on a violation of the right to truth. According to the Inter-American Court the right to truth was 'subsumed' within the victims' and relatives' rights emanating from the right to a fair trial and the right to judicial protection, of which it had already found violations.[12] This would seem to suggest that although the Inter-American system recognises the importance of a right to truth and its relationship to certain of the classic civil and political rights, it is not necessarily or explicitly founded on rights relating to freedom of expression.[13]

The right to truth has been comparatively slow to develop in the Council of Europe, although there is some recognition of its relevance in relation to disappearances. In terms of general access to state-held information, the Council of Ministers has made several important recommendations.[14] More specifically on the issue of the right to truth in post-conflict or transitional situations, in a 1987 recommendation to the Committee of Ministers concerning the situation in Cyprus, the Parliamentary Assembly called on the Committee 'to support every effort made to cast light on the fate of missing persons'.[15] In 2004, and in relation to the situation in the Balkans, the Parliamentary Assembly adopted a resolution that made the broader statement that 'the right to know the fate of missing relatives *is a fundamental right* of the families concerned and should be respected and implemented'.[16] Even more explicitly, in 2005 the Parliamentary Assembly gave advice on the content of a draft convention on enforced disappearances,[17] in which it stated that:

9 Ibid., [34] *et seq.*

10 Ibid., [39].

11 Ibid., [45].

12 Ibid., [48].

13 See also *Bámaca Velásquez v Republic of Guatemala* (Inter-American Court of Human Rights, 25 November 2000), [201].

14 Recommendation (81) 19 on Access to Information Held by Public Authorities, adopted by the Council of Ministers on November 25, 1981; Recommendation (2002) 2 on Access to Official Documents, February 21, 2002 III.

15 PACE Resolution 1056 (1987), [18(b)].

16 PACE Resolution 1414 (2004), on 'Persons unaccounted for as a result of armed conflicts or internal violence in the Balkans' [emphasis added].

17 PACE Resolution 1463 (2005).

family members of the disappeared persons should be recognised as independent victims of the enforced disappearance and be granted a 'right to the truth', that is, a right to be informed of the fate of their disappeared relatives.[18]

The jurisprudence of the European Court of Human Rights on access to official documents in general, and the right to truth as an element of post-conflict or transitional justice in particular, is fairly limited. Well before the end of the Cold War, in *Leander v Sweden*, the European Court confirmed that the Article 10 ECHR right 'to receive and impart information and ideas without interference by public authority' did not generate a free standing right of access to public information. Instead, the European Court merely observed that: '[T]he right to freedom to receive information basically prohibits a Government from restricting a person from receiving information that others wish or may be willing to impart to him.'[19]

For some time the Human Rights Chamber for Bosnia and Herzegovina had taken a more generous interpretation of the ECHR in this regard than the European Court itself. The Chamber was a judicial body established by the Dayton Peace Agreement and given jurisdiction over complaints about violations of, *inter alia*, the European Convention on Human Rights by its states' parties. In *Palic v Republika Srpska*, the Human Rights Chamber found that the fear and anguish caused by the applicant not knowing the fate of her disappeared husband, a colonel in the army of the Republic of Bosnia and Herzegovina, amounted to inhuman and degrading treatment and thus a violation of Article 3 ECHR. The Chamber also found a violation of Article 8 ECHR on the basis that the Respondent State was arbitrarily withholding information about her husband's fate or whereabouts from the applicant.[20] However, although the decision of the Human Rights Chamber in *Palic* bound the parties to the Dayton Peace Agreement, it does not constitute an authoritative interpretation of the European Convention. The European Court of Human Rights itself has not followed the Human Rights Chamber's lead in this area.

In Strasbourg, there has been some movement on this issue in recent years, with the admissibility decision in *Sdružení Jihočeské Matky v Czech Republic* recognising that the refusal to provide environmental campaigners with certain technical information they requested about a nuclear power plant could constitute a *prima facie* interference with Article 10 ECHR, although the application was declared inadmissible on national security grounds.[21] The European Court's judgment in *Társaság a Szabadságjogokért v Hungary*

18 Ibid., [10.2].

19 *Leander v Sweden* (1987) 9 EHRR 433, [74].

20 Decision of 11 January 2001, *Palic v Republika Srpska*, Case No. CH/99/3196, para. 91(5) and (6). See also Decision of 7 March 2003, "*Srebrenica Cases*", Case Nos. CH/01/8365 *et al.*

21 *Sdružení Jihočeské Matky v la République tchèque* (dec.) App no. 19101/03 (ECtHR, 10 July 2006) (available only in French), paragraphs not numbered.

confirmed that with this decision the Court had advanced 'towards a broader interpretation of the notion of "freedom to receive information" [. . .] and thereby towards the recognition of a right of access to information'.[22] It is also worth noting at this stage that national policies of lustration also have, as one of their aims, the public verification of individuals' involvement in the prior regime.[23] The European cases emanating from such lustration policies are discussed in Chapter 5.

It is also important to note that the European Court has made a series of robust judgments in cases brought against Russia concerning disappearances in Chechnya.[24] These are not so much connected to historical justice after the end of communism or the right to truth in post-conflict situations, since they concern an ongoing situation. Nevertheless, they have features in common with the circumstances giving rise to discussion of a right to truth by the Inter-American Court and Commission and the UN's Human Rights Committee. In *Imakayeva v Russia*, the European Court has found violations of the right to life and the right to liberty in relation to the actual disappearances and the right to life in relation to the failure effectively to investigate the disappearance.[25] Moreover, the Court also found that the Russian authorities' dismal handling of the applicant relative's complaint not only amounted to a violation of Article 13 ECHR on the right to an effective remedy but also amounted to inhuman and degrading treatment under Article 3 ECHR.[26] Although *Imakayeva*, the cases following it, and the earlier Turkish cases to which they make reference[27] were all, necessarily, brought by relatives rather than the disappeared, the European Court did not consolidate the issues into a relatives' 'right to truth'.

The most important recent development came in the 2011 case of *Association 21 December 1989 & Others v Romania*. The case concerned the glacially slow process of investigating the unsuccessful but violent crackdown on anti-government demonstrations in Romania in December 1989.[28] The European

22 *Társaság a Szabadságjogokért v Hungary* [2009] ECHR 618, [35].

23 A. Czarnota, 'Lustration, decommunisation and the rule of law' (2009) 1 *Hague Journal on the Rule of Law* 307.

24 E.g. *Imakayeva v Russia* (2006) 47 EHRR 4; *Musayeva v Russia* (2008) 47 EHRR 25; *Baysayeva v Russia* (2009) 48 EHRR 33; *Akhmadova v Russia* (2010) 51 EHRR 27; *Astamirova v Russia* (2010) 51 EHRR 43; see P. Leach, 'The Chechen conflict: analysing the oversight of the European Court of Human Rights' (2008) EHRLR 732.

25 *Imakayeva v Russia*, ibid.

26 This built on earlier Turkish cases, including in particular, *Çakici (Cakici) v Turkey* (2001) 31 EHRR 5.

27 Some, but not all, of the Turkish cases, such as *Kurt v Turkey* (1999) 27 EHRR 373 consider the leading judgment of the Inter-American Court of Human Rights on disappearances: the *Velasquez Rodriguez* Case, Judgment of July 29, 1988, Inter-Am.Ct.H.R. (Ser. C) No. 4 (1988).

28 *Association 21 December 1989 & Others v Romania*, App nos 33810/07 and 18817/08 (ECtHR, 24 May 2011), European Court of Human Rights, nos. 33810/07 and 18817/08 (available only in French).

Court found that Romania had failed to discharge its positive obligations under Article 2 ECHR in respect of two of the applicants. They had alleged that there had been a failure to conduct an effective investigation into the death of their son 20 years earlier. They also complained about the paucity of information they had received about the investigation. The European Court reiterated its position from *McKerr v UK*, that relatives of the victim must be involved in the proceedings to the extent necessary to protect their legitimate interests.[29] It went on to note the importance of the investigation of the events surrounding the overthrow of the Ceausescu regime for Romanian society.[30] The Court also emphasised the importance of the rights of victims and their families being able to ascertain the truth about the circumstances of events involving a large-scale violation of rights as fundamental as the right to life.[31] The Court held that this could entail the right to an effective judicial investigation and possibly also the right to compensation.[32] This does not go quite as far as deducing a fully fledged 'right to know' or 'right to truth', but the judgment at least used the terms[33] and clearly understood the importance of historical truth for the victims' families.

3.3 PACE Resolution 1096 and historical justice

The European Court's relative inertia on the right to truth may be related to the guidance it received on openness in PACE Resolution 1096 on 'measures to dismantle the heritage of former communist totalitarian systems'. The focus of PACE Resolution 1096 in relation to openness and access to information was much narrower than the broad idea of historical justice or even the right to truth. In Resolution 1096, the Parliamentary Assembly of the Council of Europe explained that it:

> welcomes the opening of secret service files for public examination in some former communist totalitarian countries. It advises all countries concerned to enable the persons affected to examine, upon their request, the files kept on them by the former secret services.

Thus the Resolution concentrated only on access to secret service files, and even then the language is hardly imperative: it 'welcomed' access to files and gave 'advice' on providing information on request. However, as we shall see, this passage of Resolution 1096 has been seized on by applicants and taken

29 Ibid., [135]; citing *McKerr v UK* [2001] ECHR 329.
30 Ibid., [142].
31 Ibid., [144].
32 Ibid.
33 Note that since the judgment is presently available only in French, and since the translation is the author's own, there is some margin for error.

into account a number of times by the European Court in its transitional jurisprudence on post-communist access to communist era secret service files.

From the outset, it is important to stress that the cases that follow are different to many of the cases discussed elsewhere in this book, since in them it is the applicant who stresses the importance of transitional justice in order to bolster their human rights claim, rather than the Respondent State arguing for some kind of transitional relativism.

3.4 The Convention as a foundation for access to secret information

The change of regime from totalitarian to democratic governance has raised difficult questions about the continued need for communist era secret files to remain secret. Although, in its early jurisprudence, the European Court seemed aloof to the extent to which gaining access to such files may assist in the delivery of historical justice, its later cases on lustration demonstrate some subtlety.

According to the facts presented in the Chamber's admissibility decision, the applicant in *Brinks v Netherlands*[34] was a Dutch academic who had lived and worked in communist East Germany from 1987 to 1990. After he returned to the Netherlands in 1990, Brinks gained the impression that he had come to the attention of the Netherlands National Security Service (BVD) and that his telephone was bugged. He claimed that his academic work had 'considerably irritated' fellow historians and politicians in the Netherlands. He felt that Dutch academics suspected he was a communist. All this led to his finding it difficult to gain suitable employment in the Netherlands, despite his having gained a *magna cum laude* doctorate degree in 1991. He left the Netherlands and went to work in Germany, the USA and the UK before returning again to the Netherlands in 1998. Shortly after his return, in early 2000, Brinks sought to gain access to the secret information that he thought the Dutch authorities held about him.[35]

The Minister of the Interior and Kingdom Relations stated that no information of a current nature held by the BVD would be disclosed to the applicant since it could give an insight into the BVD's sources, working methods and current level of knowledge. After permission was gained from a 'sister organisation' (which remains nameless in the Chamber's decision), the Minister was able to disclose outdated information. The information released to the applicant constituted of extracts from six documents, including a letter dating from 1977 from the applicant to the Public Prosecutor's Office at the West Berlin Regional Court, in which he had concluded with the phrase 'Death to the "German rule-of-law State".'

34 *Brinks v Netherlands* (dec.), App no 9940/04 (ECtHR, 5 April 2005).
35 The facts in the preceding paragraph are outlined in the decision.

The applicant appealed, largely unsuccessfully,[36] to the Groningen Regional Court and then to the Administrative Jurisdiction Division of the Council of State, claiming that the BVD held much more outdated information than it 'pretended'. In particular, he drew attention to a 1978 document suggesting that he had been the subject of an investigation and argued that the content and outcome of the investigation was also 'outdated information' to which he should be able to gain access. In both appeals, the courts had, with the applicant's permission, access to the information held about him to which he personally had no access.

The argument that Brinks made before the Administrative Jurisdiction Division of the Council of State is crucial to our discussion. Brinks stated that he failed to see how access to information collected during the Cold War could be refused on the basis that it could give insights into the present-day workings of the BVD. Thus, he was drawing specific attention to the changing democratic context of post-Cold War Europe. Unlike the classic 'right to truth' cases, he was not seeking information held by a prior totalitarian regime, but information collected by his own democratic state while it was an enemy of the former communist bloc. Brinks claimed that this violated his right to privacy under Article 8 ECHR and, since he could not find appropriate employment as an historian or journalist in the Netherlands, there was a violation of his Article 10 right to freedom of expression.

The Chamber found that there was an interference with the applicant's right to respect for his private life, but that it was necessary in a democratic society. The Chamber recognised that secret surveillance designed to protect national security must be subject to supervision because of the risk that it could undermine or even destroy the democracy that it sought to defend. Thus, in order for such surveillance to remain compatible with Article 8 ECHR it was necessary for it to be subject to procedural and judicial safeguards. The Chamber found that Brinks had benefited from such safeguards, and that consequently his application under Article 8 was manifestly ill founded. The Chamber also drew attention to the state's margin of appreciation in national security matters and found that the national security concerns, 'outweighed the individual interest of the applicant in being granted full access to any undisclosed information possibly held on him by the agency'. The Chamber also quickly found that there was nothing in the case file that could disclose a violation of Article 10 ECHR and that the complaint based on it was also manifestly ill founded.

The circumstances of, and decision in, *Brinks* are curious. The circumstances are curious because they disclose how the democratic transition of one state may have ramifications for human rights law within its neighbours. This, in turn, raises the question as to whether ideas about historical justice in the transitional context are a valid consideration in those neighbouring states.

36 The Regional Court granted access to one more document.

The decision itself is curious because, despite citing *Leander*, the Chamber did not acknowledge the possibility that there could be an infringement of Article 10 ECHR based on the right to receive information. It can be conceded that the decision was taken a year before the thawing of the Court's approach to cases brought on this ground seen in *Sdružení Jihočeské Matky v Czech Republic*, but nevertheless there was at least a *prima facie* case to answer.

It is disappointing because it fails to understand the transitional implications of gaining access to documents from a different era – in particular, the dispelling of myths and paranoia. In the light of the radical change of circumstances since the end of the Cold War and the clear advice given to former communist states in PACE Resolution 1096, the Chamber's cursory approach to reviewing the national security grounds for maintaining the secrecy of documents compiled in the 1970s is particularly problematic. The Chamber's focus on the procedural aspects of compatibility with Article 8(2) ECHR did not get to the heart of the transitional issue: that with the end of the Cold War the continuing need for certain documents to remain secret must be open to challenge.

There was a similar reluctance in *Rotaru v Romania*.[37] The applicant alleged that the Romanian Intelligence Service continued to hold information about him that had been collected in the communist era, which it could at any moment make use of and some of which was false and defamatory. The Grand Chamber found by a majority of 16 to 1 that in the case there had been a violation of, *inter alia*, Article 8 ECHR. However the majority judgment did so on the basis that the relevant domestic law did not indicate with 'reasonable clarity the scope and manner of exercise of the relevant discretion conferred on the public authorities' with respect to the secret information.[38]

The Concurring Opinion of Judge Wildhaber, joined by Judges Makarczyk, Türmen, Costa, Tulkens, Casadevall and Weber went further into the substantive issues. They noted that one of the alleged inaccuracies related to whether or not the applicant had been a member of, 'an extreme right-wing, nationalist, anti-Semitic and paramilitary movement' (which he denied). They stressed that the data had been collected by a previous regime 'in an unlawful and arbitrary way.'[39] As such the continued retention of the information pursued neither a legitimate aim nor was it necessary in a democratic society.

3.4.1 Access to secret information during lustration proceedings

The extent to which the Convention can be a foundation for access to secret information has also been tested in relation to lustration proceedings carried out in the Contracting Parties from central and eastern Europe. Lustration is

37 *Rotaru v Romania* (2000) 8 BHRC 449.

38 Ibid., [61].

39 Ibid., Concurring Opinion of Judge Wildhaber, joined by Judges Makarczyk, Türmen, Costa, Tulkens, Casadevall and Weber, paragraphs not numbered.

the practice of purging official posts of members of the previous regime.[40] It is examined in its own right in Chapter 5. In its consideration of access to information cases arising from lustration processes, the European Court has explicitly drawn on PACE Resolution 1096 to formulate a clear principle on the importance of allowing challenges to the continued need for keeping communist era documents secret.

Along with many of the former communist states, Czechoslovakia passed a lustration act with the aim of removing collaborators with the former regime from senior posts in state organs and institutions.[41] Members of and collaborators with the former Czechoslovakian State Security Agency, the StB, could be identified by being issued with a negative security clearance. The connection to historical justice is quite explicit in the Slovakian context, since, from 2002, the recording, collecting, disclosing, publishing, managing and use of documents generated by the StB is governed by the 'National Memory Act', which also established a National Memory Institute in Slovakia.[42]

The applicant in *Turek v Slovakia* had held a senior post in the state administration of the school system. The Czechoslovakian and, later, Slovak courts upheld a negative security clearance issued in relation to Turek, the consequence of which was that he resigned from his post and later felt compelled to leave his employer completely.[43]

Turek claimed that the communist authorities had wrongly classified him as a collaborator during the communist era: he claimed never to have passed on any information or to have helped the authorities at all. However, the present-day Slovakian authorities would not give Turek access to top secret guidelines dating from 1972 which defined exactly what constituted a 'collaborator' and how they could be recruited. Turek claimed that this constituted an infringement of his rights under Articles 6 and 8 ECHR.

This case was by no means the first on lustration, but it was the first to draw on paragraph 9 of PACE Resolution 1096 (on access to secret service files). Turek won on Article 6(1) ECHR, due to the unreasonable length that the proceedings in his case had taken.[44] Like the *Brinks* and *Rotaru* judgments, it was in relation to Article 8 ECHR that the European Court confronted the issue of information collected during the Cold War.

Turek argued that being labelled an StB collaborator interfered with his moral and physical integrity and with his good name and reputation.[45] He argued that the 1972 guidelines were crucial evidence in his case[46] and that,

40 See A. Czarnota, *op. cit. supra* n 23, 310.
41 *Turek v Slovakia* (2007) 44 EHRR 43, [9]; the content of the Act is detailed at [67] *et seq.*
42 Ibid., [76–77].
43 Ibid., [12].
44 Ibid., [99].
45 Ibid., [103].
46 Ibid., [106].

unless he had access to the definition of the term 'StB agent', it would be virtually impossible for him to prove he was not one.[47] Echoing *Brinks*, he argued that the necessity of the guidelines remaining top secret was 'questionable' now that it was 'years after the fall of communism'.[48]

The European Court considered PACE Resolution 1096 as a 'relevant international instrument' and cited not only the paragraphs on lustration but also the paragraph on access to secret service files.[49] The European Court appeared to have been influenced by this and, responding to Turek's argument, went on to state that:

> in proceedings related to the operations of state security agencies, there may be legitimate grounds to limit access to certain documents and other materials. However, in respect of lustration proceedings, this consideration loses much of its validity. [Lustration proceedings] are, by their very nature, oriented towards the establishment of facts dating back to the communist era and are not directly linked to the current functions and operations of the security services. Thus, *unless the contrary is shown on the facts of a specific case, it cannot be assumed that there remains a continuing and actual public interest in imposing limitations on access to materials classified as confidential under former regimes*.[50]
>
> [emphasis added]

The European Court found a violation of Article 8 ECHR on the basis that there was no procedure by which Turek could seek effective protection of his right to respect for his private life.[51]

The final part of this last quotation from *Turek* refers to 'regimes', in the plural, and suggests that the European Court's approach would not be confined to the situation in Slovakia but would be relevant in other transitional contexts as well. This proved to be the case and the same point was made in the later cases of *Matyjek v Poland*,[52] *Bobek v Poland*[53] and *Luboch v Poland*.[54] Likewise, in *Haralambie v Romania*,[55] the European Court found violations of Article 6 and Article 8 ECHR when the applicant had waited six years to gain access to information held about him.

47 Ibid., [107].
48 Ibid.
49 Ibid., [78].
50 Ibid., [115]. The Dissenting Opinion of Judge Maruste agreed with this point of principle, but argued that there had been sufficient safeguards on the facts of this case.
51 Ibid., [116]; the reason in relation to the procedural elements of Article 8 is discussed in Chapter 5.
52 *Matyjek v Poland* [2007] ECHR 317, [56].
53 *Bobek v Poland* [2007] ECHR 621, [57].
54 *Luboch v Poland* [2008] ECHR 31, [61].
55 *Haralambie v Romania*, App no 21737/0327 (ECtHR 27 October 2009) (available only in French).

In their Joint Concurring Opinion in *Petrenco v Moldova*, Judges Garlicki, Šikuta and Poalelungi went so far as to say that they would 'not exclude the possibility' that states had certain positive obligations in this regard. This would certainly benefit victims of the communist regimes as well as those who are subject to lustration.

Thus the European Court has clarified an important point of principle in these cases, albeit one that falls short of forging conceptual links with a more general right to truth or judicial developments on the Article 10 right to receive information. The approach is based on the assumption that all the secret information at issue is historical rather than current, therefore it is debatable whether the reasoning could be extended to benefit someone in the same position as Brinks (who sought to challenge whether the desired information was current or not).

3.4.2 Openness and historical research

The introduction to this chapter noted the general scepticism of central and eastern European ex-communist states towards 'official histories'. There is a resulting marked absence of truth and reconciliation processes within the Council of Europe. In this context, the construction of unofficial histories, via the media and academic research, takes on a special significance in the search for historical justice.

Kenedi v Hungary[56] concerned the attempts of an historian to gain access to certain documents he required in order to write a book about the activities of the Hungarian State Security Service in the 1960s.

The applicant's request to the Ministry of the Interior for access to the documents he needed was denied. He brought an action against the Ministry and the Budapest Regional Court found in his favour. Contrary to the wording of the judgment, in November 1999 the Ministry subsequently offered the information to Kenedi as long as he signed a confidentiality agreement. Kenedi then successfully launched an action for enforcement of the judgment in his favour and the Ministry's legal attempts to terminate the enforcement proceedings failed. Now into October 2002, the Ministry offered Kenedi a permit to access the documents, but restricted him from publishing the information contained within them to the extent that state secrets were concerned.

In June 2003 the Regional Court then fined the Ministry for non-compliance with the original judgment. In separate developments, in late 2003 all but one of the relevant documents were transferred to the national archives and made public anyway. Further proceedings were taken against the Ministry and its successor, the Ministry of Local Government and Regional Development, but at the time of the European Court's judgment the applicant still had not had access to the remaining one document.

56 *Kenedi v Hungary* [2009] ECHR 786.

Kenedi argued that the length of the enforcement proceedings constituted a violation of Article 6(1) ECHR, which guarantees that, in the determination of their 'civil rights and obligations' everyone is entitled to a hearing within a reasonable time. Somewhat disingenuously the Respondent State argued that he had contributed to the length of the proceedings by insisting on having unrestricted access to all the documents.

The European Court observed that Kenedi needed access to the documents to complete his book and that the publication fell within the applicant's freedom of expression. Freedom of expression was therefore the relevant 'civil right' for the purposes of Article 6(1) ECHR. The European Court noted that proceedings had begun back in 1998 when Kenedi had first requested access to the documents and that he had still not had unfettered access to them in spite of several judicial findings in his favour. The European Court observed that Hungary had not put forward 'any fact or convincing argument' to demonstrate that the length of the proceedings was reasonable and therefore concluded that there was a violation of Article 6(1) ECHR.

The European Court came closest to relating access to documents to the particular importance of historical research in transitional democracies during its discussion of Article 10 ECHR. Citing *Társaság a Szabadságjogokért v Hungary*, in which we saw the Court confirming it was moving towards a broader interpretation of the notion of freedom to receive information, the European Court emphasised that: '[A]access to original documentary sources for legitimate historical research was an essential element of the exercise of the applicant's right to freedom of expression.'

This statement, however, would be as valid in relation to a stable democracy.[57] In other words, the statement does not quite capture the particular importance of objective historical research to the achievement of historical justice via unofficial histories in transitional democracies. Neither does it draw on the principles contained in PACE Resolution 1096, which had guided the European Court to its useful point of principle that the continuing and actual public interest in imposing limitations on access to secret materials of the former regime cannot be assumed.

If the reasoning employed in *Kenedi* is not aimed squarely enough at the transitional context, there is at least one advantage, however. The Court has extended the role of 'public watchdog', which it has recognised the press plays, to 'social watchdogs'[58] and, in *Kenedi*, implied that academics may be another potential form of social watchdog.[59] As Buyse has eloquently observed,

57 A. Buyse, 'The truth, the past and the present', in A. Buyse and M. Hamilton (eds), *Transitional Jurisprudence and the ECHR* (Cambridge: CUP 2001), 146, argued that the case does not constitute a '*sui generis* example of transitional jurisprudence'.

58 *Társaság a Szabadságjogokért v Hungary, op. cit. supra* n 22, [27].

59 See *Kenedi v Hungary, op. cit. supra* n 56, 43, but note that the European Court did not *explicitly* state that academics were social watchdogs.

this constitutes 'a democratisation of information'.[60] Building on this we shall see later that the European Court has been more assertive on the link between historical research and free expression when it comes to the publication of materials relevant to the discussion of the past than it has been in relation to accessing previously secret materials – to draw the line at permitting 'wild' lustration.[61]

In *Karsai v Hungary*,[62] the debate was about the reputation of the pre-communist regime led by the late Pál Teleki, who as Hungary's two-time prime minister had allied Hungary with Nazi Germany at the start of World War II.[63] The debate began in 2004 because it had been suggested that a statue should be erected in Teleki's honour and this appealed to certain people on the political right.[64] The case itself arose because Karsai, a university professor of history, joined the debate by stating that Teleki had been 'one of the most reprehensible figures of Hungarian history'.[65] He alleged that Teleki had passed many anti-Semitic laws and that proponents of the statue were supporting their position by making 'overtly anti-Semitic arguments'.[66] A particularly aggrieved proponent of the statue named in Karsai's statements, and referred to in the case only as B.T., successfully sued Karsai gaining compensation and the publication of a 'rectification' from Karsai.[67]

The European Court found unanimously that the domestic courts had not provided a convincing need to prioritise the reputational rights of B.T. over free expression where issues of public interest were at stake.[68] In doing so, it reinforced the recognition that historical records and historical debate play an important role in transitional democracies.

3.5 Historical justice, memorialisation and matters of 'purely historical fact'

The cases discussed thus far in this chapter have involved situations in which the applicant's request for access to information could be seen within the paradigm of historical justice. These cases took limited inspiration from PACE Resolution 1096. However, there are also several other important ways in which the jurisprudence of the European Court of Human Rights connects with the issue of historical justice, but which are less obviously identifiable.

60 A. Buyse, *op. cit. supra* n 57, 147.
61 See Chapter 6.
62 *Karsai v Hungary* [2009] ECHR 1974.
63 Ibid., [7].
64 Ibid.
65 Ibid., [8].
66 Ibid., [9].
67 Ibid., [13].
68 Ibid., [37].

In Chapter 2, we saw that domestic successor trials deal not only in individual criminality but also take on a ritual function, delegitimising the previous regime and helping to establish the legitimacy of the successor regime.[69] If domestic successor trials play this ritual function in terms of the delivery of historical justice, then undoubtedly (and intentionally or otherwise) the judgments of the European Court of Human Rights in relation to them will take on the same ritual function.

In Chapter 2, further, it was therefore argued that the European Court's approach to the human rights cases generated by successor trials could amplify or impede the process of historical accounting that they represent. This was why the Court's apparent rejection of the Hungarian Supreme Court's findings on the facts leading up to the prosecution in *Korbely* was particularly awkward.[70]

There is, therefore, a much broader sense in which the European Court's judgments on transitional issues will be received as playing a role in historical accounting. Writing in relation to restitution policies, which are discussed in their own right in Chapter 4, Patrick Macklem has observed that international human rights law has begun to find ways in which to give expression to collective memories.[71] Macklem argued that this does not come naturally to human rights lawyers because of, the 'field's fearlessly modernist focus on the present and future at the expense of the past, and for its optimistic tendency to equate human rights with human progress'.[72] Nevertheless, he observed that law can and does play a role in the construction of collective memories. In the same way that statues or monuments may become 'memorial sites' by which groups may seek to sustain their collective identity: 'Law's memorial sites are comprised of principles, rules and procedures that invest moments in history with normative significance.'[73]

Specifically on the issue of equality claims arising from post-communist property restitution policies, Macklem went on to contrast the approach of the UN Human Rights Committee and the European Court of Human Rights and found that the latter remains 'thoroughly modernist in orientation in its steadfast resistance to engage the past.' This element of Macklem's argument is revisited in Chapter 4.[74]

There is yet another important, arguably meta-juridical, sense in which the European Court 'does' (or is asked to 'do') historical justice: the way in which it

69 Teitel, *op. cit. supra* n 1, 73.
70 *Korbely v Hungary* [2008] ECHR 847; (2010) 50 EHRR 48, discussed in Chapter 2.
71 P. Macklem, 'Rybná 9, Praha 1: restitution and memory in international human rights law' (2005) 16(1) *EJIL* 1.
72 Ibid., 13.
73 Ibid., 14.
74 Macklem's observations about the relationship between international and European human rights cases on property restitution and the construction of memory have been echoed by both Tom Allen and Istvan Pogany, among others, and these also are discussed further in Chapter 4.

presents not just the facts of the case but the broad historical context in which those facts can be placed. Indeed, the parties may attempt to enlist the European Court's assistance to settle not only contested facts directly relevant to the case at hand, but also wider historical debates. For example, the circumstances surrounding the Baltic states' incorporation into the USSR in 1940 have surfaced as background issues in several cases. We noted the so-called 'Molotov-Ribbentrop Pact' in Chapter 1. It is clear from several cases brought before the European Court that the Baltic states seek recognition that their incorporation into the USSR was unlawful, whereas Russia maintains it was not.

The 2004 Chamber and 2006 Grand Chamber judgments in *Ždanoka v Latvia* reached opposite conclusions on the alleged violation of the Convention and are discussed in detail in Chapters 6, 7 and 8 (a quotation from this case was also used the Introduction and in Chapter 1: it is a significant case). Of relevance to this chapter is that both judgments stated that the European Court would not pronounce on matters of 'purely historical fact'.[75] This chimes with Tom Allen's observations about certain restitution cases, which, he argues, show that 'there is a reluctance to allow the Court to be used as a forum for hearing disputes that have their origin in the pre-transitional era.'[76] Indeed, Allen concluded that in transitional restitution cases generally 'there is a strong (though not universal) belief [within the European Court] that there is little to be gained by investigating the stories of victims.'[77]

The restitution cases are discussed in detail in Chapter 4, when we shall also return to Macklem's observations, but at present it is Allen's reference to 'stories' that is relevant. It supports the idea that the European Court could play a role in the construction of historical narratives both within and outside its formal fact-finding role, although it is clear that Allen does not think it is doing so at present. Nevertheless, the Grand Chamber judgment in *Ždanoka* went on to observe that:

> Latvia, along with the other Baltic States, lost its independence in 1940 in the aftermath of the partition of central and eastern Europe agreed by Hitler's Germany and Stalin's Soviet Union by way of the secret protocol to the Molotov-Ribbentrop Pact, an agreement contrary to the generally recognised principles of international law.[78]

This observation formed the backdrop to legal discussion of the proportionality of a restriction placed on the applicant's right to free and fair elections, contained in Article 3, Protocol 1, ECHR. By giving recognition to the

75 *Ždanoka v Latvia* (GC) [2006] ECHR 231, [96]; *Ždanoka v Latvia* (Chamber) (2005) 41 EHRR 31, [77].

76 T. Allen, 'Restitution and transitional justice in the European Court of Human Rights' (2007) 13(1) *Columbia Journal of European Law* 1, 30.

77 Ibid., 45.

78 *Ždanoka v Latvia* (GC), *op. cit. supra* n 75, [119].

proposition that the Molotov-Ribbentrop Pact was unlawful, the European Court may have helped the transitional Baltic states in the development of an historical narrative of their experiences under communism.

In the course of its submissions in *Kuolelis, Bartoševičius and Burokevičius v Lithuania*,[79] the Respondent State explained that it had been the subject of 'annexation' and that the Lithuanian government had been 'illegally ousted by Soviet occupying forces from 1940 to 1990'. The European Court, however, did not make a finding in this regard since the legally decisive question pertained to the crystallisation of Lithuanian independence from the USSR in the early 1990s, rather than the circumstances surrounding the prior loss of its independence.[80] Nevertheless, in the introduction to the judgment the European Court had referred to the Soviet 'invasion' of Lithuania in early 1940 and the completion of the 'annexation' in August 1940.[81] These comments were made under the heading of 'historical and political background' and the European Court simply stated that the background 'was set out' in the relevant domestic courts.[82] The background materials were not therefore presented as contested domestic findings of material fact, but rather as stable propositions that merely appeared in the domestic findings. Thus the European Court seemed content to accept and to repeat the proposition that in 1940 there was an 'invasion' and 'annexation'.

Although not as explicit as *Ždanoka*, the approach to the Molotov-Ribbentrop Pact in *Kuolelis* was consistent with it. Even referring to it as 'unlawful' in the introduction, rather than in the legal findings, lends credence to the position of the Baltic states. Given this relative consistency of approach to the events of 1940, the approach of the European Court in both the 2008 Chamber judgment and 2010 Grand Chamber judgment in *Kononov v Latvia*[83] merits some discussion. In these judgments, the Court seemed to retreat from its earlier observations about the Molotov-Ribbentrop Pact.

In the Chamber decision in *Kononov v Latvia*, the parties and Russia as a third-party intervener all made submissions on whether Latvia's incorporation into the USSR in 1940 was lawful. The facts of the case related to alleged war crimes committed in 1944. The Chamber reiterated that it would not pronounce on 'matters of purely historical fact' and that for the purposes of the case before it the issues surrounding Latvia's incorporation were neither decisive nor relevant.[84] The Grand Chamber was faced with similar arguments. The applicant argued that:

> Latvia was lawfully one of the Republics of the USSR since 1940 and *it was contrary to historical fact and common sense to state otherwise*. The

79 *Kuolelis, Bartoševičius and Burokevičius v Lithuania* [2008] ECHR 152.
80 See the discussion in Chapter 2.
81 *Kuolelis, op. cit. supra* n 79, [8].
82 Ibid., [7].
83 *Kononov v Latvia* (Chamber) [2008] ECHR 695; *Kononov v Latvia* (GC) [2010] ECHR 667.
84 *Kononov v Latvia* (Chamber) [112].

> Declaration of 4 May 1990 and his conviction were designed to achieve a condemnation of the annexation of Latvia in 1940 as illegal, rather than a desire to fulfil international obligations to pursue war criminals.[85]
> [emphasis added]

The Russian government intervened in support of this position, stating that the European Court 'was not competent to re-evaluate history and notably the incorporation of Latvia into the USSR in 1940'.[86]

The government of Lithuania intervened to remind the European Court that it had already recognised that the Baltic states had lost their independence through the Molotov-Ribbentrop Pact (although it cited no cases to support this proposition) and that the Pact was 'an undisputed historical fact, an illegal agreement to commit aggression against, *inter alia*, the Baltic states and resulted in their illegal occupation by Soviet forces.'[87]

Despite its earlier finding in *Ždanoka* and the Chamber's references to 'annexation' in *Kuolelis*, the Grand Chamber in *Kononov* explicitly held that it was 'not its role to pronounce on the question of the lawfulness of Latvia's incorporation into the USSR'.[88] This is a wholesale retreat from the clear statement of the Grand Chamber in *Ždanoka* and the summary of apparently uncontested facts in *Kuolelis*.

In 1998 in *Lehideux and Isorni v France*, the Grand Chamber had held that there was a 'category of clearly established historical facts – such as the Holocaust – whose negation or revision would be removed from the protection of Article 10 by Article 17'.[89] The European Commission and Court have also made reference to more specific assertions being 'historical facts of common knowledge', such as the fact that people were gassed to death at the Struthof-Natzweiler Nazi death camp (in an inadmissible application brought by someone charged with complicity in the denial of crimes against humanity).[90]

From the *Ždanoka* and *Kuelelis* judgments, it might have appeared that the events of 1940 were on their way to becoming 'historical facts of common knowledge', rather than 'purely historical facts' outside the European Court's jurisdiction to consider. A cursory examination of basic public international law would show that the acquisition of territory by force was outlawed at least as early as 1928 through the Pact of Paris (also known as the Briand-Kellogg Pact); that the principle was affirmed with the crystallisation of the 'Stimson doctrine of non-recognition';[91] and was explicitly reaffirmed by the Assembly

85 *Kononov v Latvia* (GC) [16].
86 *Kononov v Latvia* (GC) [174].
87 *Kononov v Latvia* (GC) [179].
88 *Kononov v Latvia* (GC) [210].
89 *Lehideux and Isorni v France* (2000) 30 EHRR 665.
90 *Marais v France* [1996] ECHR 103.
91 See Q. Wright, 'The Stimson note of January 7 1932' (1932) 26 *AJIL* 342.

of the League of Nations in 1932.[92] This makes the legal quality of the Molotov-Ribbentrop Pact and its secret protocol at least questionable.[93]

The USA never recognised the incorporation of Latvia, Lithuania and Estonia into the USSR and the UK gave only *de facto* recognition.[94] In 1987 the Parliamentary Assembly of the Council of Europe passed a resolution 'on the situation of the Baltic peoples' in which it, 'recalled that the incorporation of the three Baltic states into the Soviet Union was and still is a flagrant violation of the right to self-determination of peoples'.[95] Moreover, and as the Lithuanian government pointed out in the *Kononov* case, in 1989 the Supreme Soviet of the USSR had even recognised its unlawful aggression towards the Baltic states in its 'Resolution on the Political and Juridical Appraisal of the Soviet-German Non-Aggression Treaty of 1939'.[96]

Whenever the European Court has explicitly or tacitly accepted that the incorporation of the Baltic states into the USSR was by way of annexation, and was therefore unlawful, it has undoubtedly impacted on the achievement of historical justice in those states by validating such a crucial element of their historical narrative. By contrast, its failure to continue this trend in the *Kononov* case risks undermining the delivery of historical justice in the Baltic states. It might also appear to the Baltic states that the European Court was influenced by pressure placed on it by Russia (at the time of the Chamber judgment still refusing to ratify Protocol 14).[97]

In this section, we have seen that the judgments of the European Court may play a significant role in the memorialisation of certain events. The Court's approach to major historical events forming the background to its cases may impact on the achievement of historical justice in the newer Contracting Parties from central and eastern Europe. The inconsistent approach to the Molotov-Ribbentrop Pact suggests that the European Court either does not recognise these implications or has consciously retreated from a position in which it might 'do' transitional justice by confirming the circumstances by which the Baltic states became subject to totalitarian rule.

3.6 Conclusion

The cases discussed in this chapter that have taken their inspiration from PACE Resolution 1096 have only engaged directly with a very narrow subset

92 See, generally, D.J. Harris, *Case and Materials on International Law*, 5th edn (London: Sweet & Maxwell 1997), 218 *et seq.*

93 See D. Žalimas, 'Legal issues on the continuity of the republic of Lithuania' (2006) 2 *Hawaiian Journal of Law and Politics* 73, 74 *et seq.*

94 R. Wallace, *International Law*, 5th edn (London: Sweet & Maxwell 2005), 78 and 99.

95 PACE Resolution 872 (1987) on 'the situation of the Baltic peoples', [3].

96 *Kononov v Latvia* (GC), *op. cit. supra* n 83, [179]; Žalimas, *op. cit. supra* n 93, 76; S.D. Murphy, 'Democratic legitimacy and the recognition of states and governments' (1999) 48(3) *ICLQ* 545, 557.

97 Russia ratified Protocol 14 on 18 February 2010: note the discussion of this in Chapter 1.

of issues connected to historical justice and the right to truth, namely those concerning access to information deemed secret during the communist era.

The most striking feature of these cases is that applicants were using human rights law to *seek* transitional justice rather than to *restrain* a policy implemented in its name. Where the applicant sought access to communist era information, the transitional justice consideration was one where 'doing' transitional (historical) justice would have resulted in stronger implementation of the Convention, *viz.* the rights to respect for home, family and private life and the right to receive information. There was no obvious rule of law dilemma and therefore no call for transitional relativism.

Nevertheless, within these cases the common thread of historical justice was not well recognised, with the effect that some parallels between different cases and different Convention articles were missed by the Court. The European Court has therefore not always been able to use the medium of human rights law to 'improve' transitional policies, for example by confirming procedural minima. The recognition of a presumptive right to communist-era secret information in *Turek* and the other Article 8 lustration cases citing PACE Resolution 1096 certainly showed modest recognition of the importance of historical justice. However, failure to identify the same theme of historical justice in *Brinks v Netherlands* has implications for the universality of human rights, since the contrast between it and *Turek* might support the hypothesis that the newer and older Contracting Parties may be treated differently in comparable situations. The deferential *Brinks* case emanated from an established democracy, whereas *Turek* and the cases following it did not. Of course, it could therefore be argued that it is not appropriate to analyse *Brinks* from the perspective of transitional justice at all. Nevertheless, the European Convention is a human rights system and the system as a whole must respond to all the novel circumstances presented by the end of the Cold War.

A greater recognition of the notion of historical justice would also enable some cross-fertilisation of reasoning in cases brought under different Convention articles. *Brinks* and *Turek* (and the other lustration cases cited here, which followed it) concentrated on access to communist era secret information as an element of Article 8 ECHR and so they did not tap into European judicial developments in relation the right to receive information under Article 10 ECHR. This approach sidesteps the potentially valuable relationship between these cases and developments in the post-conflict or transitional context on the right to truth. If the Court were to continue to develop a broader approach to the right to receive information, then a good starting place could be in relation to the arguably *lex specialis* of the right to truth in post-conflict or transitional contexts.

Although the application of Article 10 ECHR was decisive in *Kenedi*, it was because the information sought was to be used to write a book and therefore the element of Article 10 at issue was freedom of expression (i.e. rather than the right to receive information). Owing to the strong connection between Article 10 ECHR and the foundations of democracy itself, there is scope to allow some discussion of its *prima facie* application in cases like these even if only to test whether there are relevant and sufficient reasons to demonstrate that restricting such applicants' rights to receive communist era secret information is necessary in a democratic society. This would tap into some of the concerns expressed in the concurring opinion of Judge Wildhaber, joined by Judges Makarczyk, Türmen, Costa, Tulkens, Casadevall and Weber in *Rotaru v Romania*.

Finally in this chapter, we examined the role of the European Court where the implications for historical justice derived not from cases in which applicants sought access to historical documents, but from its approach to material and background facts. It is here where the European Court has been asked in a sense to 'do' transitional justice, but still without conceding transitional relativism.

While there is something inherently judicial about successor trials, legal systems do not necessarily have such a central role in historical accounting. Nevertheless, it is clear from the cases discussed that the European Court's approach not only to the facts of the case but also to wider issues of historical importance certainly impact on historical justice. Just as we saw in relation to access to communist era documents, it is by no means clear that human rights law presents a *prima facie* barrier to achieving historical justice (although we encountered academic commentary that argued that the European Court is reluctant to become sufficiently involved in the process of memorialisation).[98] The European Court's developing reticence towards the events of 1940 would seem also to support this hypothesis.

If human rights law does not need to be compromised by transitional relativism in order to achieve historical justice, then arguably the European Court could do more in this regard. This is not to say that courts make ideal places for findings of fact, be they material to the case or a part of its background. Legal epistemology is not great[99] and the European Court should do its best to nurture domestic narratives rather than impose internationally palatable official truths. However, and without doing this, there are at least some questions – such as those relating to the events of 1940 – that the Court is surely able to answer without compromising either its neutrality or its commitment to the universality of human rights.

98 See, e.g., Macklem, *op. cit. supra* n 71; Allen, *op. cit. supra* n 76.

99 See J.A. Sweeney, 'Credibility, proof and refugee law' (2009) 21(4) *International Journal of Refugee Law* 700, 725; J.A. Sweeney, 'The "lure" of facts in asylum appeals' in S. Smith (ed.), *Applying Theory to Policy and Practice: issues for critical reflection* (Aldershot: Ashgate 2007).

4 Reparatory justice and the restitution of property

4.1 Introduction

This chapter examines the relationship between human rights law and attempts at reparatory justice. The aim of reparatory measures is to repair, in some way, past wrongs, but as Teitel has observed, in transitional states they take on both functional and symbolic roles in the state's transformation itself.[1]

The communist regimes of central and eastern Europe were engaged in massive programmes of nationalisation and expropriation. Since the 1990s many of those states, which had now joined the Council of Europe, started to attempt policies of restitution.[2] There is guidance on good practice in relation to these policies in PACE Resolution 1096, and its observations on property restitution are quite detailed. In the cases that are discussed here, we shall see that the European Convention has been cited in order to bolster claims for restitution; to criticise the internal workings of restitution processes by dissatisfied claimants; and to oppose the process by those who have come into possession of property that was confiscated during communism.

The Court's relative inability to *require* restitution exposes – perhaps more clearly than any of the other policies examined in this book – a tension between what is 'right' and what is a human right. Although the limitations of human rights law as a means to secure reparatory justice for victims of former regimes are patent, this does not mean that the European Court has played an unimportant role. It has backed the legitimacy of restitution programmes and policed their implementation, while allowing some degree of diversity between transitional states. The question is whether in its jurisprudence on this particularly difficult transitional issue, the European Court has signalled a shift away from its previous standards such as to provide evidence of transitional relativism.

Before examining the advice of PACE and of European human rights cases on reparatory justice (and especially property restitution), we shall examine

1 R. Teitel, *Transitional Justice* (New York: OUP 2000), 7 and 119 *et seq.*

2 See the general summary in *Maria Atanasiu and Others v Romania* [2010] ECHR 1502, [85–107].

the extent to which human rights mechanisms can both constitute and deliver reparation for periods of totalitarianism.

4.1.1 International human rights law as a basis for reparatory justice

We noted in Chapter 3 that international human rights cases arising from transitional periods may, whatever their subject matter, themselves become sites of memory: they may play a role in the construction of historical knowledge and national narratives and thereby become part of the process of arriving at historical justice. Similarly, the creation of new international human rights institutions might be seen by some as a means of providing closure both for the international community and for the people that suffered under the previous regime.[3] In other words, the mere creation of international human rights mechanisms might constitute a form of reparatory justice itself. This would, however, seem a little optimistic.

International human rights mechanisms may also play a more direct role in securing reparation. It is a principle of public international law that 'every violation of an international obligation which results in harm creates a duty to make adequate reparation.'[4] However, the applicability of the general rules of international law on state responsibility to individuals, and individuals' capacity to assert their applicability, is moot.[5]

The UN's 'Basic Principles and Guidelines on the Right to a Remedy and Reparation for Victims of Gross Violations of International Human Rights Law and Serious Violations of International Humanitarian Law'[6] have gone some way to stressing the importance of reparation at the international level. Moreover, international and regional human rights courts and tribunals have the capacity to award damages for human rights abuses and so they can deliver reparatory justice by operationalising state responsibility.

Antoine Buyse[7] and Ruti Teitel[8] have both cited *Velásquez Rodríguez*, the leading Inter-American case on disappearances, in this regard. In that case, the Inter-American Court of Human Rights had to establish the circumstances

3 T. Allen, 'Restitution and transitional justice in the European Court of Human Rights' (2007) 13(1) *Columbia Journal of European Law* 1, 3: but note that Allen himself does not subscribe to this view.

4 See *Velasquez Rodriguez v Honduras (Compensatory Damages)* (1989) 7 Inter-Am. Ct. H.R. (ser. C), [25], Teitel, *op. cit. supra* n 1, 119.

5 See the discussion in A. Buyse, *Post-Conflict Housing Restitution* (Oxford: Intersentia 2008), 118 *et seq.*

6 UN, 'Basic Principles and Guidelines on the Right to a Remedy and Reparation for Victims of Gross Violations of International Human Rights Law and Serious Violations of International Humanitarian Law' adopted by General Assembly Resolution 60/147 of 16 December 2005 (UN Doc. A/RES/60/147).

7 Buyse, *op. cit. supra* n 5, 121.

8 Teitel, *op. cit. supra* n 1, 124 *et seq.*

under which violations of the American Convention could be imputed to the state of Honduras, notwithstanding that the human violations complained of had been committed by the prior regime. However, it is crucial to note that Honduras had ratified the Inter-American Convention in 1977, well before the events of the case.[9] The Inter-American Court held that:

> According to the principle of the continuity of the State in international law, responsibility exists both independently of changes of government over a period of time and continuously from the time of the act that creates responsibility to the time when the act is declared illegal. The foregoing is also valid in the area of human rights although, from an ethical or political point of view, the attitude of the new government may be much more respectful of those rights than that of the government in power when the violations occurred.[10]

Thus the Inter-American Court supported the principle that successor democracies might owe duties to victims of the former regime. In Teitel's analysis, the duties recognised in *Velásquez Rodríguez* 'transcend and bridge' the regimes.[11] The Inter-American Court divided the responsibilities under Article 1 of the American Convention into duties to prevent, investigate and compensate violations of American Convention rights.[12] Although the duty to prevent human rights abuse had fallen on the previous regime, the duties to investigate and to compensate could fall on the successor.[13] Thus, in addition to declaring that Honduras was liable as a matter of human rights law, the Inter-American Court ruled that just compensation should be paid to the next of kin of the victim.

The problem for applicants to the European Court of Human Rights has been that the alleged violations by the previous regime have taken place well before the states in question joined the European Convention system (or accepted the jurisdiction of the Court to hear individual applications). Article 28 of the Vienna Convention on the Law of Treaties represents a clear statement of the general principle of the non-retroactivity of treaties and on the basis of this principle complaints relating to the actions of the previous regime have been inadmissible *ratione temporis* (unless they constitute a continuing situation, discussed further later).[14] Attempts to use the Convention as a

9 *Velasquez Rodriguez, op. cit. supra* n 4, [11].
10 Ibid., [184].
11 Teitel, *op. cit. supra* n 1, 125.
12 *Velasquez Rodriguez, op. cit. supra* n 4, [174].
13 Teitel, *op. cit. supra* n 1, 125.
14 See, e.g., *Blecic v Croatia* (Grand Chamber) [2006] ECHR 207, [70]; the Human Rights Committee of the ICCPR has made similar findings: *Somers v Hungary* CCPR/C/57/D/566/1993. Decision of 29 July 1996; on non-retroactivity, continuing situations, and the ECHR see Buyse, 219 *et seq.*

basis for seeking reparation for such acts are similarly doomed – even where continuity between the totalitarian and democratic regimes is recognised as a matter of legal succession:

> the Convention imposes no specific obligation on the Contracting States to provide redress for wrongs or damage caused prior to their ratification of the Convention. [. . .] This also applies to the legal situation of the Federal Republic of Germany which is considered to be the continuation of the German *Reich*.

In this case, the applicants' complaint that the Federal Republic of Germany had failed to acknowledge the illegality of their and their ancestors' forced labour, detention and deportation from Italy to Germany was inadmissible *ratione materiae*.[15]

If the successor state itself chooses to investigate abuses before or during the transition, or to compensate victims of the previous regime, then the Convention compliance of the compensation scheme *will* fall within the jurisdiction of the Court.

In terms of investigation, we noted the *Association 21 December 1989 & Others v Romania* case in Chapter 3 in the context of historical justice. Recall that the case involved the very slow process of investigating the unsuccessful but violent crackdown on anti-government demonstrations in Romania in December 1989.[16] The European Court found that Romania had failed to discharge its positive obligations under Article 2 ECHR in respect of two of the applicants. The European Court held that given the importance of the investigation for Romania, and the need for the families to know what had happened, compliance with the Convention could entail the right to an effective judicial investigation and possibly also the right to compensation.[17]

As regards the process of compensation, once a state begins the process, the standards of Article 6 ECHR are particularly important. We shall see that is equally true for the property restitution schemes discussed later. For example, in 1985 the Greek government decided to allow all Greek citizens who 'were injured by or as a result of their direct involvement in the struggle against the dictatorial regime of 21 April 1967 to 23 July 1974 or as a result of their opposition to the above-mentioned regime' to apply for a state pension. In *Stamoulakatos v Greece (no. 2)*, the applicant (who had made an earlier complaint on a different basis, which was inadmissible *ratione temporis*) was successful in an application to Strasbourg alleging that domestic proceedings

15 *Associazione Nazionale Reduci Dalla Prigionia Dall'internamento E Dalla Guerra Di Liberazione and 275 others v Germany* (dec.) App no 45563/04 (ECtHR 4 September 2007).

16 *Association 21 December 1989 & Others v Romania*, App nos 33810/07 and 18817/08 (ECtHR, 24 May 2011), European Court of Human Rights, nos. 33810/07 and 18817/08 (available only in French).

17 Ibid.

concerning the 1985 pension law had, by their unreasonable length, violated Article 6 ECHR.[18]

In *Baraona v Portugal*,[19] the guarantees of Article 6 ECHR attached to domestic legal proceedings concerning Portugal's non-contractual liability for the abuses of the previous regime. *Baraona v Portugal*[20] was decided in 1987 and arose from events in 1974, when the Portuguese Estado Novo regime gave way to democracy in the so-called 'Carnation Revolution'. The Convention came into effect for Portugal in 1978. During the period of transition an arrest warrant was issued for the applicant, stating that he was a 'dangerous reactionary' and that it was thus necessary to investigate 'his reactionary activities'.[21] He and his family fled to Brazil,[22] while his employees took over his company and other assets.[23] The business became insolvent in 1976.[24] In 1981, and therefore after the Convention had become binding on Portugal, the applicant launched an action for damages against the state alleging that the arrest warrant was illegal and claiming pecuniary and non-pecuniary damages.[25] The case before the European Court was brought under Article 6 ECHR, in relation to which the applicant sought to show that the length of time taken to decide the action for damages was unreasonable. The applicant had been waiting for six years at the time of the ECtHR's judgment.[26]

The Portuguese government argued that Article 6 should not apply. They argued that the arrest warrant had no basis in law and therefore there were no 'civil rights or obligations' emanating from it. If the warrant did not give rise to such rights or obligations at all, then *a priori* there would be no dispute to which the guarantees of Article 6 ECHR could attach.[27]

In this context, the government stressed that the acts had been 'carried out against the background of a revolution' and, consequently, concerned public law relations between the individual and the state rather than the state's non-contractual liability.[28] The government went on to state that it 'did not deny all responsibility for excesses committed during the period of the revolution' but that it had 'not yet decided on the necessary measures to compensate victims of such excesses'.[29]

This element of the Respondent State's argument therefore clearly drew attention to the transitional context and hinted that at some undisclosed point

18 *Stamoulakatos v Greece (no. 2)* [1997] ECHR 96.
19 *Baraona v Portugal* (1991) 13 EHRR 329.
20 Ibid.
21 Ibid., [9].
22 Ibid.
23 Ibid., [10].
24 Ibid. These facts are also summarised at [44].
25 Ibid., [11].
26 Ibid., [46].
27 Ibid., [37].
28 Ibid., [37].
29 Ibid.

in the future it might embark on a legislative exercise aimed at providing some measure of reparatory justice. The Portuguese government went on to argue that even if there were a domestic dispute over a 'right', it was still not a 'civil right'. In this regard, the government argued that:

> the democratic State founded on the rule of law, which was established by the Constitution of 25 April 1976, cannot be held liable for excesses during the period of the revolution.[30]

This represents a clear attempt to distinguish between the democratic present and the revolutionary past. By contrast, the applicant attempted to show legal continuity between the totalitarian, revolutionary and democratic eras by demonstrating that the relevant constitutional provisions on fundamental rights and the applicable law on the state's non-contractual liability had never ceased to be in force and, thus, a putative domestic right to compensation existed at all times.[31]

In a passage that shows just how novel it was in the early 1980s for the European Court to encounter a case emanating from a High Contracting Party that was going through a period of democratic transition, the European Court stated that there was:

> no doubt that the return to democracy from April 1974 onwards caused Portugal to reorganise its social and political structure in difficult circumstances unequalled in other European countries, and tribute must be paid to the efforts made by the Portuguese people to consolidate democracy.[32]

Nevertheless, the European Court's held that the applicant 'could claim on arguable grounds' to have a right that was recognised in domestic law.[33] In other words, although the Convention itself could not impose liability for events before it came into effect for Portugal, the European Court accepted that as a matter of domestic law a claim for non-contractual liability could be based on duties that might be described as being able to 'transcend and bridge' the regimes.

The European Court applied its longstanding approach to the autonomous interpretation of the term 'civil right' and held that the applicant's claimed right to compensation fell within it.[34] The government then argued that the case was very complex and that there had been difficulties in securing necessary documentation because the facts went back to the period of revolution.[35]

30 Ibid., [39].
31 Ibid.
32 Ibid., [40].
33 Ibid., [41].
34 Ibid., [42–44].
35 Ibid., [49].

The Court dismissed this and found unanimously that the delays in the case were unreasonable and constituted a violation of Article 6 ECHR.[36]

The European Court required Portugal to pay compensation to Baraona for non-pecuniary damage (namely for the six years of uncertainty in which he had been compelled to live). However, the European Court rejected the applicant's claim that he had suffered pecuniary damage by not being able to resettle in Portugal due to the delay in his case. It held that the difficulties with the applicant's resettlement in Portugal were caused by the arrest warrant being issued *in the first place* and not by the delay in the proceedings at issue and the European Court did not want to prejudge the outcome of the (much delayed) domestic case.[37] This reiterates the careful distinction between recognising legal continuity sufficient to establish the non-contractual liability of the successor regime in domestic law and going beyond the Court's jurisdiction *ratione temporis*. The Court's receptiveness to Baraona's argument shows an often overlooked way in which the European Court has recognised the importance of reparatory justice to victims. Contrariwise, the Court did not give Portugal much leeway on the factors giving rise to the actual delay and neither did it appear influenced by the suggestion that a legislative solution to the question of reparation would be forthcoming.

A further, and slightly more prosaic, observation about the capacity of the European Court to provide adequate reparation is that, although it may be more generous than the UK courts at least on what constitutes compensatable moral damage,[38] the European Court is not particularly well known for the generosity of its 'just satisfaction' under Article 41 (ex Article 50) ECHR.[39]

4.1.2 PACE and reparatory justice

PACE Resolution 1096 on decommunisation addressed reparatory justice in two principal ways. The first concerned those who were punished for criminal offences during the communist era, in relation to which PACE recommended that:

> the prosecution of individual crimes [should] go hand-in-hand with the rehabilitation of people convicted of 'crimes' which in a civilised society do not constitute criminal acts, and of those who were unjustly sentenced. Material compensation should also be awarded to these victims of totalitarian justice, and should not be (much) lower than the compensation

36 Ibid., [57].

37 Ibid., [61].

38 D. Fairgrieve, 'The Human Rights Act 1998, damages and tort law' (2001) *Public Law* 695, 707.

39 A. Mowbray, 'The European Court of Human Rights' approach to just satisfaction' (1997) *Public Law* 647, 658; Fairgrieve, ibid., 709. paints a more mixed picture.

> accorded to those unjustly sentenced for crimes under the standard penal code in force.[40]

Some states in central and eastern Europe adopted such policies, for example, Slovakia passed the Judicial Rehabilitation Act in 1990. This might also be conceived of as a type of amnesty and one that is markedly less controversial than those aimed at facilitators, rather than victims, of the prior regime.[41] This type of reparatory policy is yet to yield any European Convention jurisprudence directly, but these policies were sometimes accompanied by attempts at reparation for actions other than convictions, and these have generated considerable jurisprudence. For example, in Slovakia, the Extra-Judicial Rehabilitations Act was adopted in 1991. This Act dealt with applications for restitution for infringements of property rights – including where property had been confiscated pursuant to criminal convictions.[42]

The second way in which PACE Resolution 1096 addressed reparatory justice was in relation to the restitution of property. PACE advised that:

> property, including that of the churches, which was illegally or unjustly seized by the state, nationalised, confiscated or otherwise expropriated during the reign of communist totalitarian systems in principle be restituted to its original owners *in integrum*, if this is possible without violating the rights of current owners who acquired the property in good faith or the rights of tenants who rented the property in good faith, and without harming the progress of democratic reforms. In cases where this is not possible, just material compensation should be awarded. Claims and conflicts relating to individual cases of property restitution should be decided by the courts.

The central feature of this passage is the clear advice that seized property 'be restituted'; in other words, that restitution *should* take place (or, as a second option, that material compensation *should* take place). Elsewhere in the Resolution, for example, in relation to lustration, the advice of PACE was about how particular transitional policies should be carried out only if a state had decided for itself to embark on them. The advice in relation to restitution went further, since it recommended the initiation of the policy itself.

Finally, and quite crucially, the advice from PACE is limited only to the restitution of property seized during the communist era. This is not surprising, given that the Resolution as a whole was aimed at decommunisation, but for the states seeking to implement restitution processes it is not so simple and has given rise to complaints of discrimination from victims of earlier injustices, which are discussed further later.

40 PACE Resolution 1096 (1996), [8].
41 Note the discussion in Chapter 2.
42 Note the discussion of this in *Kopecky v Slovakia* (2005) 41 EHRR 43.

In the sections that follow, we shall focus on the cases that have come to define the European Court's approach. We begin by examining the European Convention as a foundation for restitution claims. The cases discussed here have parallels with the cases on access to communist ere secret information, discussed in Chapter 3, since the applicant is attempting to use the Convention to gain 'transitional' justice. Later we shall examine cases where the European Court has supervised substantive and procedural aspects of restitution schemes and where, in the face of objections to the schemes by current owners, the European Court's potential to assist victims would seem tied to its willingness to recognise transitional relativism.

4.2 The European Convention as a foundation for restitution claims

The advice of PACE was clear on the political desirability for property restitution to take place in the post-Cold War era. The European Convention does not guarantee the right to property as such, but rather in Article 1, Protocol 1, enshrines a qualified right to the 'peaceful enjoyment of possessions':

> Every natural or legal person is entitled to the peaceful enjoyment of his possessions. No one shall be deprived of his possessions except in the public interest and subject to the conditions provided for by law and by the general principles of international law.
>
> The preceding provisions shall not, however, in any way impair the right of a State to enforce such laws as it deems necessary to control the use of property in accordance with the general interest or to secure the payment of taxes or other contributions or penalties.

Several applicants have sought to rely on Article 1, Protocol 1, in order to regain property that was expropriated or otherwise confiscated during the communist era, but have met with difficulties arising from both the temporal and material scope of the ECHR.

4.2.1 Temporal scope of the Convention

It is a general principle of international law, reflected in Article 28 of the Vienna Convention on the Law of Treaties, that a treaty cannot bind its parties in relation to any facts or situations that took place before it entered into force for each party. This has the effect that complaints about expropriations undertaken by the previous regime have been inadmissible *ratione temporis*.[43]

43 See, e.g., *Blecic v Croatia* [GC], *op. cit. supra* n 14, [70]; the Human Rights Committee of the ICCPR has made similar findings: *Somers v Hungary*, 29 July 1996, HRC, CCPR/C/57/D/566/1993; on non-retroactivity, continuing situations and the ECHR, see Buyse, *op. cit. supra* n 5, 219 *et seq*.

Where property was taken lawfully by the previous regime, then even if the deprivation were contrary to customary international law, it was an instantaneous act over which the European Court has no temporal jurisdiction.[44] A 'lifeline in time'[45] may exist where the European Court determines that the deprivation was contrary to domestic law and amounts therefore to a 'continuing situation' of illegality.[46] However, Judge Loucaides, writing extra-judicially, has noted that in the post-communist context, the vast majority of cases have been treated as instantaneous acts.[47]

This fairly harsh feature of the European Court's jurisprudence undoubtedly came as a disappointment to those early individual applicants who sought return or restitution simply to find that their complaint was excluded *ratione temporis*. As Aeyal Gross observed in his early assessment of European Commission decisions in relation to the new Contracting Parties: 'The Convention can reinforce the democracy the citizens of the ex-Communist countries already have. It cannot mend the past.'[48]

Antoine Buyse's exhaustive work on post-conflict housing restitution begins with the facts of *Blečić v Croatia*,[49] in which the Grand Chamber eventually held inadmissible *ratione temporis* the applicant's complaint about the termination of her protected tenancy in the town of Zadar. A rule allowed the tenancy to be terminated after six months of absence from the property. Krstina Blečić was visiting her daughter in Italy when the war in Yugoslavia reached Zadar. Blečić remained in Italy, and eventually another family broke into her house and started to live there. Her complaint was inadmissible because the Grand Chamber deemed it to relate to a decision of the Supreme Court taken in February 1996, whereas the European Convention only came into effect for Croatia in November 1997.

Tom Allen has criticised this decision and has also identified that the Croatian authorities and courts had been far more inclined to terminate tenancies of ethnic Serbs, such as Blečić.[50] Allen has gone so far as to argue that in the transitional property cases the European Court has 'gone out of its way to develop a set of jurisdictional rules that deny the victims [of communist expropriation] a hearing on the merits'.[51]

44 *Weidlich and Others v Germany* (dec.) App nos. 18890/91, 19048/91, 19049/91, 19342/92 and 19549/92 (ECommHR 4 March 1996).
45 Buyse, *op. cit. supra* n 5.
46 *Papamichalopoulos v Greece* [1993] ECHR 28 and *Loizidou v Turkey* [1996] ECHR 70.
47 L. Loucaides, 'Is the European Court of Human Rights still a principled court of human fights after the Demopoulos case?' (2011) 24(2) *Leiden Journal of International Law* 435.
48 See A. Gross, 'Reinforcing the new democracies: the European Convention on Human Rights and the former communist countries – a study of the case law' (1996) 7(1) *EJIL* 89, 102.
49 *Blečić v Croatia, op. cit. supra* n 14.
50 Allen, *op. cit. supra* n 3, 14.
51 Allen, *op. cit. supra* n 3, 6.

However, it would appear that the Court has simply applied the general principles on the non-retroactivity of the Convention, noted already, to the issue of property restitution. The problem for victims of communist expropriations is more that the European Court has *not* gone out of its way to relax its normal stance. Allen and Douglas have argued that there is a basis for such relaxation: the classic public international legal authority for the non-retroactivity of treaties arose from inter-state cases and different concerns arise in relation to individual petitions.[52] Likewise they note that the European Court has departed from other general principles of treaty law in relation to reservations.[53] Solid as these points are they can only hint at *de lega ferenda*: they do not as a matter of *lex lata* show that there is anything to compel the European Court to disrupt its adherence to the classical rules on temporal jurisdiction.[54]

4.2.2 Material scope of the Convention

The limits of the Convention's temporal scope are mirrored by the limits to its material scope. We saw that in relation to claims for reparatory justice in the form of compensation, the Court has tended to find such claims inadmissible *ratione materiae*. In relation to claims for restitution, cases have proceeded to the merits, but the Court has been clear on the Convention's limitations.

The Court has developed consistent jurisprudence in this respect, which was summarised in *Kopecky v Slovakia*.[55] During the communist regime the applicant's father was convicted of having in his possession a quantity of collectable coins.[56] In 1992 the father benefited from a posthumous pardon issued by the Supreme Court under the 1990 Judicial Rehabilitation Act.[57] The case thus has its roots in the first type of reparatory justice recommended in PACE Resolution 1096. Under the 1991 Extra-Judicial Rehabilitations Act, its beneficiaries (and their heirs) were entitled to reclaim property that had been taken from them as punishment, as long as they could identify where that property was when the act came into effect on 1 April 1991. The applicant sought restitution of the confiscated coins, but failed at every level of the domestic court system because he could not identify where the coins had been

52 T. Allen and B. Douglas, 'Closing the door on restitution: the European Court of Human Rights', in A. Buyse and M. Hamilton (eds), *Transitional Jurisprudence and the ECHR* (Cambridge: CUP 2011).

53 Ibid., 230 and 231.

54 In this regard, note the detailed discussion of the 'distinctiveness' of human rights treaties in Buyse, *op. cit. supra* n 5, 221–225.

55 *Kopecky v Slovakia, op. cit. supra* n 42.

56 Ibid., [12].

57 Ibid., [13].

on 1 April 1991. In Strasbourg, he argued that this amounted to a violation of Article 1, Protocol 1 ECHR.

In *Kopecky v Slovakia*, the European Court explained that its approach to such claims for restitution is that:

> Article 1 of Protocol No. 1 cannot be interpreted as imposing any general obligation on the Contracting States to restore property which was transferred to them before they ratified the Convention.[58]

Furthermore: 'Nor is there any general obligation under the Convention to establish legal procedures in which restitution of property may be sought.'

The Court therefore echoed its twofold general denial of a Convention right to reparatory justice: it is outside the material scope of the Convention to require restitution of the confiscated property or, second, to impose a positive obligation to create a framework within which such claims could be made. In other words, there is no Convention right to this form of transitional justice.

In *Kopecky*, the only route into a successful application under the ECHR would have been to show that the legal claim for restitution under the Act generated a 'legitimate expectation' or 'asset' that *itself* could derive protection from interference as a 'possession' under Article 1, Protocol 1, ECHR.[59]

The *Kopecky* case ultimately hinged on whether the applicant had done enough to show that the authorities themselves knew where his father's collectable coins were. The European Court confined itself to determining whether the domestic courts had acted arbitrarily in deciding that he had not. The Court found no evidence of arbitrariness, so there was not a firm enough basis in domestic law for him to claim he had either a legitimate expectation or asset that could be classed as a possession.

The Court's long recapitulation of its case law on legitimate expectations and assets obscures the simplicity of the case: the European Court allowed the applicant to be put under a considerable burden by the Respondent State in order to regain the property. This was not a jurisdictional question, either *ratione temporis* or *ratione materiae*, but rather an example of deference to the Respondent State on both the scope of its restitution laws (i.e. the exclusion of those who could not identify the location of the property in question) and in their implementation (i.e. the burden of proof that claimants would have to discharge to locate the property with sufficient accuracy). As noted later, the European Court has consistently held that there is a wide margin of appreciation with regard to the exclusion of certain categories of former owners from the scope of restitution schemes.[60]

58 Ibid., 35(d).

59 See the discussion that follows in relation to the scope of restitution schemes.

60 See *Beshiri and Others v Albania* (2008) 46 EHRR 17, 81.

4.3 The European Convention and the supervision of restitution schemes

Even though the European Court has not been able to require restitution schemes to be initiated, there is a wealth of jurisprudence on the application of European human rights law to schemes that states have chosen to initiate. These schemes have been controversial because it is not universally accepted that they contribute to a peaceful transition or are in the economic good and they may come into conflict with the rights of current owners.

4.3.1 The 'legitimacy' of restitution schemes

The European Court's strict approach to the temporal and material scope of the Convention has to be seen alongside the fact that, without being required to by the European Court, many of the former communist states in fact did set about initiating restitution schemes.[61] The Court's inability to require restitution does not mean that such policies, when they have been initiated, are *ipso facto* inimical to the aims of the Convention. Indeed, as we shall see in this section, the Court has not only supported the legitimacy of restitution processes but has also imposed positive obligations to ensure that states take timely and consistent action to address the general interest that they have been found to pursue.

This is not to say they are without their implications for human rights and the rule of law. Although restitution policies may demonstrate a clean break between regimes, symbolising a new commitment to the rule of law, they can generate a level of uncertainty that impedes progress and interferes with the rights of those who acquired confiscated property in good faith.[62] Indeed, the recommendation of PACE, that restitution should take place, was qualified to the extent that it should only take place if it were possible without violating the rights of current occupiers or harming the process of democratic reform.[63] The conflict of rights between present and former owners is particularly sensitive when the property in question is housing.[64] Secondary occupiers, that is to say, people who came into possession of property that was previously confiscated by a communist regime, have sought to challenge the interference with their property rights under Article 1, Protocol 1, ECHR. To further complicate matters, Teitel has observed that restitution policies aimed at providing reparation are not just remedial or backward looking, they play a direct and constitutive role in the construction of a society based on free market economics.[65]

61 M.L. Neff, 'Eastern Europe's policy of restitution of property in the 1990s' (1992) 10 *Dickinson Journal of International Law* 357, 374.

62 Allen and Douglas, *op. cit. supra* n 52, 210.

63 PACE Resolution 1096 (1996), [10].

64 L. Fox-O'Mahony and J.A. Sweeney (eds), *The Idea of Home in Law: Displacement and Dispossession* (Aldershot: Ashgate 2010).

65 See the discussion in Teitel, *op. cit. supra* n 1, 129 *et seq.*

In its non-transitional jurisprudence the European Court has held that restrictions on Article 1, Protocol 1, must be prescribed by law and proportionate to the relevant public interest. Unlike the qualified rights contained in Articles 8 to 11 ECHR there is no exhaustive list of 'legitimate aims' for the right's limitation: restrictions on it must simply be in the 'public interest'. The level of review that the European Court exerts as to whether measures are in the public interest has been described as 'very limited'.[66] The notion of the public interest is 'extensive' and states have a wide margin of appreciation in determining its content.[67] States have also argued that they should benefit from a wide margin of appreciation in relation to striking a 'fair balance' between the public interest and the burden imposed on the individual, since there is no requirement that the interference be 'necessary'.[68] We shall return to the notion of a fair balance in the next section, since the Court has given firm advice to ensure that secondary owners are not unfairly prejudiced.

In *Zvolský and Zvolská v Czech Republic*,[69] its first major case on restitution, the Court examined the Czech Land Act of 1991. As far as legitimacy was concerned, the Court recapitulated its position that a wide margin of appreciation is available to legislatures in implementing social and economic policies. Citing one of the major Article 1, Protocol 1, cases arising from the earlier Greek transition,[70] the Court added that: 'This necessarily applies, and perhaps to a greater extent, in the event of changes to a country's political system.'[71] The Court identified the aim of the legislation as being, 'to redress infringements of property rights that occurred under the communist regime [. . .] which it considered damaging to its democratic regime' and held that the general purpose of the 1991 Land Act could not be regarded as illegitimate because it was in the public interest.[72]

In *Pincová and Pinc v Czech Republic*,[73] the Court reiterated its position that the attenuation of violations by the communist regime was a legitimate aim in the public interest and added that it was also a means of protecting the state's socioeconomic development.[74] The Court therefore recognised that these policies are not only reparatory in their aim, but are forward looking as well. In its discussion of 'fair balance', the Court revealed deeper support for the notion of restitution:

66 P. van Dijk *et al.* (eds), *Theory and Practice of the European Convention on Human Rights* (Oxford: Intersentia 2006), 879.

67 See *James and Others v UK* [1986] 8 EHRR 123, [46].

68 See *Former King of Greece and Others v Greece* (2001) 33 EHRR 21, [91].

69 *Zvolský and Zvolská v Czech Republic* [2002] ECHR 738.

70 *Former King of Greece and Others v Greece, op. cit. supra* n 68.

71 *Zvolský and Zvolská v Czech Republic, op. cit. supra* n 69, [67].

72 Ibid., [68].

73 *Pincová and Pinc v Czech Republic* [2002] ECHR 712.

74 Ibid., [58].

> [The Court] considers it necessary to ensure that the attenuation of [. . .] old injuries does not create disproportionate new wrongs. To that end, the legislation should make it possible to take into account the particular circumstances of each case, so that persons who acquired their possessions in good faith are not made to bear *the burden of responsibility which is rightfully that of the State which once confiscated those possessions*.[75]
>
> [emphasis added]

In both of these cases, the Court ultimately found violations of Article 1, Protocol 1, but this should not detract from the statements regarding the legitimacy of restitution programmes as a tool of public policy in transitional democracies. Indeed, it is significant that in *Pincová and Pinc*, the Court went so far as to declare that the successor state 'rightfully' bore a 'burden of responsibility' regarding restitution, even though as a matter of human rights law it cannot require such restitution to take place. This gives credence to the normative argument that some duties 'transcend and bridge' changes of regime, in a similar manner to that which we saw in relation to *Velasquez Rodriguez* and *Baraona*.

In *Velikovi and Others v Bulgaria*,[76] the Court was even clearer in its support for the aims of the 1992 Bulgarian Law on the Restitution of Ownership of Nationalised Real Property:

> [The] Court has *no doubt* that the Restitution Law, which provided that the State should restore the property it had expropriated without compensation during the communist regime, pursued an important aim in the public interest. Indeed, that was not disputed by the applicants. *It is obvious* that compensating the victims of those arbitrary expropriations was an important step in the restoration of democracy in Bulgaria, after several decades of totalitarian rule.[77]
>
> [emphasis added]

The Court went on to note that section 7 of the Bulgarian Restitution Law contained a modestly punitive element as well, in that it allowed authorised persons to claim expropriated property back from private individuals where their title was 'tainted' by abuse of power or breaches of the law. The Court stated that:

> Persons who have taken advantage of their privileged position or have otherwise acted unlawfully to acquire property in a totalitarian regime, as well as their heirs, cannot expect to keep their gain in a society governed democratically through the rule of law. The underlying public interest in such cases is to restore justice and respect for the rule of law.[78]

75 Ibid.
76 *Velikovi and Others v Bulgaria* (2009) 48 EHRR 27.
77 Ibid., [170].
78 Ibid., [172].

It is worth noting in this context that there have also been cases concerning Bulgaria's 1991 Restitution of Stores, Workshops and Storage Houses Act. However, the European Court noted that the injustice that the 1991 Act sought to correct was 'less significant' than the expropriations for which redress was provided by the 1992 Act discussed in *Velikovi and Others*.[79]

The legitimacy given to the punitive element in *Velikovi and Others* was echoed in the admissibility decision in *Bieńkowski v Poland*.[80] Here the applicant had been granted the status 'veteran' for his actions as a member of the resistance movement in 1943–1945 and for his taking part in 'the armed struggle to consolidate the peoples' power' from 1945 to 1947. This status entitled him to the 'veteran's benefit': an enhanced old-age pension. The 1991 Veterans and Other Victims of War and Post-War Repression Law authorised veterans to be divested of their special status if they had served in the organs of internal security during the communist era.[81] On the basis of both his actions up to 1947 (for which he had previously been rewarded), and for his having been found to have served in the Internal Public Security Service until 1968, the applicant lost his veteran status and his entitlement to the 'veterans' benefit'. His entitlement to the remainder of his pension continued.

The European Commission explained that the right to a pension based on employment may, in certain circumstances, be assimilated to a property right such as gains protection under Article 1, Protocol 1. The Commission found that the new approach to people who had served in the public security organs during the communist era had been adopted 'in view of the political role played by such organs of the former Communist regime in combating and eliminating political opposition to the system'.

In another decision, the European Court later described the same piece of legislation as having the intention:

> to condemn the political role which the communist militia and the communist security services had played in establishing the communist regime and in repressing political opposition thereto.[82]

The Court and the Commission have confirmed that this constitutes a legitimate consideration of public policy and, in *Bienkowski*, the Commission found that since the essence of the applicant's pension right was not impaired, the interference with the applicant's Article 1, Protocol 1, rights was not contrary to the Convention. Although the reasoning was brief, the Commission clearly

79 *Manolov and Racheva-Manolova v Bulgaria* [2008] ECHR 1679, [42] (but note that the Court still found a violation of the Convention in this case).

80 *Bieńkowski v Poland* (dec.) App no 33889/96 (ECommHR, 9 September 1998).

81 The legislation has given rise to several cases, including *Skórkiewicz v Poland* (dec.) App no 39860/98 (ECtHR, 1 June 1999).

82 Ibid.

identified that actions such as these, taken against people who had benefited from their association with the previous regime, pursued a public interest.[83]

As regards discrimination, the Commission put greater emphasis on the present day priorities of the state rather than the actions of the applicant. The policy was found to have:

> aimed at the objective verification of whether certain persons, in particular those formerly employed in the organs commonly regarded as the machinery of repression, satisfy the present statutory conditions for the award of a special, honourable status.

The Polish authorities, therefore, had an objective and reasonable justification for the discrimination alleged, which pursued the legitimate aim of regulating the current system of 'granting exceptional privileges'. In a later case concerning the same legislation, a Chamber of the Court found that verifying whether people met the present statutory conditions for being awarded the honourable status was the legislation's 'primary' aim, adding that the means employed to do so 'had an objective and reasonable justification in Poland's historical experience during the Communist period'.[84]

The language used here is a little disingenuous, since it refers to the 'award' or 'granting' of a special status, whereas the applicant's complaint in *Bieńkowski* was about the revocation of it. Nevertheless, the point remains that the Court accepted that changes to the applicants' entitlements were property rights, which were so clearly trumped by the public policy at issue that the applications were manifestly ill founded.

It is clear that the European Court has supported the overall aim of restitution measures, when states have chosen to introduce them. Its support of the punitive element, however, is quite unusual when it is viewed alongside cases involving other non-criminal sanctions of measure imposed on people from the previous regime, such as lustration or prohibitions on standing for election (see, further, Chapter 5).

4.3.2 *The scope of restitution policies*

The previous section demonstrated that the European Court has been relatively supportive of the general aim of restitution policies, in the sense that it has reaffirmed that they are in the public interest in the transitional context. Once initiated, the Court has been actually quite deferential as regards the substantive scope of the policies themselves.

In the *Kopecky* case, we saw that the European Court allowed Slovakia great leeway to exclude people from the restitution scheme. Returning to this in

83 This was also confirmed in *Skórkiewicz*, ibid.

84 *Domalewski v Poland* (dec.) App no 34610/97 (ECtHR, 15 June 1999).

slightly more detail, the European Court stated that Article 1 of Protocol 1 does not:

> impose any restrictions on the Contracting States' freedom to determine the scope of property restitution and to choose the conditions under which they agree to restore property rights of former owners. [. . .] In particular, the Contracting States enjoy a wide margin of appreciation with regard to the exclusion of certain categories of former owners from such entitlement.[85]

On this basis, the European Court validated the requirement for claimants to be able to show where the property in question actually was at the time the 1991 Extra-Judicial Rehabilitations Act came into effect. Discharging this burden was always going to be a challenge when the property had been taken many years earlier by a secretive totalitarian regime. Likewise in *Beshiri and Others v Albania*, the European Court confirmed that there would be, in particular, a wide margin of appreciation with regard to the exclusion of certain categories of former owners from such entitlements.[86]

The European Court has been equally deferential on the difficult question of identifying how far back in time restitution schemes should reach in the quest to provide reparation. The Court's approach here, which is different from that of the HRC under the ICCPR, has been met with particular criticism.

There have been successive waves of expropriation and displacement in Europe, not all of which were a result of communism. Where racial, ethnic or national groups have been systematically excluded from restitution processes because their property was seized at the end of World War II rather than during the communist era, they have sought to rely on international human rights law to show that their treatment has been discriminatory.[87]

The harsh but logical extension of the wide margin of appreciation on exclusions from restitution schemes is that while people who fall within a particular restitution process may claim to have a new 'possession' such as could then be protected under Article 1 of Protocol 1,[88] those who are excluded from the outset cannot.

This has generated allegations of inequality between different classes of claimant, to which the European Court has not been receptive.[89] Where applicants have raised Article 14 ECHR alongside Article 1 of Protocol 1, it has

85 *Kopecky v Slovakia, op. cit. supra* n 42, 35(d).

86 *Beshiri and Others v Albania, op. cit. supra* n 60, 81.

87 Note the discussion of the scope of restitution schemes that follows.

88 *Beshiri and Others v Albania, op. cit. supra* n 60, [82]; see also *Broniowski v Poland* (2006) 43 EHRR 1, [125].

89 P. Macklem, 'Rybná 9, Praha 1: restitution and memory in international human rights law' (2005) 16(1) *EJIL* 1, 3; *Gratzinger and Gratzingerova v Czech Republic* (dec.) App no 39794/98 (ECtHR GC, 10 July 2002), [76].

not been of assistance to them because, since Article 14 is not autonomous, it can only be raised alongside the denial of another Convention right. If the applicants alleging discrimination have been found not have a 'possession', there is no Convention right on to which Article 14 can be attached.[90]

The approach of the European Court stands in contrast to that of the Human Rights Committee of the ICCPR.[91] In cases such as *Brok v Czech Republic*,[92] the Human Rights Committee has found a violation of the Covenant based on discriminatory exclusion from a restitution scheme. In *Brok*, the applicant was denied the benefit of a post-Cold War restitution process because the property in question (the family house) had been seized by the Nazis and then nationalised by the pre-communist, post-war, Czech authorities. The restitution scheme only allowed for restitution or compensation for either victims of racial persecution during World War II or victims of illegal confiscation carried out for political reasons during the Communist regime that began on 25 February 1948.[93] The Human Rights Committee found that this amounted to discriminatory treatment when compared to victims of Nazi confiscations whose property had not also been nationalised by the pre-communist Czech authorities.[94]

The approach of the Human Rights Committee has its outer limits, however, and in its 1997 admissibility decision in *Malik v Czech Republic*,[95] it found that the exclusion of post-war confiscations of Sudenten German property from the ongoing restitution process did not constitute discrimination. The Committee explained that, 'not every distinction or differentiation in treatment amounts to discrimination.'[96]

Both Patrick Macklem and Istvan Pogany have argued that the Human Rights Committee's failure to uphold discrimination claims by the Sudenten Germans is deeply problematic.[97] Macklem was, however, even more critical of the European Court's complete failure to engage with the issue of discrimination – especially since, he argued, the ECHR recognises a right to property (however, recall that, to be completely accurate, it is a right to peaceful enjoyment of possessions). In his view: 'While the Human Rights Committee is willing to remember certain pasts as a matter of equality, the European Court of Human Rights approaches equality with a modernist impulse to repudiate

90 See *Beshiri and Others v Albania, op. cit. supra* n 60, 91; *Polacek and Polackova v Czech Republic* (dec.) App no 38645/97 (ECtHR GC, 10 July 2002), [61–70].

91 See Buyse, *op. cit. supra* n 5, 100.

92 *Brok v Czech Republic* CCPR/C/73/D/774/1997, Decision of 31 Oct. 2001.

93 Ibid., [2.4].

94 Ibid., [7.4].

95 *Malik v. Czech Republic*, CCPR/C/D 669/1995, Decision of 21 Oct. 1998.

96 Ibid., [6.5].

97 Macklem, *op. cit. supra* n 89; I. Pogany, 'International human rights law, reparatory justice and the re-ordering of memory in Central and Eastern Europe' (2010) 10(3) *Human Rights Law Review* 397.

history.'[98] Remembering certain pasts in law is better than remembering none, according to Macklem, because 'forgetting is simultaneously an act of remembering', in the sense that by affirming the acceptability of a difference of treatment for the Sudenten Germans seeking restitution the Human Rights Committee may have assisted in the validation of a collective Czech memory of ethnic German complicity in the Nazi occupation.[99] He criticises the approach of the European Court since its conception of equality allows for deference to Contracting Parties 'in their calculations of the legal significance of certain pasts'.[100]

Pogany has built on Macklem's central argument that international human rights law can play a role in the reordering of memory in central and eastern Europe, but suggests that with its views and decisions on the Sudenten German restitution cases against the Czech Republic the Human Rights Committee may have been, 'complicit in the denial of some important collective memories'.[101]

The wide margin of appreciation seen in the European Court's exclusion cases, which consequently forestalls substantive discussion of discrimination, can be seen as another attempt to avoid being seen to 'do' transitional justice. By allowing some discrimination claims and not others, the approach of the Human Rights Committee has encountered a rule of law dilemma: an attempt to rationalise how certain people, namely the Sudenten Germans, are not equal before the law. Conversely, by deferring to the European Convention's Contracting Parties on their own choices about which restitution claims feed into an authentic post-Cold War collective history, the European Court has created maximum space within which locally relevant solutions can flourish. Indeed, put this way, the European Court is able to facilitate an element of transitional justice (local relevance and subsidiarity) without conceding transitional relativism.

Pogany's observations about the relative profiles of the Human Rights Committee and European Court are significant here also. He describes the former as 'a body that is virtually unknown outside the international human rights community', whose jurisprudence is likely to have 'a severely limited impact' compared to national and international judicial bodies.[102] The European Court, by contrast, gains much greater media scrutiny and political comment.[103] Thus, the European Court could potentially have a much greater impact on national memorialisation than could the Human Rights Committee, but precisely for this reason should be more cautious. Nevertheless, on those

98 Macklem, *op. cit. supra* n 89, 3.
99 Ibid., 19.
100 Ibid., 21.
101 Pogany, *op. cit. supra* n 97, 402.
102 Ibid., 428.
103 Ibid.

much broader elements of the historical narrative, such as whether the inclusion of the Baltic states by the USSR through the secret protocol to the Molotov-Ribbentrop pact with Nazi Germany constituted unlawful annexation, we have already seen that the European Court could do a little more.[104]

4.3.3 Proportionality and a 'fair balance': reparatory justice for victims of communism

Posner and Vermeule have downplayed the uncertainties (for current occupiers) caused by programmes of restitution, arguing that: 'In every successful market economy, people hold their property subject to uncertainties created by the government's freedom to regulate that property at any time.'[105] They go on to provide what they see as empirical evidence that restitution policies, even limited ones, actually contribute to the (economic) transition, citing post-war Germany as an example.

Whether or not the uncertainties caused by large-scale restitution programmes embody 'transitional' or ordinary justice seems to have an impact of the approach to the European Court to them. There has to be a 'fair balance' between the rights of the present owner or occupier and the aim of restituting the property in question to its original owner.

Zvolsky and Zvolská v Czech Republic and *Pincová and Pinc v Czech Republic* were, for a good while, the reading cases on this issue, but recently in *Velikovi and Others*, the European Court has revisited and altered its approach.

Zvolsky and Zvolská[106] concerned the circumstances in which 'MR' had transferred ownership of a farmhouse and adjoining plot of land in 1967. The adjoining land was transferred without consideration. By 1994 the Czech Constitutional Court was of the opinion that this type of transferral of property without consideration was a 'forced donation'.[107] The applicants in the case were the current owners of the land. At Strasbourg, the government stressed the Constitutional Court's findings that transferrals such as these were unlawful acts of compulsory expropriation without compensation that now required remedying.[108] It was noted earlier that the European Court confirmed that the Land Act permitting the redress of infringements of property rights that occurred under the communist regime pursued an aim in the public interest.[109] However, it was still necessary to determine whether there

104 See the discussion in Chapter 3.
105 E. Posner and A. Vermeule, 'Transitional justice as ordinary justice' (2004) 117 *Harvard Law Review* 761, 786.
106 *Zvolský and Zvolská v Czech Republic, op. cit. supra* n 69.
107 Ibid., [27].
108 Ibid., [59].
109 Ibid., [68].

had been a 'fair balance' struck between the demands of the general interest of the community and the applicant's rights.[110]

The European Court recognised that the Czech Republic would have a wide margin of appreciation in this regard,[111] but observed that the Land Act did not contain any mechanism whatsoever for giving compensation to the current owner in the event that their property was restituted.[112] A total lack of compensation would be very difficult to justify,[113] since it would seem perfectly possible to re-examine difficult cases to determine whether particular transferrals were against the wishes of the former owner's will.[114] A fair balance had not been struck and there was a violation of Article 1, Protocol 1.

The reasoning in *Pincová and Pinc v Czech Republic* was very similar, although in its consideration of 'fair balance' the European Court added the warning that although it accepted:

> that the general objective of the restitution laws, namely to attenuate the consequences of certain infringements of property rights caused by the communist regime, [. . .] it considers it necessary to ensure that the attenuation of those old injuries does not create disproportionate new wrongs.[115]

Without going into the facts, it suffices to say that the European Court again found a violation of Article 1, Protocol 1.

It was in *Velikovi and Others v Bulgaria* that the European Court's direction of travel on this issue became clear and in it the European Court added a significant new element to its analysis of whether, 'disproportionate new wrongs' were being created.[116] Recall that in *Velikovi*, the European Court had backed two related aims of the Restitution Law: to restore justice for persons whose property had been taken away by the communist regime *and* to sanction those who had profited from their position in the communist regime or had acted unlawfully to acquire property.[117] The judgment actually involved nine applications against Bulgaria and each of the applicants had had a different degree of association with the communist regime. In order to differentiate them, and thus to make separate findings in relation to each, the European Court stated that:

> In complex cases as the present one, which involve difficult questions in the conditions of transition from a totalitarian regime to democracy and

110 Ibid., [69].
111 Ibid.
112 Ibid., [71].
113 Ibid., [70].
114 Para 72.
115 *Pincová and Pinc v Czech Republic, op. cit. supra* n 73, [58].
116 *Velikovi and Others v Bulgaria, op. cit. supra* n 76, [178], citing *Pincová and Pinc*.
117 Ibid., [183].

> rule of law, a certain 'threshold of hardship' must have been crossed for the Court to find a breach of the applicants' Article 1 Protocol No. 1 rights.

This is a wholly new test. By applying it, the European Court found unanimously a violation of the Convention in relation to only four of the applications. It would seem, therefore, more deferential to the Czech Republic's efforts. It is also worth noting that the European Court had dismissed as separate issues *all* the applicant's complaints based on deficiencies in the quality of the law and stated that:

> The present cases concern, however, a unique period of social and legal transition in Bulgaria.
>
> [. . .]
>
> The Court cannot disregard the ensuing difficulties and would not adopt a purist approach to legal predictability. A measure of uncertainty was inevitable in respect of legislation aiming at undoing decades-old injustices.
>
> [. . .]
>
> due account must be taken of the special transitional period at the relevant time and the individual circumstances of each case.[118]

This is a remarkably generous statement. Again in the case *Padalevičius v Lithuania*, the Court applied the new test and found that the applicant's treatment under a restitution law had not passed this 'threshold of hardship' (but upheld his Article 6 complaint about the length of the proceedings).[119] Perhaps strangely, the Court has since referred to this notion of a certain 'threshold of hardship' in a general summary of its approach to cases raising complex economic questions in a case involving the UK.[120] Even if the additional hurdle were justifiable, or least explicable, in the transitional context it would seem out of place in the mainstream jurisprudence of the Court. However, were it to be confined to the specific circumstances of reviewing restitution schemes, no doubt Allen would welcome that the European Court is less 'obstructive' of the transitional states efforts than he once observed.[121]

4.3.4 Proportionality and a 'fair balance': effecting constitutional and economic reforms

The advice in PACE Resolution 1096 introduced earlier highlights that the former communist states are undergoing 'multiple transitions', in the sense

118 Ibid., Para [166].
119 *Padalevičius v Lithuania*, App no 12278/03 (ECtHR, 7 July 2009).
120 *MGN Limited v UK* (2011) 53 EHRR 2011.
121 Allen, *op. cit. supra* n 3, 44.

that not only are they undergoing transition to democracy but also to a new economic order.

There is an argument for deference here, but it is not an argument that deference is required in order to effect 'transitional justice' *per se*: it is about tackling the difficulties of democratic and economic transition. The 'fair balance' to be struck is not between victims of the former regime and present owners, but between present owners and the reforming agenda of the new democratic government. In a sense then, these cases are not about reparatory justice at all. However, they have certainly raised difficult questions about property rights in transition and there is a degree of cross-fertilisation between the cases on reparatory justice polices and constitutional or economic reforms. At the close of this section, the curious situation where economic necessity has been cited as a reason for reneging on a previous commitment to reparatory justice in the form of restitution is discussed. However, the first case examined shows that the property cases may engage with the symbolic elements of transitional justice, even where the reparatory element is absent.

The case of the *Former King of Greece and Others v Greece*[122] was always going to have a certain symbolic element to it. There was a military dictatorship in Greece from April 1967 to July 1974 and the then King left Greece in December 1968. In June 1973 the military dictatorship abolished the monarchy and all royal property was confiscated and passed to the Greek state. Some compensation was available to be claimed until 31 December 1975 but none of it was, in fact, claimed. A compromise between the former royals and the Greek state concerning the former king's property was struck in 1992, but a new government elected in 1993 invalidated the arrangement in 1994 as part of a project to restore 'constitutional legality and historical memory'.[123] After unsuccessfully challenging the 1994 law in the Greek Special Supreme Court, the former king complained to the European Court.

As to the general aim of the 1994 law, the Court explained that it:

> [did] not doubt that it was necessary for the Greek State to resolve an issue which it considered to be prejudicial for its status as a republic. The fact that the constitutional transition from a monarchy to a republic took place in 1975, namely almost twenty years before the enactment of the contested Law, might inspire some doubt as to the reasons for the measures, but it cannot suffice to deprive the overall objective of Law no. 2215/1994 of its legitimacy as being 'in the public interest'.[124]

Just as in the property cases on reparation, the European Court approved the general aim of the legislation. However, in a finding that would go on to

122 *Former King of Greece and Others v Greece, op. cit. supra* n 68.
123 Ibid., [41].
124 Ibid., [88].

influence the reasoning in *Zvolsky and Zvolská*, the European Court found that the complete absence of compensation available to the applicants upset the necessary 'fair balance'.[125]

Wider issues of economic reform were also raised in relation to Greece. The case of *Stran Greek Refineries and Stratis Andreadis v Greece*[126] concerned a contract that the applicants had concluded with the Greek state in 1972, during its period of military dictatorship. After the restoration of democracy, the new government sought to terminate the contract. The applicants eventually won an arbitral award against the Greek state, which the state then appealed at various judicial levels. However, parliament then stepped in to pass a law declaring the arbitration award void and unenforceable. The symbolic aim of the law is apparent from the government's explanation that it was part of a:

> body of measures designed to cleanse public life of the disrepute attaching to the military regime and to proclaim the power and the will of the Greek people to defend the democratic institutions. The applicants' complaints derived from a preferential contract, prejudicial to the national economy, which had helped to sustain the regime and to give the impression at national and international level that it had the support of eminent figures from the Greek business world.

However, the European Court found that the legislature had upset the fair balance to be struck between the protection of the right of property (in the arbitral award) and the requirements of the public interest.[127]

We can see from *Stran Greek Refineries* that the impugned measure was not only about protecting the economic wellbeing of the newly democratic Greece, but also about making a break with the past. The government had essentially alleged that the applicants were complicit in the actions of the military dictatorship. A more subtle issue arose in *Jahn v Germany*.[128] Here, the applicants had benefited from the non-application of a GDR law that would have prevented them from inheriting certain agricultural land. During the transition, the GDR moved to solidify its legislation on the disposition of land, and, with the so-called 'Modrow Law', allowed for the conversion of limited titles to absolute titles. Again the applicants benefited from this, even though if the earlier GDR law on inheritance of agricultural land had been applied properly they would not even have had a limited title. In 1992 the new Republic of Germany passed the Property Rights Amendment Act, under which agricultural land inherited improperly under the GDR (and over

125 Ibid., [99].
126 *Stran Greek Refineries and Stratis Andreadis v Greece* (1995) 19 EHRR 293.
127 Ibid., [74].
128 *Jahn v Germany* [2006] 42 EHRR 49.

which absolute title appeared to have been given by the Modrow Law) could be taken without compensation.

The Grand Chamber reiterated that a total lack of compensation would be justifiable only in exceptional circumstances.[129] However, it then set out to examine whether the 'unique context of German reunification' would constitute such circumstances.[130] It cited both *Kopecký v Slovakia* and *Zvolský and Zvolská v Czech Republic* as authority for there being a wide margin of appreciation in this regard.[131] This is clear evidence of cross-fertilisation between the 'pure' reparatory cases and those on wider economic reforms.

The Grand Chamber's findings on the 'fair balance' were based on three observations. First, the Modrow Law had been passed during a transition and by a parliament that had not been democratically elected.[132] Second, after only a short period of time, the newly unified Germany had moved to correct the anomalies of the Modrow Law.[133] Third, it did not seem unreasonable from a perspective of social justice that these anomalies should be resolved.[134]

In the case of the *Former King of Greece*, the European Court had conceded that the passage of time before the introduction of the impugned measure 'might inspire some doubt' about its necessity and found the lack of compensation unjustifiable. Here, less time had passed and so it seemed that the Court had found it easier to back the very strict approach to compensation. It was less symbolic and more about the complete rebuilding of the state. Allen has also observed that the European Court has taken a comparable approach in other cases on compensation for the seizure of property originally acquired as a 'windfall'.[135] Allen therefore suggested that the case is more like non-transitional ones.

It would seem equally possible to interpret the case as an example of the European Court backing unified Germany's approach to taking 'nominal law seriously', just as we saw in relation to the distinctly transitional successor trial cases: if the law of the GDR had been applied correctly, then the applicants would neither have inherited the land nor benefited from Modrow Law. This is one of the transitional responses that, paradoxically, is justified by reference to strict legal continuity and where such strictness is defended as 'ordinary' rather than transitional. Although the case is not so much about 'doing' transitional justice, the judgment may be a rare example of elements of *a transitional jurisprudence* precisely because of the approach to taking nominal law seriously. However, the certainty of this point is undermined by

129 Ibid., [111].
130 Ibid., [112].
131 Ibid., [113].
132 Ibid., [116].
133 Ibid.
134 Ibid.
135 Allen, *op. cit. supra* n 3, 36.

the European Court's reference to the Modrow Law being passed by a parliament that was not democratically elected. This would seem to suggest that the majority were calling into question the force of the law and led Judge Pavlovschi in his dissent to wonder whether every GDR law passed in its 46 years of existence, 'should be questioned or revised?' However, given that, if properly applied, the Modrow Law would not have benefited the applicants this point loses its force.

The 'taking nominal law seriously' approach is a way of defending a transitional policy while denying that it was, in fact, anything special. The dissenting judges in *Jahn* were absolutely certain that the majority's approach was both transitional and (as a result) unjustifiable. The finding that there was no violation of Article 1, Protocol 1, was made by a majority of 11 votes to 6. The most striking of the dissenting opinions was by Judge Ress, who closely re-examined whether there really was an 'exceptional situation' such as to justify a total absence of compensation:

> What is exceptional in a transitional period? There may be greater possibilities of mistakes by the legislature, which future legislatures would be inclined to correct, but does this give *carte blanche* to commit violations of human rights or to regard violations as non-violations?
>
> [. . .]
>
> If the Court is going to accept that there may be reasons for the State to disregard human rights (whether it calls them exceptional or whatever), who then will protect the individual against interferences with these rights?

He described the *Jahn* case as having 'nothing in common' with the case of *Rekvényi v Hungary*, discussed at length in Chapters 6 and 7, in which the European Court upheld a restriction on the political activities of police officers due to the special transitional context.[136] Also, and crucially, Judge Ress pointed out that this case was not about a fair balance between the rights of two people, such as where the present occupier might resist restitution of their home to a victim of communism, but one where the state perceived a distinct advantage in taking the property.[137]

Since *Jahn*, the European Court has been less generous to the transitional states. For example, in *Hutton-Czapska v Poland*, and although the European Court noted the 'exceptionally difficult housing situation in Poland, [and] the inevitably serious social consequences involved in the reform of the lease

136 *Rekvényi v Hungary* (2000) 30 EHRR 519.

137 But also note that in his conclusion Judge Ress's Opinion made a rather awkward comparison between the defence put forward by those on trial in *Streletz, Kessler and Krenz* (see Chapter 2) and the reasons for expropriation in *Jahn*.

market',[138] it found that the introduction of laws restricting the levels of rent in privately owned flats had not struck a fair balance between rights of the owners and the tenants.[139] Indeed, so serious was the situation that the European Court issued a 'pilot judgment' in the case[140] (discussed further later).

Given this post-*Jahn* assertiveness towards rights-restrictive wide-scale economic reforms that have *not* been aimed also at providing reparative justice to victims, it is perhaps unsurprising that the European Court has been critical of attempts to reduce levels of reparation on economic grounds. Indeed, this was the backdrop to the European Court's first ever pilot judgment in *Broniowski v Poland*. The case concerned compensation for people displaced by World War II: the so-called 'Bug River claimants'. During part of its transition to democracy and a free market, it was alleged that Poland had all but removed an opportunity to vindicate claims for compensation. The European Court noted Poland's wide margin of appreciation, but stated that: '[T]he exercise of the State's discretion, even in the context of the most complex reform of the State, cannot entail consequences at variance with Convention standards.'[141]

The claimants in *Broniowski* were not victims of the communist era, but of a prior injustice. In *Urbárska Obec Trenčianske Biskupice v Slovakia*, the European Court examined a complaint that the Slovakian restitution scheme for victims of communism had been abandoned in favour of land consolidation for market-led purposes.[142] The government argued its new policy promoted legal certainty and ensured optimal use of the land.[143] The applicant association gained some compensation, but the European Court found that the public interest pursued by the reforms did not justify the 'substantial difference' between the real value of the applicant's land and that of the land that it obtained in compensation.[144] There was therefore a violation of Article 1, Protocol 1.

The cases discussed here have all concerned the transition to democracy and a market-led economy, but not necessarily issues strictly of reparative justice. The European Court has nevertheless allowed a misleading cross-fertilisation of the jurisprudence – perhaps by framing the issue as being about 'possessions' rather than 'transition'. The most awkward part of the relationship between transitional justice and human rights is that, although transitional justice may be inspired by a reaction to human rights abuses of the past, it can come into conflict with contemporary human rights standards.[145] In the cases discussed here, there was no countervailing human rights consideration, but rather a

138 *Hutton-Czapska v Poland* (2006) 42 EHRR 15, [176].
139 Ibid., [225].
140 Ibid., [226] *et seq.*
141 *Broniowski v Poland, op. cit. supra* n 88, [182].
142 *Urbárska Obec Trenčianske Biskupice v Slovakia* [2008] ECHR 1894.
143 Ibid., [104].
144 Ibid., [132].
145 Note the discussion of this in Chapter 1.

general interest in economic stability or improvement. This is why the *Jahn* case was so problematic in its result and why the reasoning that likens these to the cases on reparative justice for victims of communism is unfortunate.

4.4 Procedural justice and restitution

The European Court has maintained such a close supervision of restitution policies that some would argue it has impeded their implementation.[146]

For example in *Zvolský and Zvolská v Czech Republic*, the current owner of a property was able to rely not only on Article 1, Protocol 1, but also Article 6 ECHR in his attempts to resist restitution of the property to a person who claimed that he had been forced to transfer ownership of it during the communist era.[147]

However, the cases examined here show that the European Court has played a very significant role in ensuring that, where schemes of restitution are initiated, procedural justice is observed and the process is taken to its conclusion.

4.4.1 Positive obligations

We saw earlier that the European Convention does not make a strong foundation for restitution claims. It might seem odd, therefore, to discuss the relevance of positive obligations in this context. However, in a series of cases the European Court has upheld a minimum procedural content of Article 1, Protocol 1, in order to ensure that the (sometimes rather limited) rights emanating from it are practical and effective. From this foundation, and once the state has embarked on an attempt to provide restitution, the European Court has imposed a positive obligation on states to actually deliver it.

Păduraru v Romania[148] concerned the 1995 Romania law 'on the legal status of nationalised residential property', under which the applicant had sought the restitution of two blocks of flats that were confiscated from his father during the communist era. In 'flagrant violation'[149] of a domestic judgment finding that the nationalisation was unlawful and that the applicant was the lawful owner of the building, the state sold the buildings to a third party. The applicant received no compensation for the sale.

The European Court framed the issue as one involving positive obligations under Article 1, Protocol 1. The Court recapitulated its jurisprudence on the existence of a wide margin of appreciation in relation to notions of the 'public interest', but went on to state that:

146 See Allen, *op. cit. supra* n 3.
147 *Zvolský and Zvolská v Czech Republic, op. cit. supra* n 69.
148 *Păduraru v Romania*, App no 63252/00 (ECtHR, 1 December 2005).
149 Ibid., [68].

> While the Convention does not impose an obligation on the States to restore confiscated assets, let alone to dispose of them in accordance with the elements of the right of property, once a solution has been adopted by a State, it must be implemented with reasonable clarity and coherence.[150]
>
> [Each] Contracting State must equip itself with an adequate and sufficient legal arsenal to ensure compliance with the positive obligations imposed on it.[151]

The Court found that Romania had failed to discharge its positive obligation to take 'timely and consistent action' to address the issues of general interest raised by the attempted restitution scheme.[152] The European Court has made comparable findings in, *inter alia, Viasu v Romania* and *Maria Atanasiu v Romania*.[153] In the latter, it reiterated that 'in cases involving a positive duty, there must be a legitimate justification for the State's inaction'.[154] The fact that all three of these have involved the non-enforcement of judgments about restitution in Romania rather suggests that there is something more systemic at the heart of the matter, however clear the European Court's judgments have been. We shall return to the notion of 'pilot judgments' and the final one of these cases, *Maria Atanasiu v Romania*, shortly.

In *Beshiri v Albania*, the government claimed a failure to comply with a judgment awarding the applicant's compensation in lieu of restitution was 'due to objective circumstances such as the lack of funds and its impact on the general interest of the community'.[155] The European Court declined to accept this, noting that a lack of funds cannot justify a failure to enforce a final and binding judgment on a debt owed by the state and found a violation of Article 1, Protocol 1.[156] Even more explicitly in *Nuri v Albania*, the government pleaded both in relation to Article 6 and Article 1, Protocol 1, that:

> the process of restitution and compensation could not occur overnight and spontaneously, and that the delays associated therewith were related to the transition process the country was going through.[157]

However, the European Court again found that the state had failed to make a fair balance and that there was a violation of Article 1, Protocol 1.

150 Ibid., [92].
151 Ibid., [93].
152 Ibid., [112].
153 See *Viasu v Romania*, App no 75951/01 (ECtHR 9 December 2008); *Faimblat v Romania*, App no 23066/02 (ECtHR 13 January 2009; *Katz v Romania*, App no. 29739/03 (ECtHR, 20 January 2009); and *Maria Atanasiu v Romania, op. cit. supra* n 2.
154 *Maria Atanasiu v Romania, op. cit. supra* n 2, [166].
155 *Beshiri v Albania, op. cit. supra* n 60, [96].
156 Ibid., [102].
157 *Nuri v Albania* [2009] ECHR 194, [32]; on Article 6, see [24].

These cases show that if someone can establish that they are within the scope of a restitution scheme and they can gain a decision in their favour, then the European Court's jurisprudence will assist them in gaining the reparation to which it has been shown they are entitled.

4.4.2 *The applicability of Article 6 ECHR to restitution proceedings*

Given that the European Court found what amounted to a minimum procedural standard for the vindication of rights in Article 1, Protocol 1, it will come as little surprise that the guarantees of Article 6 ECHR can also apply to restitution schemes. Indeed, in the case of *Maria Atanasiu*, discussed already, the European Court found a violation of the applicants' 'right to a fair and public hearing within a reasonable time', contained in Article 6, as well.[158]

As the European Court had explained earlier in *JS & AS v Poland*:

> once a Contracting State decides to establish legal procedures of such a kind, it cannot be exempted from the obligation to respect all relevant guarantees provided for by the Convention, in particular by its Article 6 § 1.[159]

Moreover, the judgment in *JS & AS v Poland* also confirmed the reasoning in the admissibility decision of *Malhous v Czech Republic*: namely that there is no necessary interrelation between the existence of claims covered by the concept of 'possessions' within the meaning of Article 1, Protocol 1, and the applicability of Article 6.[160] In *JS & AS v Poland*, the Court was therefore able to examine the merits of a complaint about the restitution scheme solely by reference to Article 6. Likewise, in *Malhous*, a complaint based on Article 6 was deemed admissible, even though a substantive complaint about restitution based on Article 1, Protocol 1, was inadmissible *ratione materiae*.[161]

Although supervision via Article 6 may benefit current occupiers who are resisting restitution, it is also, and equally, another way in which the European Court can support people who have a right to restitution in domestic law (even where it cannot be required by European human rights law).

4.4.3 *The effect of Article 6 ECHR on restitution proceedings*

Initially, the European Court was extremely reluctant to allow the transitional context to factor into its reasoning on the length of proceedings under

158 *Maria Atanasiu v Romania, op. cit. supra* n 2, [124].

159 *JS & AS v Poland*, App no 40732/98 (ECtHR, 24 May 2005), [53].

160 Ibid., [51].

161 *Malhous v Czech Republic* (dec.), App no 33071/96 (ECtHR GC, 13 December 2000).

Article 6 ECHR. Chapter 1 made reference to the case of *Guincho v Portugal*.[162] In it, the European Court declined to take the transitional context into account when assessing the reasonableness of the length of proceedings in a civil action for damages sought in relation to a road traffic accident. It was therefore not about restitution, but rather about a regular action for damages that happened to take place against a transitional background.

The European Court stated that it could not 'overlook that the restoration of democracy as from April 1974 led Portugal to carry out an overhaul of its judicial system in troubled circumstances which were without equivalent in most of the other European countries'.[163] However, the European Court went on to stress that in Article 1 ECHR, Portugal had guaranteed to secure to everyone the rights in the Convention, including Article 6, and that there was an unavoidable obligation to organise its legal system in compliance with the Convention.[164] Thus, the European Court seemed to be arguing that its duty to police the overarching obligation from Article 1 ECHR precluded it from allowing the transitional context to affect its assessment of Convention compliance.

As noted in the Introduction, and discussed further in Chapter 1, the *Guincho* logic could easily be applied outside the context of Article 6 ECHR. If the Court had done so, it would have considerably reduced the capacity of the newer Contracting Parties to argue that certain rights-restrictive measures were justified due to the circumstances of democratic transition. We shall see that despite *Guincho*, and especially in relation to the democratic rights discussed in Chapters 6, 7 and 8, states have been far from reluctant to test such arguments in Strasbourg.

Returning to the specific issue of Article 6 and its effect in the restitution cases, the European Court has applied it strictly in a range of cases – but has become seemingly more generous, or at least more diplomatic, than it was in *Guincho*.

When the European Court gave its judgment on the merits in *Malhous v Czech Republic*, it found that a hearing before the Mladá Boleslav Land Office on the applicant's claim for restitution did not constitute a, 'fair and public hearing [. . .] by an independent and impartial tribunal'.[165] In *JS & AS v Poland* and *Beshiri v Albania*, the Court found that the delays in the applicants' case, including the enforcement of relevant judgments, constituted a violation of Article 6.[166] The Respondent States did not make any explicitly transitional defence of their conduct in these cases, although in *JS & AS*, the European Court did consider the 'special context' and observed that the applicants' problems were, 'part of the process of transition from the former communist legal order and its property regime to one compatible with the rule of law and

162 *Guincho v Portugal* (1985) 7 EHRR 223.
163 Ibid., [38].
164 Ibid.
165 *Malhous v Czech Republic, op. cit. supra* 161.
166 *JS & AS v Poland, op. cit. supra* n 159; *Beshiri v Albania, op. cit. supra* n 60.

the market economy.'[167] However, this observation only impacted on the applicability of Article 6 and not its effect.

In *Nuri v Albania*, the government argued in respect of Article 6 that:

> the compensation process had been complex and that the difficulties with it were attributable to massive demographic movements, drastic changes to property titles during the previous communist regime, lack of experience *and the transition process*.[168]
>
> [emphasis added]

The European Court, which gave its judgment in 2009, did not accept that this could excuse the fact that a decision of the Lushnja Property Restitution and Compensation Commission awarding compensation to the applicants back in 1994 had still not been enforced. Thus, the European Court's approach was still broadly in line with *Guincho*.

It might seem as if the European Court relaxed its stance a little in *Maria Atanasiu v Romania*. In relation to the complaint under Article 6 the European Court accepted that:

> in the complex and socially sensitive context of Romania's transition to democracy and the reparation of past injustices, which entailed far-reaching economic consequences, the establishment of a legislative framework may have encountered some difficulties and delays.[169]

In making this observation, the European Court cited paragraph 162 of *Broniowski v Poland*, where the European Court had taken into account that the Polish state was, 'confronted with a difficult choice as to which pecuniary and moral obligations could be fulfilled towards persons who had suffered injustice under the totalitarian regime'.[170] However, this part of the *Broniowski* judgment concerned the width of the margin of appreciation in relation to the justification for an interference with Article 1, Protocol 1. There is very little scope for a margin of appreciation in relation to the assessment of the reasonableness of time in Article 6(1),[171] so the citation of *Broniowski* in *Maria Atanasiu* is not altogether appropriate.

167 *JS & AS v Poland, op. cit. supra* n 159, [53].
168 *Nuri v Albania, op. cit. supra* n 157, [24].
169 *Maria Atanasiu v Romania, op. cit. supra* n 2, [122].
170 *Broniowksi v Poland, op. cit. supra* n 88, [162].
171 See Y. Arai-Takahashi, *The Margin of Appreciation Doctrine and the Principle of Proportionality in the Jurisprudence of the ECHR* (Oxford: Intersentia 2002), 52; H. Yourow, *The Margin of Appreciation Doctrine in the Dynamics of European Human Rights Jurisprudence* (The Hague: Kluwer 1996), 25; and J. Schokkenbroak, 'The basis, nature, and application of the margin of appreciation doctrine in the case-law of the European Court of Human Rights (1998) 19 *Human Rights Law Journal* 30, 34.

However, the *Maria Atanasiu* judgment was the last in a series of cases concerning property restitution in Romania. Thus, far from taking its observations about the transitional context as a platform for deference, the European Court found a violation of Article 6[172] (as well as Article 1, Protocol 1);[173] observed that there were 'several hundred' similar applications pending before the Court; and went on to issue a 'pilot' judgment. The reference to *Broniowski* and the acknowledgement of the difficulties facing Romania may have played more of a rhetorical, or diplomatic, role.

4.4.4 *Reparatory justice and 'pilot judgments'*

In recent years the European Court has taken the unprecedented step of issuing so-called 'pilot judgments' in certain cases that disclose a systemic problem within a Contracting Party.[174] There is a predominance of property cases that have led to pilot judgments, including *Broniowski, Hutten-Czapska* and *Maria Atanasiu*.

These cases have already been encountered here since their substantive content touches on the issue of post-communist reparatory justice. However, the approach of the European Court to the issuing of pilot judgments merits some consideration in its own right, since this marks a development in the extent to which the European Court itself may act to ensure that states guarantee reparation for the violation of Convention rights. Combined with its substantive findings on positive obligations and Article 6, this development has equipped the European Court to require states not only to abstain from violating human rights during their attempts to provide reparation to victims of communism, but also to construct effective reparation mechanisms. On the one hand, this would seem to support the notion of subsidiarity by requiring that states resolve situations domestically, thereby protecting the European Court from an onslaught of cases, but, on the other, a massive inroad is made into the implementation discretion usually observed flowing from the Convention.

In *Xenides-Arestis v Turkey*,[175] the European Court took inspiration from its findings in *Broniowski* in its discussion of the application of Article 46 ECHR. The case was about the applicant being denied access to, as well as control, use and enjoyment of her property in the disputed 'Turkish Republic of Northern Cyprus'. The European Court found in favour of the applicant and instructed that Turkey should introduce within three months a remedy that provided 'effective redress' for the applicant and the many others in a similar situation.

172 *Maria Atanasiu v Romania, op. cit. supra* n 2, [124].
173 Ibid., [193].
174 See P. Leach, H. Hardman, S. Stephenson and B. Blitz, *An Analysis of 'Pilot Judgments' of the European Court of Human Rights and Their Impact at National Level* (Oxford: Intersentia 2010).
175 *Xenides-Arestis v Turkey* [2005] ECHR 919.

The controversial development is that subsequently, in the case of *Demopoulos v Turkey*,[176] the European Court accepted that the 'Immovable Property Commission' established by Turkey in the 'Turkish Republic of Northern Cyprus' constituted an adequate and effective remedy under Article 35(1) ECHR in relation to complaints such as those having given rise to *Xenides-Arestis*. As Nikos Skoutaris has observed, given the difficult status of the 'Turkish Republic of Northern Cyprus', the European Court has validated a transitional justice mechanism for the settlement of the property aspect of the Cyprus issue without there having been a peace settlement.[177] It is far from obvious that the pilot judgment's encouragement to settle the property issue in this way will contribute to a wider solution.

4.5 Conclusion

The European Court's jurisprudence on reparatory justice is disproportionately extensive on the issue of property restitution compared to other elements. It has largely prevented the European Convention from being a basis on which to seek reparation, although its comments in *Association 21 December 1989 & Others v Romania* were more positive. The positive obligations emanating from Article 2 ECHR were held not only to include an effective judicial investigation but possibly also the right to compensation.[178] But the case was about an investigation that had already been initiated by the successor government. *Baraona v Portugal*[179] can be confined to its facts. The issue of inadmissibility *ratione temporis* and *ratione materiae* remains.

There is perhaps a factor to consider in relation to the European Court's refusal to relax its admissibility criteria for victims of communist era expropriations. We established in Chapter 2 that the approach of the European Court in relation to successor trials was based on the understanding that states are entitled to attempt to correct misdeeds of the past. However, where those misdeeds include the deprivation of property, the advice of PACE provided a warning that there are important third-party interests that must be considered. The rule of law dilemma presented by the successor trials was that they encounter the principle of non-retroactivity. Where the dilemma is circumvented, it is only the person on trial who is affected. Teitel has argued that in reparatory justice, individual responsibility is replaced by the state's acceptance of collective responsibility for the wrongdoing.[180] It does not follow that all of those who received property without complicity in the former regime

176 *Demopoulos v Turkey* [2010] ECHR 306.

177 N. Skoutaris, 'Building transitional justice mechanisms without a peace settlement: a critical appraisal of recent case law of the Strasbourg Court on the Cyprus issue' (2010) 35(5) *European Law Review* 720.

178 Ibid.

179 *Baraona v Portugal, op. cit. supra* n 19.

180 Teitel, *op. cit. supra* n 1.

should be caught within the state's acceptance of responsibility (or, as in *Jahn*, its commitment to make sweeping economic reforms).

Nonetheless, we have seen that, where states have decided to initiate restitution schemes, the European Court has backed their legitimacy. Thus the European Court has allowed differences between transitional states, as well as reducing the potential for outright conflict between human rights norms and the motivations behind restitution. It has required a high standard of procedural justice, but that is hardly a bad thing.

5 Lustration

5.1 Introduction

The UN Secretary General has written that lustration processes are a 'vital element' of transitional justice and, done properly, are 'key to restoring public trust in national institutions of governance'.[1] It has consequently supported lustration processes both outside and within the Council of Europe, for example in both Bosnia and Herzegovina and Kosovo.[2] The United Nations has described lustration as usually entailing 'a formal process for the identification and removal of individuals responsible for abuses, especially from police, prison services, the army and the judiciary'.[3] Such processes fall within Teitel's definition of administrative justice in transition, being a form of 'politicised public law'.[4]

Roman Boed drew attention to the Encyclopaedia Britannica's definition of the term, dating back to cleansing processes in ancient Greece and Rome, identifying that the term is derived from the Latin *lustratio*, meaning 'purification by sacrifice'.[5] Teitel, meanwhile, has claimed that the term derives from the Latin *lustrare*, meaning 'to shed light' on the past.[6] Others would avoid the term completely and refer to 'vetting' or even 'purge'.[7] This fascinating etymological and semantic debate does not necessarily help us to understand its contemporary meaning, however.

Adam Czarnota has helpfully distinguished between lustration and wider measures aimed at 'decommunisation'.[8] The latter include all the political and

1 UN Secretary General, 'The Rule of Law and Transitional Justice in Conflict and Post-Conflict Societies', UN Security Council, S/2004/616, 3 August 2004, 2.

2 Ibid., 17.

3 Ibid., 18.

4 R. Teitel, *Transitional Justice* (New York: OUP 2000), 149.

5 R. Boed, 'An evaluation of the efficacy of lustration as a tool of transitional justice' (1999) 37 *Columbia Journal of Transnational Law* 357, 358.

6 Teitel, *op. cit. supra* n 4, 98.

7 See the discussion in A. Mayer-Rieckh and P. De Grieff (eds), *Justice as Prevention: Vetting Public Employees in Transitional Societies* (New York: Social Science Research Council 2007), 18.

8 See A. Czarnota, 'Lustration, decommunisation and the rule of law' (2009) 1 *Hague Journal on the Rule of Law* 307.

legal policies and practices employed to remove the legacy of communism in a social and political system.[9] This includes attempts at preventing communists from standing for election to particular public positions in the new regime. The former – lustration – is something more specific. For example, the Council of Europe's 'Guidelines to ensure that lustration laws and similar administrative measures comply with the requirements of a state based on the rule of law', state that lustration shall not apply to elected office.[10] Building on the work of Sadurski, Czarnota has identified three (often overlapping) characteristics of lustration: the *vetting* of candidates for some positions in the state according to their security credentials; *lustration* 'proper' in the sense of making public the identities of those who collaborated with the secret services of the prior regime; and the *elimination*, for some time, of those who held positions in the prior regime from public life.[11]

In this chapter, we shall examine the narrower issue of lustration and explore the wider issue of decommunisation (in the sense of restrictions on the political activity of former or present communists) in the subsequent chapters on democratic rights – although, undoubtedly, there is some overlap. It is worth noting from the outset that *all* the cases discussed in this chapter have been brought by people resisting lustration in some way. The enquiry therefore is into the extent to which Respondent States have claimed any transitional relativism in order to continue to pursue this distinctively transitional policy.

5.1.1 The European Court's early approach to lustration: pre-PACE Resolution 1096

The European Court's first major case on lustration can be traced back to events in Germany before and after reunification, in the 1995 case of *Vogt v Germany*.[12]

Dorothea Vogt was a school teacher and activist in the German Communist Party (the DKP). Vogt had been a teacher of French and German and she was held 'in high regard' by colleagues, pupils and their parents.[13] As a school teacher she was, in formal terms, a civil servant. She had held such status since 1979. She was suspended in 1986 and dismissed in 1987 on the basis that, due to her communist activities, she had not fulfilled the duty owed by every civil servant to uphold the free democratic system within the meaning of the German Basic Law.[14] Ultimately, a bitterly divided Grand Chamber found by

9 Ibid., 310
10 Explanatory Memorandum to PACE Resolution 1096 (1996), Council of Europe Doc. 7568, report of the Committee on Legal Affairs and Human Rights, rapporteur: Mr Severin, [16(e)] and [46(e)]
11 Czarnota, *op. cit. supra* n 8, 311.
12 *Vogt v Germany* (1996) 21 EHRR 205.
13 Ibid., [10].
14 See ibid., [44].

10 votes to 9 that there had been a violation of Articles 10 and 11 ECHR. The judgment makes no reference to the term 'lustration' at all, in spite of its subject matter. It has, however, gone on to be influential on the development of the jurisprudence on lustration laws in central and eastern Europe.

In *Vogt*, the Court found that there was an interference with Article 10 ECHR,[15] which was both prescribed by law[16] and in pursuit of a number of legitimate aims: protecting national security, preventing disorder and protecting the rights of others.[17] The reasoning in relation to the legitimate aims bears quotation in full, since it draws attention to the special circumstances of the Respondent State and makes a conceptual connection to the notion of 'self-defending' or 'militant' democracy. The Court began by noting that civil servants' duty of loyalty was founded on the notion that civil servants were guarantors of the German constitution and of democracy itself:

> This notion has a special importance in Germany because of that country's experience under the Weimar Republic, which, when the Federal Republic was founded after the nightmare of nazism, led to its constitution being based on the principle of a 'democracy capable of defending itself' (*wehrhafte Demokratie*).[18]

This was not the first time that the European Court had been influenced by Germany's attempts to insure against democratic failure. In the examination of democratic rights in Chapters 6, 7 and 8 we shall frequently encounter the 1957 admissibility decision in *Germany Communist Party and Others v Germany*, which found a complaint about the dissolution of the party in question to be inadmissible by virtue of Article 17 ECHR.[19]

In *Vogt*, the Respondent State made reference to the notion of self-defending democracy again when it argued that the interference was 'necessary in democratic society'.[20]

The European Court accepted the principle of self-defending democracy and stated that the German historical and present-day experiences 'lent extra weight' to the notion.[21] Nevertheless, the measure at issue imposed a duty that was 'striking' in its absolute nature.[22] It applied equally to public service as to private life and went beyond comparable measures elsewhere in Europe.[23]

15 Ibid., [44].
16 Ibid., [48].
17 Ibid., [51].
18 Ibid.
19 *German Communist Party and Others v Germany*, App no. 250/75 (ECommHR, 20 July 1957).
20 *Vogt v Germany, op. cit. supra* n 12, [54].
21 Ibid., [59].
22 Ibid.
23 Ibid.

The Court found that Vogt's dismissal was a very serious measure, not least of all because of the harm to her reputation; that her post did not carry any intrinsic security risks; and that, as the DKP had not been banned, the applicant's activities, for which she was being punished, were wholly lawful.[24] In the light of all this, the reasons put forward by Germany were found to be relevant but not sufficient to justify the interference.[25] This reasoning applied *mutatis mutandis* to the alleged violation of Article 11 ECHR.[26]

Articles 10 and 11 ECHR were applicable because the only way that Vogt could have continued in her position was to curtail her political expression and association. The Court distinguished Vogt's situation from the facts of the earlier case of *Glasenapp v Germany*, in which the Court found *no* violation of Article 10 in a case concerning *appointment* to a teaching post. Again the applicant had connections to a communist organisation but, crucially, the European Court found for the Respondent State on the basis that a right of access to the civil service is specifically excluded from the European Convention.[27]

In *Vogt*, the Joint Dissenting Opinion of Judges Bernhardt, Gölcüklü, Matscher, Loizou, Mifsud Bonnici, Gotchev, Jungwiert and Kuris made a clear and concise point of principle that states should be able to dismiss extremists from their civil service. They also argued that the circumstances of the case warranted a 'different emphasis' from that placed on them in the judgment of the majority. They drew attention to the fact that the DKP was supported by the communist regime and its governing party in East Germany and that there existed 'confrontation and antagonism' between the democratic FRG and communist GDR. They would have granted Germany a wider margin of appreciation.

Likewise, the Dissenting Opinion of Judge Jambrek placed greater emphasis both on the vulnerability of West Germany at the relevant time and the role that the DKP played as 'a means of infiltration and dissemination of communist propaganda in Germany': the party aimed to overthrow the democratic order of West Germany. Judge Jambrek also took a different view on the extent of the applicant's cooperation with the DKP and the absoluteness of the impugned measure. The supplementary Dissenting Opinion by Judge Gotchev took a different approach altogether, arguing simply that Article 10 did not apply to the case at all.

The case is interesting for at least three reasons. First, the Court was sharply divided on the outcome. This suggested that future cases on lustration would likewise be challenging. Second, the majority accepted the notion of self-defending democracy as arguable in Convention law, and saw it as the

24 Ibid., [60].
25 Ibid., [61].
26 Ibid., [68].
27 See *Glasenapp v Germany* (1987) 9 EHRR 25, [48 and 49]; note the Glasenapp case is discussed in more detail again in Chapter 7 because of its implications for freedom of association.

principle underpinning the narrower notion of lustration. In a separate line of cases self-defending democracy has continued to play a very important role in the Court's reasoning on Article 11 ECHR and Article 3, Protocol 1.[28] Third, the majority's support for the *notion* of self-defending democracy and acknowledgement of the distinctive German situation did not translate into deference. The majority and minority clearly split according to the weight that each group of judges placed on the distinctive experience of Germany. This is the essential fault line identified in Chapter 1: how much deference is due to states in periods of transition without sliding into transitional relativism.

5.1.2 PACE Resolution 1096 and lustration

The *Vogt* case was decided in September 1995. PACE Resolution 1096 (1996) was adopted nearly a year later, in June 1996. By this time the Council of Europe was prepared to use the term 'lustration' explicitly and to offer guidance on the legitimate aims, scope and procedural safeguards of lustration schemes. Notably, the Resolution uses the terms 'lustration' and 'decommunisation' interchangeably, but from the content it is clear that the Resolution relates to the narrow definition of lustration used earlier – not least of all because, as noted, the accompanying 'Guidelines to ensure that lustration laws and similar administrative measures comply with the requirements of a state based on the rule of law' state that lustration shall not apply to elected office.[29]

The guidance from PACE began thus:

> 11. Concerning the treatment of persons who did not commit any crimes that can be prosecuted in accordance with paragraph 7, but who nevertheless held high positions in the former totalitarian communist regimes and supported them, the Assembly notes that some states have found it necessary to introduce administrative measures, such as lustration or decommunisation laws. The aim of these measures is to exclude persons from exercising governmental power if they cannot be trusted to exercise it in compliance with democratic principles, as they have shown no commitment to or belief in them in the past and have no interest or motivation to make the transition to them now.

PACE went on to explain good practice in the conduct of such administrative processes:

> 12. The Assembly stresses that, in general, these measures can be compatible with a democratic state under the rule of law if several criteria are

28 See Chapter 8.

29 Explanatory Memorandum to PACE Resolution 1096 (1996), *op. cit. supra* n 10, [16(e)] and [46(e)].

> met. Firstly, guilt, being individual, rather than collective, must be proven in each individual case – this emphasises the need for an individual, and not collective, application of lustration laws. Secondly, the right of defence, the presumption of innocence until proven guilty, and the right to appeal to a court of law must be guaranteed. Revenge may never be a goal of such measures, nor should political or social misuse of the resulting lustration process be allowed. The aim of lustration is not to punish people presumed guilty – this is the task of prosecutors using criminal law – but to protect the newly emerged democracy.
>
> 13. The Assembly thus suggests that it be ensured that lustration laws and similar administrative measures comply with the requirements of a state based on the rule of law, and focus on threats to fundamental human rights and the democratisation process.

Several important features can be extracted from this guidance. First, it took on the principal rule of law dilemma presented by lustration by clarifying that it must not be based on collective guilt or presumptions of guilt. The rather awkward language concerning the punishment of 'people presumed guilty' being the task of prosecutors can be dismissed as drafting *faux pas*: it is clear that the Council of Europe believes in the presumption of innocence until proved guilty.

Second, it noted the relationship between administrative measures like lustration and criminal justice. Paragraph 11 stated that lustration may apply to people who did not commit any crimes. An alternative view, put forward by the UN, is that since only a fraction of the persons complicit in the actions of the previous regime will ever be brought to trial, lustration is important in order to bridge the 'impunity gap'.[30] Thus it may be initiated not only against people who did not commit crimes, but against whom it is impossible to bring charges. The UN guidance has identified that this may have certain advantages in a post-conflict or post-authoritarian context where resources are scarce, since although there are costs associated with lustration processes, they are procedurally less complex than criminal prosecutions.[31] It is therefore notable that, as we shall see shortly, the European Court has applied the criminal limb of Article 6 ECHR to lustration processes. These procedural guarantees are far more rigorous than the principles put forward in paragraph 12 of the Resolution.

The third key feature of the PACE guidance is on the aim of lustration. According to PACE, such measures are aimed at restricting 'governmental power'. We shall see in the case law that there has been discussion of the extension of lustration into the private sector. Perhaps more importantly, the

30 UN OHCHR, *Rule-of-Law Tools for Post-Conflict States: prosecution initiatives* (New York: United Nations 2006), 9; UN OHCHR, *Rule-of-Law Tools for Post-Conflict States: vetting – an operational framework* (New York: United Nations 2006), 5.

31 UN OHCHR, *Rule-of-Law Tools for Post-Conflict States: vetting – an operational framework*, ibid., 5.

Resolution seemed to link lustration to the present situation and the future more than to the past, in the sense that it saw lustration as being about protecting the new democracy from threats. It was not about 'revenge' or even punishment, according to paragraph 12: the latter, it clarified, was exclusively for the criminal law.

This guidance is slightly naive, and at odds with the UN's recognition that 'Exclusions from public service have a punitive effect as they take away or pre-empt employment, public authority, and other privileges and benefits.'[32] The UN guidance was clear, however, that lustration should not be used as pretext for avoiding criminal prosecutions.[33]

The reality is that lustration has both formal and informal aims and that within the states that have attempted it there are very different models. They include forward-looking aims that are protective of democracy, as well as a certain element of retribution or punishment – whether formally acknowledged or not. For example, the Polish parliamentary debates focused on historical truth, minimal justice and state security, while, in addition to these aims, the Czechoslovak parliamentary debates identified three further aims including 'the protection of rights and the need to regulate the [lustration] process by law', 'territorial integrity' and 'trust'.[34] However, Roman David's analysis showed that opponents of the Czechoslovakian law alleged that it constituted a form of institutionalised retaliation.[35]

Resolution 1096 has had a moderate influence on the development of the European Court's jurisprudence on lustration, being cited by the parties to the case as well as in decisive parts of the judgments. In the next section, we shall continue to examine the aims of lustration processes, this time from the perspective of the 'legitimate aim' cited for their *prima facie* interference with Convention rights.

5.2 The European Convention and the 'legitimacy' of lustration processes

There are essentially two main challenges that European human rights law has presented to states pursuing lustration processes. Persons subject to lustration have attempted to challenge it on procedural grounds under Article 6 ECHR and also on substantive grounds, under Article 14 in conjunction with Article 8. The issue of 'legitimacy' arises particularly in relation to the latter

32 Ibid.

33 Ibid.

34 R. David, 'Lustration laws in action: the motives and evaluation of lustration policy in the Czech Republic and Poland (1989–2000), (2003) 28 *Law and Social Inquiry* 387, 392, citing original research by M. Los in relation to the debates in the Polish Sentate: M. Los, 'Lustration and truth claims: unfinished revolutions in central Europe' (1995) 20(1) *Law and Social Inquiry* 117.

35 David, ibid., 406.

group of cases, since these more explicitly challenge the notion of lustration itself. Typically, the applicant has argued that there has been a difference in treatment compared to people who are not associated with the prior regime and that Article 8 is engaged because the impact of lustration on their employment has interfered with their home, family and private life.

Since the allegation is of a violation of Article 14, the question is whether the alleged difference of treatment is objectively and reasonably justified, in the sense that there is a 'legitimate aim' for it and that there is a 'reasonable relationship of proportionality between the means employed and the aim sought to be realised'.[36] This is a slightly different formulation to that seen in other qualified Convention articles in which the legitimate aims are listed exhaustively and where restrictions must be 'necessary in a democratic society'. Whatever the political aims of lustration measures, it is clear that their aims must also be 'legitimate' from a Convention standpoint if their interference with Convention rights is to be justified by the transitional state.

The leading case of *Sidabras and Džiautas v Lithuania*[37] concerned restrictions on working in the private sector imposed on two individuals who had previously worked for the KGB. One had since become a public prosecutor, the other a tax inspector. Their complaint, however, was not based on their dismissal from these jobs in 1999, but rather on the prohibition on their seeking a broad range of professions in the public and private sector until 2009.

We shall return to the question of whether the Lithuanian legislation was 'proportionate' later. For now, we shall concentrate on the aims of the legislation. The Lithuanian government argued that the 'KGB Act' pursued the legitimate aim of protecting national security.[38] The employment restrictions imposed on the applicants were not for their actions in the KGB *per se*, but were by reason of their having shown a lack of loyalty to the state.[39] Presumably, it would have actually been more accurate to argue that it was their demonstrable loyalty to the state in its communist manifestation that was the problem.

The European Court stated that it 'must' have regard to Lithuania's experiences under communist rule.[40] The Court again recognised the notion of self-defending democracy, this time as a principle underpinning the new Lithuanian Constitution.[41] In the light of this, the Court accepted that the lustration measure 'pursued the legitimate aims of the protection of national security, public safety, the economic well-being of the country and the rights and freedoms of others'.[42] Indeed, in all the other lustration cases examined

36 see *Belgian Linguistic* (1979–1980) 1 EHRR 252, [10].
37 *Sidabras and Džiautas v Lithuania* (2004) 42 EHRR 104.
38 Ibid., [34].
39 Ibid., [53].
40 Ibid., [54].
41 Ibid., [54].
42 Ibid., [55].

under Article 14, the Court has never denied that the measure has pursued a legitimate national security aim (although it has found that several have been disproportionate).[43] Whatever the complexity of the academic and political debate on the formal and informal aims of lustration, the European Court has accepted the broad national security ethos behind them, taking into account the post-communist context.

The clearest challenge to this developing orthodoxy was made by the applicant in the 2008 decision of *Chodynicki v Poland*.[44] Unlike the others discussed thus far, this case was brought under Article 6 ECHR. The applicant challenged the principles of the 1997 Polish Lustration Act, arguing that it was not compatible with a democratic state under the rule of law and, quite specifically, that it was contrary to the principles outlined in PACE Resolution 1096. The applicant had been elected as an MP in Poland. Legal proceedings subsequently established that he had lied in his lustration declaration. The European Court acknowledged that there was 'no uniform approach' among Contracting Parties as to how to deal with the former totalitarian apparatus. This language is significant since it echoes the classic rationale give for the recognition of a margin of appreciation.[45] The Court again accepted that at the relevant time the Respondent State had an 'interest' in carrying out lustration in respect of important positions. The Court noted that 'from an ethical standpoint' someone might be treated differently if their work with the previous regime was in the open, on the one hand, and secret, on the other. Therefore, given the state's margin of appreciation, there could be no violation of the right to a fair trial and the application was deemed manifestly ill founded.

The case is interesting because of the explicit attempt to challenge the notion of lustration and the Court's equally explicit support of it. From a doctrinal point of view it is notable because it is not common to see discussion of 'uniform' approaches and the margin of appreciation in relation to Article 6 ECHR.[46]

43 In *Rainys and Gasparavičius v Lithuania* [2005] ECHR 226, the emphasis of the reasoning in the case was on the measure's lack of proportionality, but the Respondent State had clearly cited the national security aim of the impugned lustration measure ([32]); in *Turek v Slovakia* [2006] ECHR 138, even the applicant accepted that lustration could pursue a legitimate national security aim (although he challenged the basis on which the process had been applied to him). These cases are discussed further later.

44 *Chodynicki v Poland* (dec.) [2008] ECHR 930.

45 For example, that there is 'no uniform European conception of morals': see the discussion of *Handyside* in Chapter 1.

46 This is noted also in Chapter 4. See See Y. Arai-Takahashi, *The Margin of Appreciation Doctrine and the Principle of Proportionality in the Jurisprudence of the ECHR* (Oxford: Intersentia 2002), 52; H. Yourow, *The Margin of Appreciation Doctrine in the Dynamics of European Human Rights Jurisprudence* (The Hague: Kluwer 1996), 25; and J. Schokkenbroak 'The basis, nature, and application of the margin of appreciation doctrine in the case-law of the European Court of Human Rights (1998) 19 *Human Rights Law Journal* 30, 34.

The only real limitation on the aims of the lustration process was clarified in the case of *Ādamsons v Latvia*.[47] The case is one that, following the definitions produced earlier, can be considered as being more about decommunisation than lustration: the case concerned the applicant's removal from the electoral list because of his communist past and was brought under Article 3, Protocol 1 ECHR (it is discussed in more detail in Chapter 8). Nevertheless, the Respondent State argued that the case should be seen in the context of lustration measures adopted elsewhere in central and eastern Europe.[48] Consequently, the European Court was moved to summarise its jurisprudence on lustration, and clarified that 'lustration proceedings must not only serve the purpose of punishment or vengeance'.[49] This is broadly in line with PACE Resolution 1096.

From the jurisprudence examined thus far we can see that the European Court has not distinguished particularly between the different forms of lustration identified in the scholarship when it has looked at their legitimacy: it has essentially given blanket approval to their legitimacy. In this way, it has allowed some differences between lustration policies, but has not negatively affected the universality of human rights.

5.3 Proportionality in the lustration process

Assuming that an allegedly discriminatory measure is in pursuit of a legitimate aim, it is still necessary for the Respondent State to show that in each case the lustration measure displays a 'reasonable relationship of proportionality between the means employed and the aim sought to be realised'.[50]

The UN's 'Vetting: An Operational Framework' stressed that lustration measures should be individually applied rather than collectively administered.[51] Not only can a blanket approach be too wide, it risks missing certain people who are equally tainted but did not belong to whichever broad class is chosen to disqualify.[52] PACE Resolution 1096, likewise, stressed that valid lustration measures must be based on individual rather than collective guilt.[53] With such international guidance in mind, several applicants have sought to challenge the breadth of lustration measures.

The 2004 case of *Sidabras and Džiautas v Lithuania* has been noted briefly already in relation to the question of legitimacy. The proportionality of the measure hinged on three factors. First, the European Court noted that although

47 *Ādamsons v Latvia*, App no 3669/03, (ECtHR, 24 June 2008) (available only in French).

48 Ibid., [96].

49 Ibid., [116] (author's translation).

50 *Sidabras and Džiautas v Lithuania, op. cit. supra* n 37, [51].

51 UN OHCHR, *Rule-of-Law Tools for Post-Conflict States: vetting – an operational framework, op. cit. supra* n 30, 4.

52 Ibid., 14.

53 PACE Resolution 1096 (1996), [12].

loyalty to the state was an inherent condition of employment in the public sector, it was not inevitable that the same should apply in the private sector.[54] The European Court made a clear statement that:

> State-imposed restrictions on a person's opportunity to find employment with a private company for reasons of lack of loyalty to the State cannot be justified from the Convention perspective in the same manner as restrictions on access to their employment in the public service.[55]

Second, the Court found that the measure was ambiguous, in the sense that it did not explain the link between its potential legitimate aim and the precise list of prohibited private sector positions listed in the legislation. Third, the Court noted that the KGB Act came into force a decade after Lithuania had declared its independence. The Court described the measure as 'belated' and stated that the timing of it was relevant to, but not decisive of, its proportionality.[56] This last point is particularly interesting because it implies that a broader lustration measure might have been Convention compliant had it been introduced earlier.

We noted in relation to successor trials that it seemed as if the European Court took into account the transition context when determining whether the judicial clarification of certain concepts was foreseeable.[57] In Chapter 8, we shall also see that in cases on Article 3, Protocol 1, the European Court has likewise recognised a relationship between the precision of restrictive measures and the proximity of their imposition to the start of the transition.[58]

Rainys and Gasparavičius v Lithuania[59] was decided in 2005 and confirmed the approach in *Sidabras and Džiautas*. As in that case, the applicants alleged that their treatment under the 1998 KGB Act violated Article 8 ECHR taken in conjunction with Article 14. The facts were similar to the earlier case, but here the applicants were not only complaining about their inability to apply for jobs in the private sector until 2009 but had also been dismissed from positions in that sector.[60] The European Court reiterated that 'even having regard to the legitimacy of the measure', namely the 1998 KGB Act, it was disproportionate and discriminatory.[61]

The two Lithuanian cases both dealt with substantive violations of Article 8 ECHR taken in conjunction with Article 14. In *Turek v Slovakia*,[62] the

54 *Sidabras and Džiautas v Lithuania, op. cit. supra* n 37, [57].
55 Ibid., [58].
56 Ibid., [60].
57 See Chapter 2.
58 See Chapter 8.
59 *Rainys and Gasparavičius v Lithuania, op. cit. supra* n 43.
60 Ibid., [34].
61 Ibid., [36].
62 *Turek v Slovakia, op. cit. supra* n 43.

European Court examined the procedural safeguards implicit in Article 8 ECHR taken alone and noted that the different purposes of Article 8 and Article 6 ECHR meant that the same facts could be examined under both.[63]

We encountered the *Turek* case in the context of gaining access to communist era information in Chapter 3. Turek had claimed that the communist authorities themselves wrongly classified him as a collaborator. He claimed never to have assisted them. When he attempted to challenge his classification as a collaborator, the Slovakian authorities refused Turek access to the top secret guidelines dating from 1972, which defined exactly what constituted a 'collaborator' and how they could be recruited. The applicant argued explicitly that his treatment was contrary to the principles set out in PACE Resolution 1096.[64]

The case engaged Article 8 because Turek argued that being labelled an StB collaborator interfered with his moral and physical integrity and with his good name and reputation.[65] The European Court examined whether the procedural safeguards available to Turek were sufficient to ensure that the right to respect for his Article 8 rights was 'practical and effective'.[66] It was in relation to this discussion that the European Court made the point of principle noted already, namely, that there could be no assumption of 'a continuing and actual public interest' in refusing access to communist era information.[67]

The European Court noted that in the domestic proceedings the applicant had to prove that the interference with his rights was contrary to the applicable rules, but that those rules were still secret. According to the Court, this placed Turek under an 'unrealistic burden' and did not respect the principle of equality.[68] There was, therefore, a violation of Article 8 on the basis that there was a lack of procedure open to the applicant to guarantee effective protection of his rights.

The message to the transitional states has been fairly clear: although lustration measures may pursue a legitimate aim in the post-communist context, they must not be so broad as to constitute discrimination in the enjoyment of Article 8 rights. Thus the principle of proportionality has prevented excessive transitional relativism. Moreover, in the next section we shall see that lustration processes must also have sufficient procedural safeguards to ensure effective protection of Article 8 rights.

63 Ibid., [112].
64 Ibid., [81] (Helsinki Foundation); ibid., [107] (applicant).
65 Ibid., [103].
66 Ibid., [113].
67 Ibid., [115]; see also Chapter 3.
68 Ibid., [116].

5.4 Procedural justice and lustration

5.4.1 The applicability of Article 6 ECHR to lustration processes

Article 6 ECHR guarantees people a fair and public hearing in a reasonable time in the determination of their civil rights and obligations and in the determination of any criminal charge brought against them. Article 6(2) enshrines the presumption of innocence for persons charged with a criminal offence. Article 6(3) sets down additional minimum rights for persons charged with a criminal offence. In the Grand Chamber judgment in *Pellegrin v France*, the European Court held that 'no disputes between administrative authorities and employees who occupy posts involving participation in the exercise of powers conferred by public law attract the application of Article 6(1).'[69]

The lustration cases have therefore been contentious because the applicant has sought the full application of Article 6 to their case, including the criminal limb, whereas the Respondent States have argued that the application of Article 6 is excluded altogether.

In the *Turek* case, the Helsinki Foundation intervened to argue, purportedly by reference to PACE Resolution 1096, that lustration was 'punitive in nature' and that the whole range of guarantees in Article 6 therefore applied to it.[70] The reliance on PACE Resolution 1096 is intriguing, since as we noted earlier it states that: 'The aim of lustration is not to punish people presumed guilty [. . .] but to protect the newly emerged democracy.'[71] At both the admissibility and merits stage, the European Court found that the application did not concern the applicant's employment in the public sector, but rather his personal integrity.[72] For this reason, the application of Article 6 was not excluded by the *Pellegrin* line of cases.[73] The applicant relied on the guarantee of a hearing within a reasonable time, which applies equally to civil and criminal charges. The proceedings had taken seven years and five months[74] and the European Court therefore found a violation of Article 6(1) ECHR.[75]

Since *Turek* had established that Article 6 could apply to lustration, it then fell to be determined whether persons subject to lustration gained access to the greater range of minimum rights under Article 6(3): the criminal limb. In *Matyjek v Poland*,[76] the applicant had made a declaration required by the 1997 Lustration Act, in which he denied having collaborated with the communist

69 *Pellegrin v France* (2001) 31 EHRR 26, [67].
70 *Turek v Slovakia, op. cit. supra* n 43, [81].
71 PACE Resolution 1096 (1996) [12], discussed earlier.
72 *Turek v Slovakia, op. cit. supra* n 43, [82].
73 See the discussion at the admissibility stage, *Turek v Slovakia* App no. 57986/00 (ECtHR, 14 December 2004).
74 *Turek v Slovakia, op. cit. supra* n 43, [96].
75 *Turek v Slovakia, op. cit. supra* n 43, [99].
76 *Matyjek v Poland* [2007] ECHR 317.

era secret services. Following this, in 1999, the Commissioner of the Public Interest launched proceedings against him alleging that he had falsified his lustration declaration.

The case went up through the Warsaw Court of Appeal acting as both first and then second instance lustration court and then to the Supreme Court *twice* before in May 2003 the appeal against being classified as a lustration liar failed. The Supreme Court had found that the first set of proceedings were fatally flawed due to a serious procedural error: the applicant's motion to hear two additional witnesses had been disregarded.[77] At the second attempt, however, there was no such error and the charge stuck. From February 2000 the applicant lost his mandate as an MP.[78] Nevertheless, the applicant applied to the European Court on the basis that during the whole process he had been prevented from taking any notes on the materials he had been allowed to see, which he could have then used in his own defence. We will re-examine the substance of this complaint in the next section. Here, we shall concentrate on the question of whether Article 6 could apply and, if so, whether its application would include the guarantees of Article 6(3). The Respondent State argued that following the *Pellegin* line of cases the application was inadmissible *ratione materie*.[79]

In the leading 1976 judgment in *Engel v Netherlands*, the European Court had determined that the word 'criminal' in the phrase 'criminal charge' was an autonomous concept,[80] in the sense that it would be defined by the European Court rather than be tied to the domestic classification of the charge in question. In doing so, the Court established three tests for the determination of whether a measure was criminal and in *Matyjek*, it went on to apply these to the Polish lustration measure.

Applying *Engel*, the Court assessed the domestic classification of the measure, as a starting point (noting that the lustration process was based on the model of a Polish criminal trial and that the rules of the Code of Criminal Procedure were directly applicable to lustration proceedings),[81] and moved on to the nature of the offence and the nature and seriousness of the punishment. In relation to the first, it drew parallels with the notion of perjury, which is usually punishable by criminal law.[82] In relation to the last, it stated that, however 'well deserved' the deprivation the applicant's ability to continue a professional life might be 'in the historical context of Poland', this did not affect the Court's assessment of the seriousness of the sanction. In the light of all this, it held that the criminal limb of Article 6 applied. The 2007 Chamber

77 Ibid., [8].
78 Ibid., [26].
79 Ibid., [41].
80 *Engel and Others v Netherlands* [1976] ECHR 3, [81].
81 *Matyjek v Poland, op. cit. supra* n 76, [50].
82 Ibid., [52].

judgment on the merits accepted this decision in its entirety, and concentrated solely on compliance with Article 6. The application of the criminal limb of Article 6 to the Polish lustration legislation was confirmed in the 2011 case of *Moscicki v Poland*.[83]

The European Court's approach here is interesting because, as noted above, the UN's guidance has observed that: 'While vetting processes also require significant resources, they are procedurally less complex than criminal prosecutions.'[84] For this reason, the UN argued that they can help fill the 'impunity gap' left by the sheer impossibility of prosecuting everyone who was complicit in the former regime.

By equating lustration to a criminal trial, the European Court has imposed a very high standard of procedural justice on states seeking to embark on lustration. Therefore, to an extent, we can see again that the standards of the European Convention are not quite aligned with the received wisdom on the aim and implementation of transitional justice policies. This is less an issue of transitional relativism and more an issue of impeding transitional justice.

5.4.2 The effect of Article 6 on lustration processes

In Chapter 1, and again in Chapter 4 in relation to restitution, we encountered the 1984 judgment in *Guincho v Portugal*. In *Guincho*, the European Court conceded that the 'restoration of democracy as from April 1974 led Portugal to carry out an overhaul of its judicial system in troubled circumstances which were without equivalent in most of the other European countries'[85], but declined to take the transitional context into account when assessing the reasonableness of the length of proceedings in a civil action for damages sought in relation to a road traffic accident. The Court stressed Portugal's overarching obligation to guarantee the rights in the Convention, derived from Article 1 ECHR. Likewise, the conventional wisdom is that there is no margin of appreciation in relation to Article 6.[86]

In the light of this background, it is therefore surprising that, in *Chodyniki*, the Court's finding that the application was inadmissible rested on the conclusion that: 'Given the margin of appreciation afforded to the State, the Court does not find that such domestic regulation could amount to a breach of the applicant's right to a fair trial.'[87]

However, the reasoning in this decision seems to have been an exception and cases decided on the merits have given few concessions to the transitional

83 *Moscicki v Poland* [2011] ECHR 929.
84 UN OHCHR, *Rule-of-Law Tools for Post-Conflict States: vetting – an operational framework, op. cit. supra* n 30, 5.
85 *Guincho v Portugal* (1985) 7 EHRR 223, [38].
86 Note the discussion at *supra* n 46.
87 *Chodynicki v Poland, op. cit. supra* n 46.

context. For example, we have already seen that in the *Turek* case, the Court found that lustration proceedings lasting seven years and five months[88] violated the principle of a fair hearing within a reasonable time, reasonableness being assessed 'in the light of the circumstances of the case'[89] and the Respondent State stressing the complexity of the proceedings notwithstanding.[90]

The Polish cases on access to documents within the lustration proceedings have likewise maintained a strict approach to equality of arms. There was a systemic problem with Polish law, which meant that several applicants complained that they had inadequate access to materials essential to their defence. For example, in *Matyjeck*, which was judged on its merits in 2007, the applicant complained that although he had been able to read his file, held in the secret registry of the lustration court, he was not allowed to make any copies of them; to take the notes that he made in the registry away with him; to show the notes to anyone; or even to use them at the hearings.[91] The European Court emphasised that there could be no assumption of a continuing and actual public interest in keeping communist era documents secret, and stated that:

> If the party to whom the classified materials relate is denied access to all or most of the materials in question, his or her possibilities of contradicting the security agency's version of the facts will be severely curtailed.

The Court held that it was incompatible with the concept of the equality of arms for the Head of the State Security Bureau to have complete discretion over whether and when to lift the confidentiality rating of the relevant documents.[92] The Court also dismissed the rather fanciful argument that the Commissioner of the Public Interest was in the same position as the applicant in respect of access to the documents.[93] The Court also noted that even the reasoning in earlier judgments in Matyjek's case had been subject to access restrictions.[94]

The post-communist context of the case was certainly considered by the Court, however. It accepted that 'at end of the 1990s' there had been an interest in carrying out lustration and that there could be situations where even documents produced by the previous regime could justifiably remain secret.[95] However, given the passage of time since the creation of those

88 *Turek v Slovakia, op. cit. supra* n 43, [96].
89 Ibid., [97].
90 Ibid., [94]
91 *Matyjeck v Poland, op. cit. supra* n 76, [46].
92 Ibid., [56].
93 Ibid., [60].
94 Ibid., [61].
95 Ibid., [62].

documents it would have to be an exceptional case.[96] The Court concluded that the applicant was placed at a clear disadvantage[97] and that the defects of the lustration process could not be adequately remedied by the appeal processes that had been open to him.[98] There was therefore a violation of Article 6(1) ECHR taken in conjunction with Article 6(3). The same approach was taken in the very similar 2007 case of *Bobek v Poland* and the 2011 case of *Mościcki v Poland*. The former is notable for its further criticism of the secrecy surrounding the legal and factual content of the lustration judgments, since apparently:

> Neither the findings of fact nor any reference to the evidence on which the courts had based their findings were to be found therein. Likewise, the parts of the judgments accessible to the public did not contain any judicial reasoning specifying the grounds on which the courts had reached their decisions.

5.5 Conclusion

It would seem from all these cases, taken together, that the European Court has a fairly advanced jurisprudence on the substantive and procedural human rights standards applicable to lustration. This makes its recent summary of the jurisprudence in *Ādamsons v Latvia* more than a little intriguing. In it, the European Court put forward four conditions for a lustration procedure to be compatible with the Convention.[99] First, a lustration law must meet the basic requirements of accessibility and predictability inherent in the concept of 'legality'. Second, the procedure must not only serve the purpose of punishment, since that is the role of criminal law. Third, the procedure must be capable of being applied with sufficient precision to individualise the responsibility of the persons involved, and must contain adequate procedural safeguards. It is the fourth condition that is the most interesting, because the European Court had not been as explicit in the earlier cases. The Court stated that:

> Finally, national authorities must keep in mind that lustration measures are, by their nature temporary, the objective necessity of a restriction of individual rights resulting from this procedure decreases with time.[100]

Recall that in the earlier *Sidabras and Džiautas v Lithuania*, the European Court expressly held that the passage of time was 'not in itself decisive'.[101] We

96 Ibid.
97 Ibid.
98 Ibid., 64.
99 *Ādamsons v Latvia, op. cit. supra* n 47, [116].
100 Ibid. (author's translation).
101 *Sidabras and Džiautas v Lithuania, op. cit. supra* n 37, [60].

saw that in every case the European Court has backed the broad aim of lustration measures (thereby accommodating differences *between* transitions), but has reserved the right to test them for proportionality and to apply the criminal limb of Article 6. Taken together with the (admittedly exceptional) statement in *Chodyniki* that the Court recognised a margin of appreciation in relation to Article 6, the summary in *Ādamsons v Latvia* could certainly give the impression that the European Court must have recognised a certain transitional relativism in relation to lustration.

From the very outset, this chapter has noted that defining lustration is difficult and that, in any event, it has close connections to the wider issue of decommunisation and the restriction of democratic rights in transition. It may be these close connections that have given rise to the relative flexibility seen in this chapter. The next three chapters of this book examine democratic rights in transition in more detail.

Section B

Democratic rights in the transitional context

B.1 Introduction

The previous four chapters of this book focussed on the European Court's jurisprudence on the policies specifically identified as embodying 'transitional justice'. We looked at transitional criminal justice, historical justice and access to documents, reparation and restitution, and lustration. We have seen that there are several ways in which these policies may come into conflict with the rule of law and international human rights law. Thus states have occasionally asked for special treatment, and the European Court has sometimes granted it (sometimes explicitly, sometimes implicitly). This has implications for the universality of human rights, since it might amount to a form of transitional relativism. The European cases arising from these clearly identifiable policies are not the only ones that have raised complex issues of transitional justice, however.

Ruti Teitel identified 'constitutional justice' as one of the core categories of transitional justice.[1] She would see 'militant constitutional democracy', sometimes referred to as 'militant democracy' or 'self-defending democracy', as one of the markers of transitional constitutionalism.[2] It derived historically from concerns about how vulnerable the pre-war Weimar Republic had proven to being overrun by totalitarianism, and posits that states should be able to protect themselves from such risks. It is known in German as *wehrhafte Demokratie* and is reflected in several linked provisions of the German Basic Law. For example, Article 21 of German Basic Law states that:

> [Political] Parties that, by reason of their aims or the behavior of their adherents, seek to undermine or abolish the free democratic basic order or to endanger the existence of the Federal Republic of Germany shall be

1 R. Teitel, *Transitional Justice* (New York: OUP 2000), 191 *et seq.*

2 R. Teitel, 'Militating democracy: comparative constitutional perspectives' (2007) 29 *Michigan Journal of International Law* 29; but note that in her 2000 book, Teitel examined militant democracy within her discussion of 'administrative justice', *op. cit. supra* n 1, 177–179.

unconstitutional. The Federal Constitutional Court shall rule on the question of unconstitutionality.

Crucially, it is not just a constitutional principle, but one over which *judicial* rather than political oversight is envisaged. In a 1957 admissibility decision, discussed in detail in Chapter 8, the European Commission confirmed that the motives behind Article 17 ECHR and Article 21 of the German Basic Law were similar.[3]

For Teitel, the central dilemma of self-defending democracy is 'the restriction of democracy in the name of democracy'.[4] However, the process of judicial constitutional interpretation and the fact that the repression of communist parties in both Germany and the USA took place for a limited time after World War II mitigate some of its effects.[5] Teitel, among others, has since expressed concern that the thinking behind 'self-defending' or 'militant' democracy has seeped into discourse surrounding the 'war on terror', so that a steady state of transitional justice is apparently established in order to justify illiberal moves to protect the state.[6]

With this in mind, it is significant that the European Court affirmed, in the *Vogt* case on lustration, that the notion of self-defending democracy was a valid principle within European human rights jurisprudence. Notably that was a case that was not on the precise issue of dissolving a political party, but on other associated steps that a democracy might take to protect itself. Thus in this part of the book we will examine the extent to which the European Court has been called on to endorse, and to apply for itself, transitional constitutionalism including self-defending democracy. The cases would seem to imply the existence of a form of self-*consolidating* democracy, which can only really be interpreted as evidence for the existence of a kind of transitional relativism in the jurisprudence of the European Court.

The European Court is grappling with these issues of transitional constitutionalism precisely at the time when its role in delivering 'constitutional justice' is becoming more dominant.[7] We shall therefore be particularly concerned with those cases where the Respondent State has cited the necessities of transition as a distinctive reason for restricting human rights in particular cases, including, but certainly not exclusively, those on the dissolution of political parties. Moreover, just as Teitel observed that the paradigmatic communist party dissolution cases occurred within a limited period after World War II, we shall see that the European Court has had to grapple with the issue not only of whether a transitional, or self-defending, democratic

3 *German Communist Party and Others v Germany*, App no. 250/75 (ECommHR, 20 July 1957).
4 Teitel, *op. cit. supra* n 1, 178.
5 Ibid.
6 R. Teitel, 'Transitional justice genealogy' (2003) 16 *Harvard Human Rights Journal* 69.
7 See Chapter 1.

response *is* required, but whether it is *still required* some time after the end of a state's totalitarian era.

If the European Court is, inevitably, being asked to play a role in transitional constitutionalism, then its international supervisory role is not only to give leeway to the transitional states but also to facilitate the transition, by highlighting problems in the reception of democratic norms. Thus, after an introduction to democracy in the European Convention and an explanation of the choice of Convention rights to be examined, each of the substantive chapters in this part of the book is divided between those cases where the Respondent State has made claims about the necessities of transition, and those where the European Court appears to have played a role in facilitating the transition to democracy by identifying systemic or structural problems in the reception of democratic norms. As noted in the conclusion to Chapter 1, it is readily conceded that the division between these two broad groups of cases is not watertight: several of the cases in which the Respondent State has cited the transitional context as a reason for restriction might also seem to display systemic problems and some judges have come to different conclusions as to whether particular restrictions are due to the content, or the application, of particular laws.[8] Links are therefore made between the broad categories.

B.2 The centrality of democracy in the ECHR

The notion of a 'democratic society' permeates the entire European Convention system.[9] In the preamble to the 1949 Statute of the Council of Europe, participating states reaffirm:

> their devotion to the spiritual and moral values which are the common heritage of their peoples and the true source of individual freedom, political liberty and the rule of law, principles which form the basis of all genuine democracy.[10]

Likewise, the Preamble to the 1950 European Convention on Human Rights itself states that fundamental freedoms:

> are best maintained, on the one hand by an effective political democracy and, on the other, by a common understanding and observance of the human rights upon which they depend.

8 In this respect, note the Concurring Opinion of Judge Malinverni, joined by Judges Vajić and Kovler in *Seyidzade v Azerbaijan* [2009] ECHR 1983.

9 See S. Greer, *The European Convention on Human Rights* (Cambridge: CUP 2006), 199 *et seq.*

10 *Statute of the Council of Europe*, ETS 01.

Despite the concerns about the Council of Europe's apparent relaxation of its accession standards noted in Chapter 1, at a political level the Council of Europe has continued to stress its vision of democracy, for example, in the 1980 Resolution 'On the Principles of Democracy'; 1992 Resolution 'On Citizens' Participation in Politics'; 1997 Resolution 'On Instruments of Citizen Participation in Representative Democracy'; 1998 Resolution 'On the Democratic Functioning of National Parliaments'; and 2003 Resolution 'On the Future of Democracy: strengthening democratic institutions'. In 2004 the Council of Europe published an 'analytical summary' of the Council's *aquis* on democracy, containing suggestions about the future directions that it might take.[11] Disappointingly, the summary made virtually no reference to the jurisprudence of the European Court of Human Rights.[12] This is regrettable since the European Court has played an important role in this regard.

In *United Communist Party of Turkey v Turkey*, the European Court summarised its position as follows:

> Democracy is without doubt a fundamental feature of the European public order. [. . .] That is apparent [. . .] firstly, from the Preamble to the Convention. [. . .] [The Court] has pointed out several times that the Convention was designed to maintain and promote the ideals and values of a democratic society. [. . .] In addition, Articles 8, 9, 10 and 11 of the Convention require that interference with the exercise of the rights they enshrine must be assessed by the yardstick of what is 'necessary in a democratic society'. The only type of necessity capable of justifying an interference with any of those rights is, therefore, one which may claim to spring from 'democratic society'. Democracy thus appears to be the only political model contemplated by the Convention and, accordingly, the only one compatible with it.[13]

The centrality of democracy to the Convention system does not mean that the precise form of democracy implied by the Convention is particularly clear. Wheatley has argued that the Court has failed to guarantee against the 'tyranny of majority', by insufficiently promoting deliberative democracy.[14] Both Marks[15] and O'Connell[16] have divined characteristics of representative

11 L. Pratchett and V. Lowndes, *Developing Democracy in Europe – an analytical summary of the Council of Europe's acquis* (Strasbourg: Council of Europe 2004).
12 There is a brief discussion of the cases on freedom of expression. Ibid., 58.
13 *United Communist Party of Turkey v Turkey* (1998) 26 EHRR 121, [145].
14 S. Wheatley, 'Minorities under the ECHR and the construction of a "democratic society"' (2007) *Public Law* 770, 791.
15 S. Marks, 'The European Convention on Human Rights and its "democratic dociety"' (1995) 66 *British Yearbook of International Law* 209.
16 R. O'Connell, 'Towards a stronger concept of democracy in the Strasbourg Convention' (2006) 3 *European Human Rights Law Review* 281.

democracy in the European Court's approach, with the latter stressing the possibilities for greater engagement with participatory democracy.

The precise relationship between rights and democracy remains moot both in the abstract and within the Convention system. For example, Gearty has claimed that the European Court has the ability to interfere with the *status quo* in a state not only on issues of substantive rights but also where it is found to have failed, 'the Court's test of what its version of democracy requires'.[17] In relation to this, he observed:

> There is irony as well as paradox in this: an unelected judicial body standing outside the democratic dialogue it purports to foster, determining not only what rights should matter but also, *a priori* in the name of democracy, setting out how such a dialogue should be conducted.[18]

Both Wheatley and O'Connell have identified that this goes to the historical tension between rights and democracy, classically conceived as the 'counter-majoritarian difficulty'. While O'Connell has observed that a more positive relationship between rights and democracy has been claimed since the 1990s[19] and has always been inherent in the Convention system,[20] Wheatley has argued that the international counter-majoritarian difficulty is exacerbated by the absence of any possibility of legislative override of the European Court's decisions or amendment of the treaty without all states agreeing.[21] Although the European Court has promoted a liberal conception of justice, for example, in cases on gay rights,[22] according to Wheatley these judgments were 'a loss for democracy'.[23] Instead, and avoiding what he would deem a rather defective margin of appreciation doctrine, Wheatley would have the Strasbourg institutions more aggressively promote deliberative democracy.[24]

Gearty has argued that the European Court's use of the margin of appreciation doctrine has some 'conceptually attractive side effects' in this regard, since it can temper the absolutist tendencies of rights talk; although he has lamented that the European Court has not developed the doctrine in a sufficiently democratically sensitive way.[25] Indeed, the margin of appreciation, noted in Chapter 1 as a potential vehicle for transitional relativism, is most frequently used in the discussion of the priority between the first and second

17 C. Gearty, 'Democracy and human rights in the European Court of Human Rights: a critical appraisal' (2000) 51 *Northern Ireland Legal Quarterly* 381, 388.

18 Ibid.

19 O'Connell, *op. cit. supra* n 16, 282.

20 Ibid., 283.

21 Wheatley, *op. cit. supra* n 14, 783.

22 *Dudgeon v UK* (1982) 4 EHRR 149; *Norris v Ireland* (1991) 13 EHRR 186.

23 Wheatley, *op. cit. supra* n 14, 783.

24 Ibid., 791.

25 Gearty, *op. cit. supra* n 17, 387.

paragraphs of Articles 8 to 11 ECHR, a textual division that replicates the counter-majoritarian difficulty. The first paragraph specifies the right, but the second allows for it to be overridden by the imperatives of a democratic society. But herein lies the problem in relation to cases hailing from the transitional states: is the Respondent State truly arguing that the restriction is necessary in a *democratic* society or is it instead arguing that the restriction is necessary in a *transitional* society? We noted in Chapter 1 that the reference to a democratic, rather than transitional, society in the qualified rights might appear to be an impediment to any accommodation of transitional justice.

It has been argued that the European Convention offers protection from human rights abuses at two levels.[26] First, it protects against 'naked, bad faith abuse of power'.[27] In this sense, the European Convention clearly required from the outset a standard of human rights to be set in response to the recent horrors of World War II. However, in protecting human rights the Court also has to deal with restrictions imposed in the name of the general, democratic majoritarian, interest and which, while impacting disproportionately on the individual, are imposed in good faith. The European Court's engagement with these types of restriction affects its reasoning and in particular its recourse to the margin of appreciation doctrine. According to Mahoney:

> It is only in this second context, once the first degree of protection has been assured, that the doctrine of the margin of appreciation comes into play, that is to say, only if the preliminary conditions of normal democratic governance have been shown to exist.[28]

This was for many people, this author included, how the margin of appreciation doctrine was understood to work.[29] However, the cases discussed in this part of the book demonstrate that the margin of appreciation has been an attractive proposition to the transitional states and that the European Court has allowed states to benefit from it even when explicitly transitional motives have been cited for the restrictive measure at issue.[30]

B.3 Democratic rights in the European Convention

Even if the counter-majoritarian difficultly remains unsolved and the concept of democracy promoted by the European Convention and the Strasbourg

26 See P. Mahoney, 'Marvellous richness of diversity or insidious cultural relativism' (1998) 19(1) *Human Rights Law Journal* (1998), 2 and 3.

27 Ibid., 4.

28 Ibid., 4.

29 For example in J.A. Sweeney, 'Margins of appreciation, cultural relativism, and the European Court of Human Rights' (University of Hull, unpublished PhD thesis 2003).

30 *Rekvényi v Hungary* (1997) 23 EHRR CD63 being one of the more notable ones: See Chapter 6, 7 and 9 for discussion of this case.

institutions remains opaque, the substantive rights that are said to comprise the concept of democracy are relatively easily identified. Along with the reference to a 'democratic society' in relation to the qualification of rights, the substantive content of Articles 10 and 11 ECHR and Article 3, Protocol 1, combine to give a democratic backbone to the Convention system.[31] These are the rights to free expression, free assembly and association and the right to free elections. The European Court has explained that: 'There is undoubtedly a link between all of these provisions, namely the need to guarantee respect for pluralism of opinion in a democratic society through the exercise of civic and political freedoms.'[32]

The European Court has also recognised a strong link between these rights and Article 9 ECHR on freedom of thought, conscience and religion. According to the Court: 'Freedom of thought, conscience and religion is one of the foundations of a democratic society within the meaning of the Convention. The pluralism indissociable from a democratic society, which has been dearly won over the centuries, depends on it.'[33]

In this way, Article 9 is often interpreted in the light of other Convention rights, such as the Article 11 right to freedom of association and peaceful assembly.[34] Thus, in the discussion of free assembly and association, we shall also examine Article 9 cases on the registration and dissolution of religious organisations.

B.4 Article 17 and 'gatekeepers' of the democratic rights

To these substantive rights we can also add Article 17 ECHR. This article prohibits the use of Convention rights from implying:

> any right to engage in any activity or perform any act aimed at the destruction of any of the rights and freedoms set forth herein or at their limitation to a greater extent than is provided for in the Convention.

The Article may be raised at the admissibility or the merits stage and the European Court therefore may consider purported interferences with Convention rights in the light of Article 17.

The Article is relevant to the following discussion because it serves to limit reliance on the Convention by anti-democratic actors. Article 17 has been used, for example, to prevent extreme right-wing views from benefiting from protection under Article 10 ECHR.[35] It is one of several 'gatekeepers' to

31 Alasdair Mowbray, 'The role of the European Court of Human Rights in the promotion of democracy' [1999] *Public Law* 703.

32 *Ždanoka v Latvia* (GC) (2007) 45 EHRR 17, [115].

33 *Hasan and Choush v Bulgaria* (2002) 34 EHRR 55, [60].

34 Ibid., [62].

35 For example in *Kuhnen v Germany* (dec.) App no 12194/86 (ECommHR, 12 May 1988).

reliance on the democratic rights and in the transitional context it has been tempting to some of the Respondent States to rely on Article 17 to restrict certain points of view that might hamper the transition, even where they are not anti-democratic *per se*.

Other gatekeepers include that freedom of assembly only extends to 'peaceful' assembly[36] and so, often alongside Article 17, it has been suggested that some points of view are inherently incompatible with 'peaceful' assembly during the transitional period – such as, for example, calling for secession of a part of the state. Likewise, and invoking the notion of self-defending democracy, the European Court has recognised that restrictions on freedom of association might be necessary where there is evidence of violent intentions. Thus the question of whether particular viewpoints are inherently 'violent' (such as contemporary communism or denying that a particular ethnicity actually exists as a matter of fact) has become a gatekeeping question for reliance on freedom of association.

In the following chapters we shall examine freedom of expression, freedom of assembly and association (two rights which, although contained in the same Convention article, have raised rather different issues), and the right to free elections.

36 See, e.g., *Ezelin v France* (1992) 14 EHRR 362.

6 Freedom of expression

6.1 Introduction

In the introduction to Chapter 5, the overlap between cases on lustration and broader issues of de-communisation was raised. At the crossroads of these two issues sits *Vogt v Germany*,[1] since it concerned the impact on a person's democratic rights of a restriction on what political activities were compatible with their continued employment as a teacher. Recall that the applicant's dismissal led to a violation of Articles 10 and 11 ECHR. Crucially, the case made conceptual links between the impugned restriction and the notion of self-defending democracy. These links are explored in relation to freedom of assembly and association and the right to free elections in Chapters 7 and 8. In this chapter, we shall examine the importance of this thinking in the context of cases concerning restrictions on the media or other political speech during transition.

6.1.1 The media and political speech: a recipe for reservations?

The European Court has long recognised that the press and political speech more generally deserve a high level of protection in the Convention system.[2] In a case brought against Slovakia (discussed further later), the European Court emphasised that:

> the promotion of free political debate is a very important feature in a democratic society. It attaches the highest importance to the freedom of expression in the context of political debate and considers that very strong reasons are required to justify restrictions on political speech. Allowing broad restrictions on political speech in individual cases would

1 *Vogt v Germany* (1996) 21 EHRR 205.

2 See P. Mahoney, 'Universality versus subsidiarity in the Strasbourg case law on free speech: explaining some recent judgments' (1997) *European Human Rights Law Review* 4, 364.

> undoubtedly affect respect for the freedom of expression in general in the state concerned.[3]

Likewise, in a case brought against Hungary, also discussed shortly, the European Court stated that: '[W]hen freedom of expression is exercised as political speech – as in the present case – limitations are justified only in so far as there exists a clear, pressing and specific social need.'[4]

There is some debate as to whether it is desirable to have a hierarchy of free expression in the Convention system, not least of all because of the sheer difficulty of taxonomising free expression.[5] Assuming, briefly, that it is possible to identify political expression, the jurisprudence seems to show fairly clearly that the media have an important role to play in relation to it.[6]

The European Court first explained in *Barthold v Germany* that the task of the press was to be a 'purveyor of information and public watchdog'.[7] In *Observer and Guardian v UK*, the European Court further clarified that:

> Not only does the press have the task of imparting such information and ideas: the public also has a right to receive them. Were it otherwise, the press would be unable to play its vital role of 'public watchdog'.[8]

We have seen that in recent years that the European Court has acknowledged that the role of 'public watchdog' stretches further than that played by the mass media and may include other types of social actor such as NGOs.[9]

Since the media and political speech have this special status in the Convention system, and since the communist states were less than inclined to protect such interests, it might have seemed likely that the Convention system could be at risk from questionable reservations about the mass media emanating from the new Contracting Parties from central and eastern Europe. It has transpired that only Azerbaijan has attempted to make a reservation to Article 10 ECHR specifically in relation to the media.[10] Its reservation attempts to subordinate Article 10 ECHR to Article 14 of the Law of the Republic of Azerbaijan 'on mass media' of 7 December 1999. This provision concerns foreign ownership of mass media outlets and requires that the establishment of mass media outlets with more than 30 per cent foreign ownership

3 *Feldek v Slovakia* [2001] ECHR 463, [83].
4 *Vajani v Hungary* (2010) 50 EHRR 44, [51].
5 See A. Lester, 'Universality versus subsidiarity: a reply' (1998) *European Human Rights Law Review* 1, 73.
6 See Mahoney, *op. cit. supra* n 38, 371.
7 *Barthold v Germany* (1985) 7 EHRR 383, [58].
8 *Observer and Guardian v UK* (1992) 14 EHRR 15, [59(b)].
9 See *Társaság a Szabadságjogokért v Hungary* [2009] ECHR 618, [27]; note also the discussion of academics as social watchdogs in Chapter 3.
10 See http://conventions.coe.int/Treaty/Commun/ListeDeclarations.asp?NT=005&CM=8&DF= 06/06/2011&CL=ENG&VL=1 (accessed 20.5.2012).

shall be regulated by interstate treaties. Thus it does not appear to strike at the very essence of Article 10 and, even if it did, the severance doctrine outlined in *Belilos v Switzerland* would apply.[11]

We shall now turn to those cases in which the Respondent States have put forward distinctively transitional reasons for restricting particular instances of free expression and afterwards to those that reveal more systemic problems or 'echoes' of totalitarianism. This pattern is followed in Chapters 7 and 8.

6.2 Freedom of expression: 'transitional' arguments by the Respondent State

In *Rekvényi v Hungary*,[12] decided in May 1999, the applicant was a police officer who complained that a Hungarian law prohibiting police officers from engaging in political activity unduly restricted his rights to free expression and association under Articles 10 and 11 of the ECHR.[13] With respect to Article 10, the state agreed that there had been an interference with the applicant's right, but argued that the interference was justified under Article 10(2).[14] We shall discuss the claim in respect of Article 11 in Chapter 7, since it raises some distinctive legal issues relating to the particular wording of the final sentence of Article 11(2) ECHR.

The Respondent State argued that the impugned measure's aim was to depoliticise the police in a period when Hungary was in the process of transformation from a totalitarian regime to a pluralistic democratic society.[15] The Court noted that some other democratic states lawfully restrict police officers' political activities, believing that the public should expect their police to be above political considerations in their operations. Citing the *Vogt* case, the European Court went on to state that this objective took on:

> a special historical significance in Hungary because of that country's experience of a totalitarian regime which relied to a great extent on its police's direct commitment to the ruling party.[16]

As a result, the Court held that the interference *did* pursue one or more of the legitimate aims listed exhaustively in the Convention, namely the protection of national security, public safety and the prevention of disorder.[17] It is notable

11 *Belilos v Switzerland* (1988) 10 EHRR 466.

12 *Rekvényi v Hungary, op. cit. supra* n 30.

13 Ibid. The Court held by 16 votes to 1 that there had been no violation of Article 11. It held unanimously that there was no violation of Article 14, on which the applicants had also sought to rely in conjunction with Article 11 (but not Article 10).

14 Ibid., [25].

15 Ibid., [39].

16 Ibid., [41].

17 Ibid.

from a doctrinal perspective that the transitional context played a role in the determination of whether the measure pursued a 'legitimate aim'. Much of the flexibility in the Convention system is assumed to have been facilitated by the use of the margin of appreciation doctrine, attaching to the question of necessity. Indeed, this was the principal vehicle by which cultural and, by extension, transitional relativism was identified as being able to encroach on the universality of human rights in Chapter 1. In this case, there was an element of flexibility at both stages: legitimate aim *and* necessity.

When it came to discuss whether the interference actually met a pressing social need, the Court reiterated the Respondent State's view of Hungary's transition to democracy. It was acknowledged that there had been no purge of officials during that time, as had been the case in some of the other central and eastern European states[18] (and note that *none* of the cases discussed in Chapter 5 of this book was brought against Hungary). Given this, the state argued, police neutrality was particularly important so that the public should come to trust the police as defenders of democracy rather than tools of the state.[19] The Court accepted in principle that such a position towards police neutrality was justifiable:

> In view of the particular history of some Contracting States, the national authorities of these States may, so as to ensure the consolidation and maintenance of democracy, consider it necessary to have constitutional safeguards to achieve this aim by restricting the freedom of police officers to engage in political activities and, in particular, political debate.[20]

This was already a fairly clear statement that the transitional milieu was having an effect on its reasoning. It was still necessary to examine the particular restriction at issue, however, and so the Court detailed for itself the recent history of Hungarian moves towards democracy. The Court then went on to state:

> Regard being had to the margin of appreciation left to the national authorities in this area, the Court finds that, especially against this historical background, the relevant measures taken in Hungary in order to protect the police force from the direct influence of party politics can be seen as answering a 'pressing social need' in a democratic society.[21]

As to proportionality, the Court noted that the law in question did not prohibit political participation absolutely and gave a long list of ways in which, under Hungarian law, a police officer could exercise his or her political will. As a result

18 Ibid., [44].
19 Ibid.
20 Ibid., [46].
21 Ibid., [48].

of this, the interference did not seem disproportionate. Combined with the findings just examined, the Court therefore concluded unanimously that the interference was necessary in a democratic society and there had been no violation of Article 10[22] (Judge Fischbach dissented in relation to the finding that there was no violation of Article 11: this is discussed in Chapter 7). This judgment is one of the strongest examples of transitional relativism in the European Court's jurisprudence, since it clearly allowed a degree of exceptionalism, or non-idealism on transitional grounds,[23] the very few in which the European Court seemed to have been influenced to a considerable degree by the transitional context.

Given the degree of impact that the transition appeared to have on the judgment in *Rekvényi*, much has been made of a later case in which the Hungarian government also cited the transitional context but was rebuffed, apparently due to the passage of time.[24] *Vajnai v Hungary* concerned the applicant's conviction for wearing a five-pointed red star during a lawful demonstration, which he attended as the vice-president of the Workers' Party, a registered left-wing political party.[25] The prosecution and conviction were based on a provision of the Criminal Code that outlawed the use of totalitarian symbols, of which the authorities considered the five-pointed red star to be one. The conviction had been upheld by the Constitutional Court, which based much of its reasoning on *Rekvényi* and also drew parallels with the German experience.[26]

At the European Court, the government reiterated that in its view the red star symbolised totalitarian ideas and practices directed against the Convention's underlying values and argued, therefore, that Article 17 ECHR should apply.[27] The Court disagreed and therefore proceeded to the merits. It found there was an interference,[28] prescribed by law,[29] that pursued a legitimate aim.[30] In relation to the latter, it was only the applicant that drew attention to the passage of time, pointing out that nearly 20 years had passed since Hungary had begun its transition.[31] The government did not attempt to defend the provision on grounds that could be described as transitionally relativist, but on the basis that wearing the symbols of dictatorships was a demonstration against any pluralist democracy.[32]

22 Ibid., [50]. The applicant's arguments under Articles 11 and 14 also failed, [62] [68].
23 In the Teitel, *op. cit. supra* n 1, sense, see Chapter 1.
24 See A. Buyse, 'The truth, the past and the present: Article 10 ECHR and situations of transition', in A. Buyse and M. Hamilton, *Transitional jurisprudence and the ECHR* (Cambridge: CUP 2011), 133–138: M. Varju, 'Transition as a concept of European human rights law' (2009) *EHRLR* 170, 176.
25 *Vajnai v Hungary, op. cit. supra* n 40, [6].
26 Ibid., [17].
27 Ibid., [20–22].
28 Ibid., [29].
29 Ibid., [31].
30 Ibid., [34].
31 Ibid., [32].
32 Ibid., [33].

On the question of necessity, the European Court immediately distinguished *Rekvényi* by reference to Vajnai's being a politician and to the passage of time. The European Court's distinguishing of *Rekvényi* was not solely based on the passage of time, the Court stated that there was no evidential basis from which to conclude that there was any longer a 'real and present danger' of any political movement or party restoring the communist dictatorship.[33]

Moreover, the European Court's central finding was that, although it was 'aware that the systematic terror applied to consolidate Communist rule in several countries, including Hungary, remains a serious scar in the mind and heart of Europe',[34] the ban was too broad in the light of the multiple meanings that the five-pointed red star can posses.[35]

It can be observed that the judgment in *Vajnai* did *not* go so far as to say that, *but for the passage of time*, the restriction would have been justifiable: the measure would still have been overbroad because the five-pointed star was not exclusively a totalitarian symbol. In fact, it did not even go as far as it had a month earlier in *Ādamsons v Latvia* or in *Sidabras and Džiautas v Lithuania* in 2004, where it was implied that there was a balance to be struck between the precision of the restrictive measure and temporal proximity to the transition. By contrast, when the European Court found a violation of the Convention in relation to a prohibition on dual nationals standing for election to the Moldovan parliament, it said it 'did not exclude' that the restriction could have been justified in the immediate aftermath of independence in 1991.[36] That the Court *has* been able to make such statements shows that the *Vajnai* case is not quite as groundbreaking on closing the era of transition as it first appears.

6.3 Freedom of expression: 'echoes' of totalitarianism and systemic problems

Cases such as *Rekvényi* and *Vajnai*, in which the Respondent State has explicitly cited the transition as a reason for interfering with Article 10 are in something of a minority. There are far more cases in which the transitional issue is revealed more subtly within potentially systemic problems.

6.3.1 Press intimidation and censorship

In *Dalban v Romania*, the applicant journalist had been convicted in 1994 of criminal libel after writing several articles alleging a named senator and a chief executive of a state-owned company had been engaged in corruption

33 Ibid., [49].
34 Ibid., [57].
35 Ibid., [54].
36 *Tănase v Moldova* (GC) App no. 7/08 (ECtHR, 10 March 2010), discussed further in Chapter 8.

regarding taxation. His appeals failed and he subsequently claimed in 1995 that his convictions violated, *inter alia*, his rights under Article 10 of the ECHR.[37] However, in 1998, shortly before the Court of Human Rights was to hear his case, Dalban died.[38] The Romanian Supreme Court then quashed his convictions and ordered the discontinuation of further proceedings. The Romanian government argued that this meant the applicant had lost his victim status and the European Court should dismiss the application.[39] The European Court disagreed – not least of all because it was only the applicant's death that triggered the discontinuation of further proceedings.[40]

In its recapitulation of the facts, the European Court noted that many Romanian newspapers took up the story and described the applicant's conviction as an attempt to intimidate the press.[41] In the European Court's discussion of the merits of the case, it confirmed that Dalban's articles concerned matters in the public interest.[42] The European Court cited its earlier case law on the importance of allowing the press to perform its rightful role of public watchdog[43] and reiterated that it was unacceptable for a journalist to be barred from expressing critical value judgments unless he or she can prove their truth.[44] Although the government had contested the case's admissibility, it did not challenge the European Commission's conclusion that the applicant's conviction was not necessary in a democratic society.[45] Finding a violation of Article 10, the European Court likewise concluded that although the restriction was prescribed by law and in pursuit of the legitimate aim of protecting the reputation of others,[46] it was unnecessary and disproportionate.[47]

Press intimidation and censorship were also an issue in the *Ukrainian Media Group*[48] case. Although the parties had apparently reached a friendly settlement, it was rejected by the Court in October 2004 and the Court gave its judgment in March 2005. This decision suggests that the Court was concerned about the implications that this case would have for attitudes toward freedom of the press in Ukrainian democracy from the outset.

37 *Dalban v Romania* (2001) 31 EHRR 39, [31]. Dalban had also argued before the Commission that his right to a fair trial had been violated. The Commission's report of 22 January 1998 opined that there had been a violation of Article 10 and that it would not be necessary for the Court to examine the complaint under Article 6. The Court disagreed, [32], [55].
38 Ibid., [1].
39 Ibid.
40 See ibid., [44] and [45].
41 Ibid., [26].
42 Ibid., [51].
43 Ibid., [49].
44 Ibid., [56] (citing *Lingens v Austria* (1986) 8 EHRR 407).
45 Ibid., [51].
46 Ibid., [46].
47 Ibid., [60–61].
48 *Ukrainian Media Group v Ukraine* (2006) 43 EHRR 25.

The Ukrainian Media Group owned a daily newspaper in which it published articles criticising two politicians, Petro Symonenko and Natalia Vitrenko, leaders of the Communist Party and the Progressive Socialist Party, respectively. The articles, both published in 1999, expressed negative opinions about the politicians' likely relationship to the administration of President Kuchma during presidential elections later that year. The applicant group was successfully sued in defamation and subsequently complained to the European Court under Article 10 ECHR.

The applicants argued that the interference was not necessary in a democratic society, because the articles expressed value judgments, which are not susceptible of proof.[49] Ukrainian law, however, did not distinguish between factual statements and value judgments. Further, the Ukrainian Media Group claimed that the Ukrainian Court's decisions were 'in fact a form of political censorship'.[50] Ultimately, the European Court found that both the Ukrainian media law in the abstract[51] and its application to the case at hand[52] were contrary to Article 10 ECHR.[53]

The Court did not explicitly confirm the allegations of press intimidation in either *Dalban* or *Ukrainian Media Group*, but its unambiguous presentation of existing case law on the role of the press gave a very clear message. The implications of the restrictions at issue were clearly linked to regressive practices more commonly associated with totalitarianism and the European Court was well aware of the chilling effect that such restrictions could have.[54] Interestingly, neither Respondent State made strong arguments for special treatment in the transitional context. Romania did not contest the Commission's findings on necessity at all and Ukraine attempted to argue that the Ukrainian law in general and the particular restriction were 'in full compliance' with the standards set in the non-transitional cases.[55]

These two cases can be contrasted with those in which the applicant has unsuccessfully sought to link their own case to wider issues of democratic transition.

Janowski v Poland[56] concerned a claim by a journalist that his rights under Article 10 ECHR had been violated. Janowski was convicted of insulting two municipal guards in a public square. Janowski had seen the municipal guards attempting to move some street vendors from the square because it was not an authorised place for retail. Janowski interjected on behalf of the vendors,

49 Ibid., [37].
50 Ibid., [64].
51 Ibid., [62].
52 Ibid., [69].
53 Ibid., [70].
54 *Cumpănă and Mazăre v Romania* (GC), App no 33348/96 (ECtHR, 17 December 2004) [114], [116].
55 *Ukrainian Media Group, op. cit. supra* n 48, [57].
56 *Janowski v Poland* (2000) 29 EHRR 705.

arguing that the guards had no authority to move them. In the course of his advice, Janowski called the municipal guards 'dumb' and 'oafs'.[57]

The applicant argued that his rights under Article 10 ECHR[58] had been violated by his conviction for insulting the guards. The Court held that there had been an interference with the applicant's rights under Article 10,[59] that the interference was prescribed by law[60] and that the restriction pursued the legitimate aim of preventing disorder.[61] The real area of debate was on the question of whether the interference was 'necessary in a democratic society'. Following the European Court's well-established methodology, in order to be 'necessary', the interference would have to answer a 'pressing social need', be proportionate to the legitimate aim invoked and be supported by reasons that were both relevant and sufficient.

Significantly, Janowski argued that, since he was a journalist, his conviction had been taken by others as a sign that the authorities were reintroducing censorship such as had been common under communism. He felt that this might mean that future criticism of the state and its apparatus would be discouraged.[62] Such an argument clearly invited the Court and Commission to be especially vigilant of restrictions on free expression in the newly democratic Poland.

The European Commission in *Janowski* had acknowledged that civil servants such as the municipal guards acting in their official capacity were, like politicians, subject to wider acceptable limits of criticism than private parties. In the context of the heated exchange, the Commission formed the view that those limits had not been overstepped by the applicant.[63] The government responded to this, arguing before the Court that the applicant's comments had not formed part of a public debate, but were confined to the particular situation. In the light of this, they argued that the applicant's profession as a journalist was irrelevant. The European Court agreed.

The Court noted that it did not even have to balance public order against a wider public interest in political criticism because Janowski's remarks were not made in his professional capacity.[64] In other words, the European Court

57 The words used were *głupki* and *ćwoki*, respectively.

58 The applicant had also alleged violations of Articles 3, 6 and 7(1), but the European Commission declared those complaints inadmissible.

59 *Janowski v Poland, op. cit. supra* n 56, [22–23].

60 Ibid., [24].

61 Ibid., [25–26]. The government also contended that their aim was to protect the 'reputation and rights of others', namely the municipal guards. Having examined the facts of the case and the reasoning of the domestic courts, the European Court felt the aim of preventing disorder was the dominant aim.

62 Ibid., [27].

63 It should be noted that the Commission was split 8:7 in favour of finding a violation of the Convention. There was therefore a significant minority of Commissioners that felt the boundaries of the state's margin had not been overstepped in this case: *Janowski v Poland* (dec.) App no 25716/94 (ECommHR, 27 November 1996).

64 *Janowski, op. cit. supra* n 56, [32].

did not consider it a political speech case, such as would deserve special scrutiny. Both national courts that had heard the case had confirmed that Janowski had been convicted on the basis of his use of insulting words, not simply for making critical remarks,[65] and therefore the European Court was not convinced the Polish authorities' actions could be likened to censorship. Moreover, the applicant's sentence had been reduced on appeal and his prison sentence quashed. For these reasons, the European Court concluded that the national authorities had not overstepped their margin of appreciation in assessing the necessity of the contested measure. There was no violation of Article 10.[66]

It is difficult not to have some sympathy with Janowski, who clearly felt his intervention on behalf of the street vendors was for the public good. Indeed, the Grand Chamber that decided the case was by no means unanimous in its decision to contradict the Commission. A majority of 12 to 5 found no violation of Article 10 and the President of the Court, Judge Wildhaber, was in the minority. The core of the dissenters' argument was that the criminal legislation applied to Janowski was overbroad in that it protected civil servants from criticism even where they exceeded their lawful authority – which these guards undoubtedly had.

The Dissenting Opinion of Judge Sir Nicolas Bratza, joined by Judge Rozakis, placed its emphasis on the public issues raised by the case. They argued that the case concerned what the applicant perceived as an abuse or excess of authority on the part of public officials and was, to this extent, 'clearly a matter of public concern which merited the protection of Article 10'. Judge Bonello was particularly concerned about the outcome of the case:

> I wonder what the Court would have found had the applicant insulted the guards while witnessing accidentally the torture of a third person. Would the Court have said that the guards were carrying out their official duties and were therefore entitled to special protection? The difference between torture and any other official abuse is only one of degree, not of substance.

These arguments are compelling, and rightly stress the importance of free expression in nascent democracies in which official authority has frequently been used in the past to disguise repression.

In *Constantinescu v Romania*, the applicant was convicted of criminal libel, after referring in a newspaper article to certain people on trial for theft, misappropriation and fraudulent conversion as being guilty of the crimes.[67] The context of the case was that of a dispute between successive leaders of a

65 Ibid.
66 Ibid., [35].
67 *Constantinescu v Romania* (2001) 33 EHRR 33.
68 Ibid., [8–13].

teachers' trade union in Romania in the early 1990s.[68] Constantinescu, the new president of the union, alleged that previous union leadership had failed to return certain items of the union's property and that they were using the items in question to form a new trade union organisation.[69] Interviewed for a newspaper article, Constantinescu complained that by taking so long to try the former leadership for their alleged crimes, the police and the public prosecutor's office were engaged in premeditated anti-union practices.[70]

The legal process in *Constantinescu* had been complex and flawed and the Court found a violation of Article 6.[71] However, it also had to consider whether there was an unjustified interference with Constantinescu's free expression. It reasoned that Constantinescu's conviction was only in relation to his statements about the previous leadership of the union and not his allegation that the police and prosecution did not want to conclude their investigation.[72] Thus, in this case, the applicant's suspicion of the state apparatus did not form part of the findings on Article 10. In other words, as in *Janowski*, the restricted speech was held not to relate to political matters and so the restriction was to be examined only insofar as it was designed to achieve the legitimate aim of protecting the 'reputation or rights of others'.[73]

Looking at the precise words used, the Court felt that in respect of the former trade union leaders, Constantinescu had gone beyond the limits of acceptable criticism when he used the word *delapidatori*, which apparently refers to persons found guilty of the offence of fraudulent conversion.[74] Since the trade union leaders had not been found guilty of anything, the authorities had not overstepped their margin of appreciation in attempting to protect their rights and reputations as permitted by Article 10(2) and therefore no violation of Article 10 was established.[75]

Like the 'wild' lustration cases discussed later, the judgment in *Constantinescu* took a very narrow reading of the material facts of the case, which perhaps does not do full justice to the complexities of the transitional context. However, there is another element that the *Janowski* and *Constantinscu* cases have in common in addition to the fact that the applicant did not win their case: in both cases, the European Court gave signs of concern about the precise words used by the applicants and took it under advisement from the Respondent State that those words were particularly harsh.

In *Constantinscu*, the word was a technical legal one, the definition of which the Respondent State merely supplied. However, in *Janowski* the applicant had used the words *głupki* and *ćwoki*, which were translated as 'dumb' and

69 Ibid., [9].
70 Ibid., [13].
71 Ibid., [61].
72 Ibid., [71].
73 Ibid., [72].
74 Ibid., [73].
75 Ibid., [75–78].

'oafs' respectively.[76] The applicant argued that the words he used should be considered appropriate,[77] whereas the government suggested that they constituted a 'destructive attack' on the municipal guards.[78] The European Court merely observed that the domestic trial and appeal courts had found these words to be offensive[79] and thus in its summary referred to the applicant as having resorted to abusive and insulting language.[80] There was therefore certainly a sense in which the European Court took advice on the meaning of the words in question and the level of insult or offence inflicted by them.

A similar issue arose in *Tammer v Estonia*,[81] in which the applicant journalist's conviction for criminal libel was held not to violate Article 10, since the words that he had used to describe someone had, according to the Estonian government:

> [a] very special meaning in the Estonian language, and that they had no equivalent in English. When interpreting the words and their meaning their specific nature within the Estonian language and culture should also be taken into account.[82]

The journalist referred to Vilja Laanaru (who had had an affair with Estonian prime minister and had entrusted the care of their child together to her parents) as *abielulõhkuja* and *rongaema*. According to the European Court, these can be translated as, 'unfit and careless mother who had deserted her children' and 'someone who was willing to break up another's marriage'. A footnote to the case report explained that the translation of these words was descriptive, since no one-word equivalent exists in English.

In addition to the perception of censorship or press intimidation, the approach to the words at issue in *Janowski* and *Tammer* might seem problematic from the perspective of maintaining the universality of human rights. The apparent willingness of the European Court to take into account the transitional states' interpretation of the words' connotations demonstrates that the relationship between cultural and transitional relativism is particularly close.

6.3.2 Political expression about the transition itself

Despite these overtures to transitional relativism, the European Court has observed that some expression is directly relevant to the transition itself and

76 The terms used were *głupki* and *ćwoki*, respectively.
77 *Janowski, op. cit. supra* n 92, [27].
78 Ibid., [29].
79 Ibid., [32].
80 Ibid., [34].
81 *Tammer v Estonia (No. 2)* (2003) 37 EHRR 43.
82 Ibid., [53].

should therefore be protected. In *Marônek v Slovakia*,[83] the applicant wrote an open letter to the Slovakian prime minister, which was reprinted in several newspapers. The letter concerned a property dispute in which the applicant was engaged. He gave the full names and addresses of the Public Prosecutor and her husband,[84] whom he alleged were illegally occupying a house that he had been allocated in 1991. The Public Prosecutor and her husband successfully sued Marônek for defamation. Marônek then unsuccessfully petitioned the Constitutional Court, alleging a violation of his constitutional rights. Marônek claimed before the European Court of Human Rights that his rights under Article 10 ECHR had been violated.[85] The Court observed that Marônek's open letter was not simply designed to resolve his own situation:

> In fact, at the end of his letter the applicant called upon other persons with a similar problem, with a view to taking joint action. He expressed the view, apparently in good faith, that the resolution of the problem *was important for strengthening the rule of law in the newly born democracy*.[86]

Given this, the applicant's statements did not appear excessive and so the limits of acceptable criticism had not been overstepped.[87] The Court held that the measures taken against the applicant (a very large fine) were disproportionate[88] and that there had therefore been a violation of Article 10.[89]

By looking at the Concurring Opinion of Judge Rozakis, joined by Judges Baka and Lorenzen, it seems that there was disagreement as to whether Marônek's letter really did engage with wider issues of democratic transition. Judge Rozakis characterised the dispute that gave rise to the open letter as essentially one concerning private rights rather than 'wider social concerns'. With this in mind, Judge Rozakis only agreed to find a violation of the Convention on grounds of proportionality (in the sense that even though he felt that the applicant's criticism of the public prosecutor and her husband was excessive, the punishment was disproportionate). The Concurring Opinion, however, is based on a questionable presentation of the law on free expression; it states that: 'The freedom of journalists to express their opinions

83 *Marônek v Slovakia* (2004) 38 EHRR 5.

84 Ibid., [23].

85 Ibid., [46].

86 Ibid., [56].

87 Ibid., [57]. The Court also found it very important that the amount of damages that the applicant was ordered to pay to the state prosecutor and her husband was excessive. Interestingly, a separate concurring opinion of three judges was prepared to find a violation of Article 10 only on the basis that the sum demanded from Marônek was excessive. These judges, Rozakis, Baka, and Lorenzen, took less notice of the local context than the majority. Judge Bonello partly dissented in this case, but only on the ground that the majority had not awarded just satisfaction to the applicant under Article 41.

88 Ibid., [59].

89 Ibid., [60].

freely through the media is, for example, different from that of a private individual.' This puts too great an emphasis on the nature of the speaker and not enough on the nature of the *speech*.

In *Feldek v Slovakia*, the relevance of the restricted speech to the transition played an even clearer role in affecting the European Court's assessment. In 1992 the applicant, Feldek, contributed his views to a number of scathing newspaper pieces about the Slovakian Minister for Culture and Education, Dušan Slobodník.[90] The general theme was that Slobodník was unsuitable to be a politician because he had allegedly been involved with the Nazis in World War II. The applicant had also published a poem that, without naming Slobodník, implied he had been a member of the SS.[91] Slobodník brought defamation proceedings against Feldek.[92] Slobodník had served time in a Soviet prison camp for his contact with the Nazis but denied he had ever been a fascist. Such details were given in Slobodník's autobiography. Moreover, the conviction for which Slobodník was imprisoned had now been quashed. On appeal, Feldek's statements were therefore found to be defamatory, so he subsequently claimed that his rights under Article 10 had been violated.[93]

The European Court found it 'clear and undisputed' that there had been an interference with Feldek's free expression.[94] Argumentation again focused on Article 10(2). The applicant argued that his conviction was not sufficiently foreseeable as to constitute being prescribed by law, although the European Court disagreed.[95] It was not disputed that the aim of the restriction was legitimate, inasmuch as it sought to protect Slobodník's reputation and personal rights.[96] Once again the case hinged on whether the interference was necessary in a democratic society. Here, the Respondent State cautioned that:

> the case attracted the attention of the public at large in Slovakia and underlined that the Court's decision on the merits of the present application was of prejudicial importance for the Slovakian courts when deciding on similar issues.[97]

Despite its alleged relevance to the wider democratic context, the case did not concern a transitional justice *policy* so much as it concerned the decision of the Slovakian Court of Cassation.

After setting out the general principles relating to Article 10, the European Court reiterated that the state's margin of appreciation was circumscribed by

90 *Feldek v Slovakia, op. cit. supra* n 3.
91 Ibid., [15].
92 Ibid.
93 Ibid., [50].
94 Ibid., [51].
95 Ibid., [52–57].
96 Ibid., [58].
97 Ibid., [67].

the interest of maintaining a free press.[98] Here the European Court certainly took the transitional context into account, but showed that it can be a reason for strict scrutiny rather than deference:

> The applicant's statement was clearly made in a very political context and one that was crucial for the development of Slovakia. It contained harsh words, but was not without a factual basis. There is nothing to suggest that it was made otherwise than in good faith, and in pursuit of *the legitimate aim of protecting the democratic development of the newly established State of which the applicant was a national.*
>
> The Court finds that the applicant's statement was a value judgment the truthfulness of which is not susceptible of proof. It was made in the context of a free debate on an issue of general interest, *namely the political development of Slovakia in the light of the country's historical background.*[99]
>
> [emphasis added]

As a result of this, the European Court held that the reasons given by the Slovakian Court of Cassation were not sufficient to justify limiting Feldek's free expression in such a context and thus there was a violation of Article 10.[100] Judges Fischbach and Lorenzen dissented and, in their Dissenting Opinion reminded the majority that it was not for the European Court to take the role of a domestic court assessing the factual background of the case. Implicitly, therefore, their argument was that even if the case invoked broad questions of transitional justice or democratic transition, it should be for the domestic court to determine their impact on the case.

In these cases, the European Court's approach is more akin to the approach[101] in *Guincho* and the early view of the judges that suspected the new Contracting Parties to the European Convention might need a certain level of tuition, rather than deference.

6.3.3 'Wild' lustration and the relationship between Articles 8 and 10 ECHR

In the *Feldek* case, we encountered not just political expression about the transition, but a particular form of political expression: the public scrutiny of a political figure's suitability for office. Statements in the media were being used to convey a message about the relationship between Slobodník's past and his current political role in the emergent Slovakian democracy. To this extent,

98 Ibid., [78].

99 Ibid., [84–8].

100 Ibid., [88–90]. This was a majority decision of five votes to two. The Court also held unanimously that there was no violation of Article 14 in this case.

101 *Guincho v Portugal* (1985) 7 EHRR 223: note the discussion of the case in Chapter 1 and Chapter 4.

Feldek's statements were opening a debate that has much in common with formal processes of lustration. Such unconstrained, media-driven discussion of public figures' pasts has been described as 'wild' lustration.

The relationship between statutory lustration and 'wild' lustration is not always clear. It has been suggested that 'wild' lustration has enabled the identification of collaborators who were not detected through the formal processes.[102] To others, it was necessary to introduce statutory lustration laws such as those discussed in Chapter 5 precisely to bring 'wild' lustration under control.[103]

Since the phenomenon of 'wild' lustration is non-statutory from the outset, the human rights cases have derived from people taking issue with the behaviour of the domestic courts either in relation to their failure to protect free expression (such as in *Feldek*) or, by contrast, in relation to Article 8 claims that publicity surrounding stories about their alleged collaboration has interfered with the applicant's home, family and private life. The question is whether transition is best facilitated by prioritising Article 8 or Article 10.

The Court first dealt with 'wild' lustration in its Admissibility Decision in *Tudor v Romania*.[104] The applicant was a well-known Romanian senator who had published several controversial articles in the journal *România Mare*, of which he was the editor. In addition to being generally very critical of other named politicians, the articles by Tudor alleged that certain of them had cooperated with the communist secret services. Tudor was convicted of insult and ordered to pay a fine and give compensation. He was acquitted of the criminal charges on appeal to the Supreme Court but was still obliged to pay the compensation. He complained that the obligation to pay compensation still violated Article 10 ECHR.

In determining the necessity of the interference, the European Court explained that it would be 'mindful' of the context. This included not only that the comments were part of a political debate of general interest, but also that cooperation with the former communist security services was socially and morally sensitive in the specific historical context of Romania. The European Court found that the applicant's statements were not value judgments: they were specific enough to require some degree of factual basis to them, which he had not taken steps to provide (indeed, the available evidence contradicted the allegations). With this in mind, the European Court found that the applicant's statements went further than the level of exaggeration and even provocation protected by Article 10 ECHR and thus that there were relevant and sufficient reasons for the interference and the level of compensation demanded.

102 H. Born and M. Caparini (eds), *Democratic Control of Intelligence Services: containing rogue elephants* (Aldershot: Ashgate 2007), 77, discussing Poland.

103 See J. Priban, 'Oppressors and their victims: the Czech Lustration Law and the rule of law', in A. Mayer-Rieckh and P. de Grieff (eds), *Justice as Prevention: vetting public employees in transitional societies* (New York: Social Science Research Council 2007).

104 *Tudor v Romania* (dec.) App no 6928/04 (ECtHR, 15 June 2006).

The application was therefore declared inadmissible. This case has been influential on other cases concerning 'wild' lustration in the way that it: treated allegations of communist collaboration as particularly sensitive; characterised criticism based on perceived association with the communist regime as factual allegations rather than value judgments; and in its apparent sensitivity to the interests of those who were being 'wildly' lustrated.

The European Court encountered an element of 'wild' lustration again in the 2007 case of *Klein v Slovakia*. Klein had made various critical remarks about Archbishop Monsignor Ján Sokol in the context of contrasting views about the morality or otherwise of the 1996 feature film *The People vs. Larry Flint*[105] and its publicity material. Klein disputed the Archbishop's moral integrity and drew attention to his alleged collaboration with the communist secret service. From the text of the judgment it is not clear whether the allegations were based on a positive lustration finding[106] or on Klein's receipt of allegedly incriminating documents.[107] It is the latter possibility that gives the case the air of 'wild' lustration.

The remarks offended both the Archbishop and members of the Catholic Church. The Archbishop eventually withdrew from pursuing the case, but the applicant was convicted of the offence of 'defamation of nation, race and belief'. Klein's complaint to the European Court alleged that his conviction constituted a violation of Article 10 ECHR. The European Court found for the applicant on the basis that although he had been prosecuted for statements about Catholicism, the applicant's criticisms were actually directed specifically to the Archbishop. Thus the European Court found unanimously that the reasons for prosecuting him for 'defamation of nation, race and belief' were 'narrow and insufficient'. Although it cited *Feldek*,[108] the European Court did not deem it necessary to check the allegations of communist collaboration that the applicant had levelled at the Archbishop and so it did not elaborate on its view of these types of allegation in the post-communist states.

It was therefore not until *Petrina v Romania* (in 2008) that the European Court had to confront the issue of 'wild' lustration head-on in a judgment on the merits. It took exactly the same approach in the similar case, *Petrenco v Moldova*, in 2010, which suggests that the European Court now has a clear methodology on this issue. However, even if from the similar analytical approach taken in these two cases it can be said that the European Court has developed a methodology to understand cases arising from 'wild' lustration, the cases show that it can be difficult to apply the methodology to the facts. Judge Thór Björgvinsson, who had been part of the seven-judge Chamber that

105 See http://www.imdb.com/title/tt0117318/ (accessed 20.5.2012).

106 This is what the quotation at [12] would suggest.

107 At [16], it is reported that the applicant, 'had learned that [the Archbishop] had been registered in the files of the former communist secret police'.

108 *Tudor v Romania, op. cit. supra* n 140, [49].

declared the *Tudor* case manifestly ill founded, disagreed with the majority judgment's characterisation of the facts in *Petrenco* and his Dissenting Opinion will be discussed shortly.

Both *Petrina* and *Petrenco* concerned newspaper articles that made allegations of collaboration with the previous regime against public figures. The applicants to the European Court, however, were the subjects of the articles and not their authors and so the orientation of these cases was different to *Feldek* and *Tudor* from the outset. The applicants in both of these cases had launched unsuccessful domestic legal actions to protect their reputation.

In *Petrina*, the applicant, a senior politician, was named by a journalist both in a television programme and in a weekly journal as being a collaborator, with the rank of captain in the former Securitate. The television programme and article both alleged that the National Peasant Party had been infiltrated by 'moles' such as the applicant. It was also alleged that within the National Peasant Party there were 'false heroes' who, far from having been political prisoners, had been in prison for ordinary crimes. A later article by a different journalist alleged that Petrina had, in fact, been a major in the Securitate. Petrina brought actions against the two journalists for making these allegations, but both journalists were acquitted on consideration of Article 10 ECHR.

In *Petrenco v Moldova*, statements in a government-owned newspaper were taken to state that Petrenco's success as a postgraduate student and subsequent career as an historian were due to his having cooperated with the Soviet secret services.[109] Petrenco likewise launched an unsuccessful action in domestic law to protect his reputation.

The European Court analysed both cases from the perspective of whether in its handling of the domestic cases the Respondent State had complied with its positive obligations under Article 8 ECHR to protect the applicants' reputation.[110] In doing so, the European Court confined its role to determining whether there had been a 'fair balance' between the applicant's Article 8 rights and the journalists' Article 10 rights.[111] We shall return to the doctrinal implications of this approach shortly.

Following the approach in *Tudor*, the European Court in both *Petrina* and *Petrenco* held that allegations of collaboration were not mere value judgments.[112] The Court found that there was no evidence to support the allegations in either case.[113] Indeed, in *Petrina* the European Court stated that the case involved 'a misrepresentation of reality, devoid of any factual basis'.[114]

109 *Petrenco v Moldova* [2010] ECHR 419, [6].
110 *Petrina v Romania* [2008] ECHR 1899, [34 and 35].
111 Ibid., [28]; *Petrenco v Moldova, op. cit. supra* n 109, [52].
112 See *Petrina, op. cit. supra* n 110, [42]; *Petrenco, op. cit. supra* n 109, [65].
113 *Petrenco, op. cit. supra* n 109, [66]; *Petrina, op. cit. supra* n 110, [58].
114 *Petrina, op. cit. supra* n 110, [48] (author's translation).

Again, following *Tudor*, the European Court reiterated the allegations of collaboration with the former regime were especially serious in the context.[115] As the European Court put it in *Petrenco*:

> [The] issue of the collaboration with the Soviet secret services of Moldovan citizens, particularly those holding positions of power or held in high esteem, was a particularly sensitive social and moral question in the specific context of Moldova.

In its conclusion in *Petrenco*, the European Court again stressed the 'gravity of the allegation'.[116] The European Court found in both cases that the domestic courts had not provided sufficient reasons for protecting free expression at the expense of the applicants' rights.

In the cases on 'wild' lustration, contextual reasoning by the European Court is subject to two competing impulses. The first, seen in *Feldek*, promotes free expression in the context of public debate about the past and the role of prominent politicians within it. The second, seen in *Petrina* and *Petrenco*, recognises that the allegation of collaboration with the communist security services takes on a special significance and is particularly detrimental to the right to protection of reputation.

From a doctrinal perspective, this second approach is troubling. Both *Petrina* and *Petrenco* acknowledged the main principles of Article 10, but the applicable case law was hardly rigorously applied. In *Petrina*, the conclusion was merely that there was not a 'reasonable relationship of proportionality' between the competing interests. This is an unfortunate symptom of approaching the case from the perspective of Article 8 ECHR: had the jurisprudence on Article 10 been applied in detail, the European Court would presumably have been moved to recall that, 'when freedom of expression is exercised as political speech [. . .] limitations are justified only in so far as there exists a clear, pressing and specific social need.'[117]

In *Petrenco*, the impugned article 'exceeded the acceptable limits of comment in the context of a debate of general interest' because it *implied* that the applicant had collaborated with the Soviet secret services. This is the real distinction between these two cases. The judgments in both are based on the legal approach taken in *Tudor*, but having established that these types of allegation are serious, the European Court may have been to ready to see 'wild' lustration in *Petrenco* when the comments made were not, in fact, very explicit at all.

Indeed, it was that the impugned article merely *implied* collaboration that led to the strong dissent from Judge Thór Björgvinsson. The majority stated that the national courts were, 'in principle, *better placed* than an international

115 *Petrenco, op. cit. supra* n 109, [59]; *Petrina, op. cit. supra* n 110, [43].
116 *Petrenco, op. cit. supra* n 109, [68].
117 *Vajani v Hungary, op. cit. supra* n 4, [51].

court to assess the intention behind the impugned phrases in the article and, in particular, to judge how the general public of Moldova would interpret, and react to, such phrases'.[118] Via an allusion to the margin of appreciation doctrine (the use of the 'better placed' formula), this seems to put more weight on reactions to the statements than on what they actually contained. According to Judge Björgvinsson, the statements did not by their precise wording state as a matter of fact that the applicant had been a KGB collaborator: 'At best they contain[ed] an innuendo that the applicant was well regarded by the KGB.'

Judge Björgvinsson also took a different approach to the role of the relationship between judicial protection of reputation and public debate in transitional democracies. He stated that:

> [As] an active participant in a public debate the applicant has had every opportunity to answer any insinuations which allegedly were directed at him. This is how a media-driven public debate in a democratic society works and should work.

In other words, it was preferable to encourage people in the public eye to settle these disputes via public debate rather than in the courts. This was particularly so in relation to allegations of collaboration, precisely because of their ubiquity. Judge Björgvinsson continued:

> The relevance and seriousness of the statements for the applicant's reputation must also be assessed in light of the whole social and political context in which they were made. In many of the former communist countries, including Moldova, insinuations similar to those in the present case are not uncommon in everyday political and social debate. *True or false*, they should be viewed as *an unavoidable part of the public debate* when a new political system is being established on the ruins of an oppressive regime, with which many of the present players in the public debate were associated in one way or another.
>
> [emphasis added]

This passage suggests that, as an element of transitional jurisprudence, free expression should be given higher priority than private rights on these very specifically transitional issues. This goes even further than *Feldek*, since, in that case, the allegations were not without a factual basis. The approach of the majority, while taking the specificity of the type of allegation into account, prioritised a different interest – namely, that of dealing with allegations of collaborations via formal lustration processes.

118 *Petrenco, op. cit. supra* n 109, [58].

The Concurring Opinion of Judges Garlicki, Šikuta and Poalelungi in *Petrenco* clarified the reasoning of the majority and explicitly identified that the case involved 'wild' lustration. In arguably slightly hyperbolic language, they explained that although public debate can be harsh for those who choose to participate in it, 'neither the press nor political opponents can be granted a licence to kill.' They conceded that the pre-democratic life of public figures 'may' be of legitimate interest to public opinion and that the press should play a 'prominent' role in debates on this topic. In contrast to Judge Björgvinsson, they drew attention not to the specificities of the transition, but to parallels between 'wild' lustration and earlier ECtHR cases concerning unfounded allegations of corruption made against politicians. However, they tempered this stance with their call to open state archives, including the suggestion that there might even be a developing positive obligation to do so (as discussed in Chapter 3).

The cases on 'wild' lustration are intriguing because in them (unlike many of the cases discussed in this part of the book) the Respondent State was not arguing for a restriction of democratic rights on transitional grounds. Quite the opposite. The Respondent State was in favour of an extensive interpretation of freedom of expression in the transitional context. It remains debatable whether they would have done so were it not for the fact that they were defending against the allegation of a violation of Article 8.

6.4 Conclusion

This chapter has encountered a range of cases in which both states and applicants have cited transitional issues to strengthen their case. The most significant of the cases in which the Respondent State cited the transition was *Rekvényi v Hungary*, which is described elsewhere in this book as being one of the most transitionally relative in the European Court's jurisprudence.[119] It certainly influenced the arguments of the Hungarian government in *Vajnai*, but the European Court was able to distinguish the cases (but not, as it might first appear, exclusively on the passage of time).

It is the applicants, however, who seem to have been more successful in citing the transitional context in relation to freedom of expression. However, this was equally the case when applicants subject to 'wild' lustration referred to the transitional context to bolster their claim under Article 8 ECHR at the expense of Article 10.

119 See Chapter 9.

7 Freedom of assembly and (religious) association

7.1 Introduction

Freedom of assembly and association are brought together under Article 11 ECHR, unlike for example in the ICPPR, where they are contained in Articles 21 and 22, respectively. As a result, this is essentially a double chapter. The two rights have much in common, but the jurisprudence of the European Court shows that they have given rise not only to very different cases, but also different forms of argumentation and judicial reasoning in relation to them. In particular, the cases on freedom of association have been far more explicit in their engagement with the transitional context than the cases on freedom of assembly. They are, therefore, more fertile ground for discerning the existence or otherwise of transitional relativism in the jurisprudence of the European Court.

These rights are closely connected to freedom of expression, such that the European Court has treated Article 10 as a *lex generalis* and Article 11 as a *lex specialis*.[1] Protecting personal opinions is one of the aims of protecting freedom of peaceful assembly.[2] In this way, Article 11 is often considered 'in the light of' Article 10.[3] Frequently, having discussed Article 11, the European Court declares that it is not necessary to examine the same complaint under Article 10.[4] Likewise, the European Court has explained that it would be very difficult to enjoy freedom of expression or freedom of thought, conscience and religion, without the ability to share views with other people through freedom of association.[5] We shall thus see that many of the freedom of association cases concern religious associations and therefore engage both Articles 9 and 11 ECHR.[6]

1 *Ezelin v France* (1992) 14 EHRR 362, [35]; *Ashughyan v Armenia*, [2008] ECHR 640, [71].
2 *Ezelin v France*, ibid., [37].
3 Ibid.
4 See, e.g., *United Communist Party of Turkey v Turkey* (1998) 26 EHRR 121, [62].
5 *Chassagnou v France* (1999) 29 EHRR 615, [100].
6 See, e.g., *Barankevich v Russia* [2007] ECHR 648.

An example of the overlapping democratic rights at stake is given by *Vogt v Germany*, cited several times already in the course of this book.[7] The applicant teacher successfully argued that both her Article 10 *and* Article 11 rights were violated when she was dismissed from her post for not ceasing her activities with the German Communist Party.[8] It was noted in Chapter 5 that the case is particularly significant not just for its illustration of the relationship between Convention rights, but also because, in it, the European Court accepted that the requirement of political loyalty could be viewed within the paradigm of self-defending democracy and thus pursued a legitimate aim in the context of Germany's history.[9] Even though the interference with both Articles 10 and 11 was disproportionate,[10] the validation of self-defending democracy as an applicable framework for examining rights-restrictive measures in transitional democracies was an important step.

The suggestion that the transitional context, or states' recent history, may play a particular role in the consideration of democratic rights is crucial since it implies a need for the European Court to accommodate a form of transitional relativism. The newer Contracting Parties to the European Convention are engaged in the reconstruction of public space[11] after totalitarianism, but the cases show that there have been real difficulties in coming to terms with the democratic standards expected by the European Court. It is here where the judgments of the European Court perhaps most directly impact on the process of democratic consolidation – but that is not to say that transitional justice (in the sense of 'non-ideal' rule of law compromises) are absent from the jurisprudence.

7.2 Freedom of peaceful assembly

7.2.1 *Freedom of assembly: 'transitional' arguments by the Respondent State*

Stankov and the United Macedonian Organisation Ilinden v Bulgaria[12] involved restrictions placed on an organisation designed to unite ethnic Macedonians in Bulgaria and to protect their rights as a minority. The organisation claimed that by failing to grant permission for them to hold meetings, their rights under Article 11 of the ECHR were unjustifiably restricted. The Bulgarian courts had found that the association advocated ethnic and national hatred and was dangerous for Bulgaria's territorial integrity.[13]

7 See Chapters 5 and 6.
8 *Vogt v Germany* (1996) 21 EHRR 205.
9 Ibid., [51].
10 Ibid., [61 and 68].
11 See M. Hamilton, 'Freedom of assembly, consequential harms and the rule of law: liberty-limiting principles in the context of transition' (2007) 27(1) *OJLS* 75.
12 *Stankov & United Macedonian Organisation Ilinden v Bulgaria* [2001] ECHR 567.
13 Ibid., [12].

In response to the case against it, the Bulgarian government took the relatively unusual step of explicitly stressing that 'knowledge of the historical context and of the current situation in Bulgaria and in the Balkans was essential for the understanding of the issues in the present case.'[14]

In its submissions, the Bulgarian government argued that the idea of a Macedonian nationality was a creation of the Communist International (sometimes known as 'Comintern') in 1934 and that after World War II, communist Yugoslavia likewise proclaimed the concept of a separate Macedonian nation.[15] 'A massive assimilation campaign accompanied by brutalities' was instigated, the Bulgarian government continued, including the forced imposition of Macedonian identity on the population of Pirin Macedonia, which the local population attempted to resist.[16] In other words, it would seem that the Bulgarian had suspicions about the association not just because of its stated aims, but because those aims were reminiscent of a particular, and controversial, policy or project of the former communist regime.

With all this in mind, the government cast doubt on the extent to which the restricted assemblies could be considered 'peaceful' (and asserted that some members of the association were armed).[17] The European Court rejected these arguments, finding no evidence that the people involved in organising the prohibited meetings had violent intentions.[18]

If there had been an 'interference' with Article 11, then in order to justify it, the government stressed that the applicant association 'was a separatist group which sought the secession of the region of Pirin from Bulgaria. It posed a direct threat to national security and the territorial integrity of the country.'[19] Again, the government stressed not just the local but also the transitional context in an argument that merits quotation at length:

> In the context of *the difficult transition from totalitarian regimes to democracy*, and due to the attendant economic and political crisis, tensions between cohabiting communities, where they existed in the region, were particularly explosive. The events in former Yugoslavia were an example. The propaganda of separatism in such conditions had rightly been seen by the authorities as a threat to national security and peace in the region.
>
> Moreover, the national authorities were *better placed* to assess those risks. It was conceivable that the same facts might have different implications in other States, depending on the context. The facts of the present case had to be seen, however, against the background of the difficulties in the region.[20]

14 Ibid., [47].
15 Ibid., [47].
16 Ibid., [47].
17 Ibid., [66].
18 Ibid., [77].
19 Ibid., [71].
20 Ibid., [73].

The argument is interesting because at the same time as stressing the exceptional transitional situation, there is an attempt to use the existing, non-transitional 'better placed' rationale for a domestic margin of appreciation to legitimate it.

The European Court accepted that the restriction pursued a legitimate aim, but its reasoning was not detailed. It is implicit, however, that the specific context of the case contributed to the aim's legitimacy (if not its necessity). In several of the freedom of association cases, discussed further later, the European Court has discussed in detail the relationship between the 'legitimate aim' of a restrictive measure and the transitional context.[21]Instead, the emphasis in *Stankov* was on giving guidance on content-based restrictions and the relationship between democracy and violence.

As to necessity, the Court recognised that states possess a 'certain' margin of appreciation, but reiterated that it would examine the restriction's aim and the reasons put forward for it, as well as whether the relevant decisions were based on an acceptable assessment of the facts.[22] In other words, given that there was little scope for the restrictions on political speech, the Court took a fairly strict approach.

The Court observed that the restrictions at issue were 'at least in part, in reaction to views held or statements made by participants or members'. This judgment is one of the strongest examples of transitional relativism in the European Court's jurisprudence, since it clearly allowed a degree of exceptionalism, or non-idealism on transitional grounds.[23]

> One of the principal characteristics of democracy is the possibility it offers of resolving a country's problems through dialogue, without recourse to violence, even when those problems are irksome.[24]

These comments about violence were directed to the respondent government and, in a statement that may have resonance within many of the former communist states, the Court explained further that: 'Demanding territorial changes in speeches and demonstrations does not automatically amount to a threat to the country's territorial integrity and national security.' The Court cautioned that:

> Sweeping measures of a preventive nature to suppress freedom of assembly and expression *other than in cases of incitement to violence or rejection of democratic principles* – however shocking and unacceptable certain views or words used may appear to the authorities, and however illegitimate the demands made may be – do a disservice to democracy and often even endanger it.[25]
>
> [emphasis added]

21 See, e.g., *Rekvényi v Hungary* (1997) 23 EHRR CD63.
22 *Stankov, op. cit. supra* n 12, [87].
23 Ibid., [85].
24 Ibid., [88].
25 Ibid., [97], emphasis added.

The mere probability that separatist statements might be made could not justify banning the assemblies.[26] The Court's approach demonstrates that there are effectively only two valid ways in which restrictions on political expression through an assembly will be Convention compliant: where Article 11 does not apply at all or where the principle of self-defending democracy can be relied on.

There have been several related applications to the ECHR based not just on freedom of assembly but also on freedom of association, most recently resulting in a judgment in October 2011 which found that a third successive refusal[27] to register the 'United Macedonian Organisation Ilinden' was in violation of Article 11. This time the European Court pointed to its June 2009 judgment in *Etxeberria and Others v Spain*, in which it had confirmed that the expression of separatist ideas cannot be regarded as in itself threatening a state's territorial integrity and national security.[28] These cases are discussed in more detail later, in relation to freedom of association.

The first *Stankov* judgment is certainly the most explicit in terms of the European Court being asked to apply what can be termed transitional relativism, but the issue of the Respondent States' concerns about the fragility of the transitional state runs behind several other cases that go to the issue of whether the assembly in question is 'peaceful'.

7.2.1.1 Clarifying 'peaceful' assembly in transition

The European Convention's protection of freedom of assembly is limited to 'peaceful' assemblies.[29] Not surprisingly, therefore, Respondent States may contest whether Article 11 is applicable at all to the assembly in question, by alleging that the assembly was not 'peaceful'.[30] This has exposed contrasting points of view as to what characteristics a 'peaceful' assembly may possess in transitional states and the correct place to discuss this issue within the reasoning of the European Court's decisions and judgments.

The admissibility decision in *Osmani and Others v Former Yugoslav Republic of Macedonia*[31] concerned the actions of the mayor of Gostivar. The mayor had attempted to require that the Turkish and Albanian flags be displayed alongside the Macedonian flag outside the town hall and on public holidays. The Macedonian Constitutional Court granted the government an interim order

26 Ibid., [98].
27 *United Macedonian Organisation Ilinden and Others v Bulgaria (No. 2)*, App no 34960/04 (ECtHR, 18 October 2011, [27].
28 Ibid., [37].
29 See, e.g., *G v Germany* (dec.) [1989] ECHR 28.
30 See *Ezelin v France, op. cit. supra* n 1, [53].
31 *Osmani and Others v the former Yugoslav Republic of Macedonia*, App no 50841/99 (ECtHR, 11 October 2001).

suspending the validity of the mayor's decision and later found that the local council had exceeded its power by regulating the display of flags.

In response to the interim order, the mayor gave a speech at a meeting indicating that 'we [apparently meaning all ethnic Albanians] are going to reply to a slap with a slap' and promising that Gostivar 'would become an Albanian town'.

When a group of citizens attempted to remove the Albanian flag, the mayor organised armed shifts for its defence, as well as a central and several regional 'crisis headquarters'. According to the Foreign Ministry, after the Constitutional Court's ruling on the merits the police removed the flag and confiscated weapons and emergency medical supplies from the town hall, but were then attacked by a group of up to 200 people. The police were subjected to physical violence, including assault by Molotov cocktails and other projectiles, smoke bombs and automatic-weapons fire. There was an hour of 'intensive firing' from both sides, during which three people apparently died and over 200 were injured.

The applicant was convicted of, *inter alia*, 'stirring up, as a public official, national, racial and religious hatred, disagreement and intolerance'. Although his appeals were dismissed by the Supreme Court and his constitutional complaint was dismissed by the Constitutional Court, the applicant was later granted an amnesty and released after serving just over a year in prison. The applicant complained of violations of Articles 10 and 11 ECHR, although the Court focused on Article 11 as the *lex specialis*. The government argued that Article 11 should not be applicable to the case, since the applicant's intention had not been to organise and hold a peaceful political debate.

The government's argument would seem to have had some basis: after all, the applicant had organised armed resistance to the enforcement of a ruling of the Constitutional Court. Strangely, then, the European Court found that there had in this case been an interference with the right to freedom of '*peaceful*' assembly. Instead, the Court examined whether, in the light of the state's margin of appreciation, the interference was in pursuit of a pressing social need; was supported by relevant and sufficient reasons; and was proportionate. In other words, the Court proceeded to Article 11(2) when it could have resolved the case by reference solely to Article 11(1).

The only clue as to the reasoning behind this choice of approach is given by the Court's reiteration that the 'freedom of expression of an elected representative calls for the closest scrutiny on the part of the Court'.[32] It was, therefore, a case that apparently required close analysis and where the Court said that 'special attention [was] to be given to the content of the applicant's speech and its context'.[33] The Court went on to find that the interference was

32 Ibid., [4c].
33 Ibid.

fully justified and therefore declared the application manifestly ill founded. The facts of the case certainly arose within the context of difficult ethnic tensions in the Balkans, the resolution of which the European Court may well have deemed essential to the transition to peace and democracy, but this does not explain why the Court left the ambit of Article 11 so wide in the case. It may be that the rhetorical value of making a finding on the content rather than the applicability of Article 11 was deemed more important, but this runs the risk of trading doctrinal coherence for democratic tutelage of the sort that, as we noted in Chapter 1, prompted Deputy Secretary General of the Council of Europe Peter Leuprecht to resign.[34]

More helpfully the European Court has stressed that where the authorities allege that an assembly was not peaceful, they will have to substantiate the claim. In *Christian Democratic People's Party v Moldova*, which concerned apparently unauthorised protests against the introduction of compulsory Russian-language study to schools in Moldova, and which as a consequence led to a temporary ban on the party's activities, the government again argued that Article 11 should not apply at all since the gatherings had not been peaceful.[35] The applicant pointed out that video evidence submitted by the government itself gave no signs of violence and the European Court noted that the government had failed to substantiate the allegation.[36] Thus, the government's objection to the application of Article 11 was dismissed. Likewise, on the question of whether the interference with Article 11 was justified the Court found that singing a mildly cheeky student song could not constitute a call to violence and so the government's reasons for consequently banning the party's activities were not relevant and sufficient.[37]

Taken together these cases at least imply that the European Court is keeping the ambit of 'peaceful' assembly relatively wide, with a need for real proof of violence if Article 11 is to be excluded and thereby allowing for a full discussion of necessity in a democratic society. However, the reference to *Etxeberria and Others v Spain* in *United Macedonian Organisation Ilinden and Others v Bulgaria (No. 2)* shows that the European Court is keen to downplay the extent to which its approach is a distinctively transitional one (the Spanish transition having begun with the death of Franco in 1975) – even though the forms of separatism at stake in *Stankov* and *Osmani* were particularly closely related to the post-Cold War, post-communist, political settlement.

34 This was discussed in Chapter 1.
35 *Christian Democratic People's Party v Moldova* (2007) 45 EHRR 13, [43].
36 Ibid., [44–45].
37 Ibid., [75].

7.2.2 *Freedom of assembly: 'echoes' of totalitarianism and systemic problems*

7.2.2.1 *A culture of popular protest*

We saw earlier that some Respondent States have attempted to take a very narrow view of what 'peaceful' protest resembles and have as a result attempted to challenge the application of Article 11. This may have a lot to do with some of the former totalitarian states being somewhat lacking in a culture of popular protest. The European Court has, therefore, on occasion given, further guidance to the newer Contracting Parties on what a 'peaceful' protest might resemble.

Both *Galystan v Armenia* and *Ashughyan v Armenia* concerned administrative sanctions imposed by the same judge, on the same day, for participation in the same opposition demonstration, which took place on Mothering Sunday 2003 (the *Ashughyan* case also related to the applicant's behaviour at a second demonstration). In both cases, the applicant had been subject to either administrative detention or a fine because they had, among other things, 'violated public order by making a loud noise'.[38] In *Galystan*, the European Court helpfully explained that:

> [as] to the loud noise made by the applicant, there is no suggestion that this noise involved any obscenity or incitement to violence. The Court, however, finds it hard to imagine a huge political demonstration, at which people express their opinion, not generating a certain amount of noise.[39]

Likewise, in *Ashughyan*, the European Court explained that irrespective of disruption to ordinary life, including disruption of traffic, authorities must show a 'certain degree of tolerance' towards peaceful gatherings if the freedom of assembly guaranteed by Article 11 of the Convention is not to be deprived of its substance.[40] We shall return to these cases later insofar as they also engage issues pertaining to the right to a fair hearing.

7.2.2.2 *A culture of popular protest and content-based restrictions*

It is not only where the European Court has faced potentially non-peaceful protests about the future composition of the state that it has dealt with content-based restrictions. The case of *Hyde Park v Moldova (no. 3)* involved the Moldovan authorities' refusal of authorisation to hold a demonstration

38 See *Galystan v Armenia*, App no 26986/03 (ECtHR, 15 November 2007), [18]; *Ashughyan v Armenia, op. cit. supra* n 1, [17].

39 *Galystan*, ibid., [116].

40 *Ashughyan v Armenia, op. cit. supra* n 1, [90].

outside the parliament about the apparently 'non-transparent' organisation of voting in the Eurovision Song Contest in 2006.[41] The authorisation was refused on the basis that the competition had already taken place and, in any event, it had been held in Ukraine so the Moldovan parliament had no responsibility for it.[42]

Although the circumstances might at first glance seem a little more trivial than the ethnic and separatist issues at stake in *Osmani* and *Stankov*, the restriction in this case took place against a backdrop of a series of serious acts of intimidation against the applicant association, 'Hyde Park', which was an NGO campaigning for free expression and freedom of assembly. Indeed by the time the authorisation for the 2006 Eurovision demonstration was refused, the organisation had ceased to be registered with the authorities and several of its members had sought asylum in other states.[43] The case is therefore emblematic of much wider problems with freedom of assembly in Moldova.

The crucial part of the European Court's judgment in the case stressed its scepticism of content-based restrictions.

> The Court finds it unacceptable from the standpoint of Article 11 of the Convention that an interference with the right to freedom of assembly could be justified simply on the basis of the authorities' own view of the merits of a particular protest.

The interference, therefore, did not pursue a pressing social need and there was a violation of Article 11.

Content-based restrictions have also engaged Article 14 ECHR. In *Baczkowski and Others v Poland*,[44] the 'Foundation for Equality' intended to hold a march and several static assemblies in Warsaw to highlight the problem of discrimination against sexual, national, ethnic and religious minorities, women and disabled persons.[45] Permission was given only to hold assemblies concerning discrimination against women. Although the authorities initially agreed that a march could take place, permission was later withdrawn. Just prior to taking his decision on the static demonstrations, the mayor of Warsaw gave an interview in which he indicated that he would ban all demonstrations that he perceived as supportive of homosexuality. He stated that, in his view, 'propaganda about homosexuality is not to the same as exercising one's freedom of assembly.'[46]

41 *Hyde Park v Moldova (No. 3)* [2009] ECHR 1695, [7].
42 Ibid., [8].
43 Ibid., [5].
44 *Baczkowski and Others v Poland* (2009) 48 EHRR 19 (2007).
45 Their language, as reported in the case.
46 *Baczkowski, op. cit. supra* n 44, [27].

The mayor then proceeded to allow demonstrations on certain other topics to take place on the same day, some of which might appear to be a little more socially conservative, including on topics of 'Against any legislative work on the law on partnerships', 'Against propaganda for partnerships', 'Education in Christian values, a guarantee of a moral society', 'Christians respecting God's and nature's laws are citizens of the first rank' and 'Against adoption of children by homosexual couples'. It is possible to discern a certain pattern here.

The government claimed that there was no link between the mayor's expressed opinions and the reasoning behind the official decisions in the applicant's case.[47] Nevertheless, the European Court found that it could be 'reasonably surmised' that the mayor's opinions could have affected the decision-making process and therefore impinged on the applicant's freedom of assembly in a discriminatory manner.[48]

Taken together with the cases on 'peacefulness', these cases show that the European Court has maintained its scepticism of content-based restrictions on freedom of assembly, even in circumstances where the Respondent State has attempted to argue that the subject of the assembly takes on a special significance in the transitional context.

7.2.2.3 *Notification regimes and spontaneous assemblies*

The case of *Ziliberberg v Moldova* concerned the applicant's prosecution for taking part in an unauthorised demonstration, which began peacefully but became more violent, against the abolition of urban transport privileges for students. In its 2004 admissibility decision, the European Court stressed that Article 11 could be applicable in the case of such prosecutions, where the applicant had remained peaceful in their own intentions or behaviour.[49] This follows the earlier non-transitional case of *Ezelin v France*[50] and shows again that the European Court is reluctant to allow the exclusion of Article 11 outright.

The decision in *Ziliberberg* is disappointing, however, in the way that it dealt with the issue of notification procedures. The leading European Commission decision on notification processes established that insofar as meetings on public thoroughfares are concerned, their subjection to an authorisation procedure does not normally encroach on the essence of the right.[51] The European Court has gone on to clarify that such procedures should not represent a 'hidden obstacle' to the exercise of the right.[52] In the *Ziliberberg* admissibility decision, the Court eventually dismissed the complaint relying on Article 11 by reasoning that:

47 Ibid., [87].
48 Ibid., [100].
49 *Ziliberberg v Moldova* (dec.) App no 61821/00 (ECtHR, 4 May 2004).
50 *Ezelin v France, op. cit. supra* n 1.
51 *Rassemblement Jurassien v Switzerland* (dec.) [1979] ECHR 7, [3].
52 *Balcik v Turkey* [2007] ECHR 1002, [49].

> [S]ince States have *the right to require authorisation*, they must be able to apply sanctions to those who participate in demonstrations that do not comply with the requirement.
>
> [emphasis added]

The OSCE's 'Guidelines on Freedom of Peaceful Assembly' draw a distinction between notification and authorisation, stressing that although domestic law may require advance notification it should not require a request for permission.[53] The language in *Ziliberberg* turns the presumption of legality on its head and appears to give great latitude to transitional (and other) states to frame freedom of assembly legislation restrictively.

It is certainly the case that states may use proportionate measures to deal with participation in unlawful assemblies and that the penalty imposed on the applicant for participating in the unauthorised demonstration in *Ziliberberg* itself was modest (around €3.00),[54] but the reference to a state's right to 'require' authorisation is troubling. (It is worth noting that the applicant's complaint under Article 6 was declared admissible and that he won his case before the European Court in relation to that article of the Convention: we shall examine the relationship of Article 11 to other rights shortly.)

The European Court appears to have changed its stance somewhat now. In *Baczkowski*, discussed earlier in relation to content-based restrictions, the European Court explained that the presumption of assemblies' legality constitutes 'a vital aspect of effective and unhindered exercise of freedom of assembly and freedom of expression'.[55] In the same case, the European Court also stressed that where authorisation has been refused there may be an 'interference' even if the event subsequently goes ahead, on the basis that the refusal of authorisation may have had a 'chilling effect' on possible attendees.[56] Likewise, in the 2009 case of *Sergey Kuznetsov v Russia*, which involved a picket of the Sverdlovsk Regional Court, the European Court repeated this approach.[57] The picket protested against alleged violations of the right of access to a court and also distributed leaflets and news clippings about the President of the Court's alleged involvement in corruption.[58] The applicant had been refused permission for the picket, but held it anyway.

The European Court explained that authorisation or notification processes do not normally impinge on the essence of the right, 'as long as the purpose

53 OSCE ODIHR, *Guidelines on Freedom of Peaceful Assembly*, 2nd edn (Warsaw: ODIHR 2010), 65.

54 But note that at both the admissibility and the merits stage, it was noted that this amounted to more than 50% of the applicant's monthly income relation to Article 6 ECHR, it was observed that this sum constituted 60% of the applicant's monthly income: *Ziliberberg v Moldova* [2005] ECHR 51, [34].

55 *Baczkowski, op. cit. supra* n 44, [67].

56 Ibid.

57 *Sergey Kuznetsov v Russia* [2008] ECHR 1170.

58 Ibid., [5 and 8].

of the procedure is to allow the authorities to take reasonable and appropriate measures in order to guarantee the smooth conduct of any assembly, meeting or other gathering'.[59] This is actually a slight development of the case law, since, although the European Court has long accepted that Article 11 generates positive obligations, in this case, it was saying that notification processes were tied to the facilitation of assemblies rather than the protection of public order. Likewise the European Court also held that 'the *only* necessity capable of justifying an interference with the rights enshrined in [Article 11] is one that may claim to spring from "democratic society"' (emphasis added). This language suggests that a restriction must not only be compatible with a democratic society but must also 'spring from it', in the sense of pursuing an equal or greater democratic purpose than the restricted assembly. This is a forceful approach, but it is consistent with the OSCE's guidelines on freedom of assembly mentioned earlier.

The more forceful approach is mirrored by the European Court's approach to the difficult issue of spontaneous assemblies which, by definition, are non-notified. These may be particularly challenging for states without an established culture of popular protest.

The 2007 case, *Bukta and Others v Hungary*,[60] concerned the police disbandment of a peaceful but spontaneous demonstration against the Hungarian Prime Minister's attendance at a reception held by the visiting Prime Minister of Romania, in commemoration of the transferral of Transylvania from Hungary to Romania in 1918. The Hungarian Prime Minister had only announced his intention to attend the reception the day before it was due to take place. On the day of the reception, around 150 people assembled in front of the hotel in which the reception was taking place. After a 'sharp noise' was heard, the police disbanded the assembly.[61] The applicants in the case had unsuccessfully pursued domestic judicial review of the decision to disperse the assembly.[62]

The European Court drew attention to the Hungarian Prime Minister's late indication of his intention to attend the event[63] and explained that:

> [I]n the Court's view, in special circumstances when an immediate response, in the form of a demonstration, to a political event might be justified, a decision to disband the ensuing, peaceful assembly solely because of the absence of the requisite prior notice, without any illegal conduct by the participants, amounts to a disproportionate restriction on freedom of peaceful assembly.

59 Ibid., [42].
60 *Bukta and Others v Hungary* [2007] ECHR 610.
61 Ibid., [7–10].
62 Ibid., [11–17].
63 Ibid., [35].

This does not do away with the jurisprudence on the permissibility of notification regimes altogether: it is an exception to the norm. This was confirmed in the 2008 case, *Eva Molnár v Hungary*, in which the European Court stated that 'the right to hold spontaneous demonstrations may override the obligation to give prior notification to public assemblies *only in special circumstances*.'[64] In that case, the Court found that such circumstances did not exist.[65]

7.2.2.4 *The quality of domestic law and freedom of peaceful assembly*

Where an interference with the freedom of peaceful assembly is legally flawed, the European Court will step in. For example, in *Zeleni Balkani v Bulgaria*, the European Court confirmed that where a restriction had been made in violation of the applicable domestic legislation, it could not be 'prescribed by law' for the purposes of Article 11 ECHR.[66]

The European Court's statements about the quality of the domestic freedom of assembly legislation in the 2007 *Mkrtchyan v Armenia* case, *en route* to a conclusion that the alleged interference was likewise not 'prescribed by law', merit some attention because of the extent to which the Court acknowledged the transitional context.

The case concerned the applicant's participation in an authorised demonstration and subsequent spontaneous procession. He was charged with an administrative offence for his participation in the latter; was fined by the District Court; and failed to have the Civil Court of Appeal and Court of Cassation set aside any of the relevant decisions.[67]

The government argued that the administrative offence was governed by the 1985 Code of Administrative Offences in conjunction with the 1998 Decree of the Chairmanship of the Supreme Soviet of the USSR on 'Rules for Organising and Holding of Assemblies, Rallies, Street Processions and Demonstrations in the USSR'. The applicant drew attention to the 1990 Armenian Declaration of Independence and the 1991 CIS Convention – both of which would seem to suggest that the *laws of the former USSR* would no long apply in Armenia. By contrast, the Armenian government argued that the USSR law on assemblies had been converted into a *law of the Republic of Armenia* as a result of the 1991 Constitutional Law on the Foundations of Independent Statehood and had continued to operate as such after the new full Constitution came into effect in 1995.[68]

64 *Eva Molnár v Hungary* [2008] ECHR 1027, [38].
65 Ibid., [39].
66 *Zeleni Balkani v Bulgaria* [2007] ECHR 272.
67 See *Mkrtchyan v Armenia* (2009) 49 EHRR 16, [7–19].
68 Ibid., [30–36].

The European Court reiterated that measures taken after an assembly can constitute an 'interference' with Article 11[69] and went on to examine whether the interference was 'prescribed by law'. The Court examined the various possible interpretations of Armenian and USSR law and accepted:

> that it may take some time for a country to establish its legislative framework in a transition period, but it cannot accept the delay of almost thirteen years to be justifiable, especially when such a fundamental right as freedom of peaceful assembly is at stake.[70]

The application of domestic law was not foreseeable enough and so the interference was not prescribed by law and thus a violation of Article 11 followed.

The interesting part of this reasoning is the apparent acceptance that states might need some time to organise their legislation, even after joining the Council of Europe. The Court's statement implies an evaluation of this type of flexibility by reference to the passage of time and the right at stake. Given the early jurisprudence such as *Guincho v Portugal*,[71] in which the European Court invoked Article 1 ECHR to deny any transitional flexibility to states, this is an unusual statement – suggesting that the European Court may more readily concede a level of transitional relativism than it did previously.

7.2.2.5 *Procedural justice and freedom of peaceful assembly*

Where the domestic law on notification procedures or wider issues of peaceful assembly is defective, the European Court has been able to apply the procedural safeguards emanating from Articles 5 and 6 ECHR. In Chapters 4 and 5, we saw that the procedural rights in the European Convention played an important role in relation to the Court's supervision of restitution and lustration and it is no different here.

For example, in the admissibility decision in *Ziliberberg v Moldova*, already discussed, we saw that the European Court found the applicant's complaint under Article 11 ECHR manifestly ill founded on somewhat awkward grounds related to the state's 'right to require authorisation'.[72] However, the European Court *did* hold that Article 6 applied to the case and the complaint based on that article of the Convention proceeded to the merits.

At the merits stage, in relation to the applicability of Article 6, the Respondent State argued that the offence committed by the applicant was 'administrative' rather than 'criminal' because, first, that was how it was characterised in domestic law and, second, it was punished with a sanction that

69 Ibid., [37].
70 Ibid., [43].
71 *Guincho v Portugal* (1985) 7 EHRR 223.
72 *Ziliberberg v Moldova* (dec.), *op. cit. supra* n 49.

had an 'educational' and 'preventive' purpose.[73] Applying the *Engel* criteria,[74] the European Court felt that the 'preponderance' of aspects to the case suggested that a criminal charge was involved,[75] including that the applicant had been detained by the police and that, in its view, the fine was 'punitive and deterrent' in nature (and, were it not to be paid, could have resulted in imprisonment for 20 days).[76] Whether or not this consequence would necessarily follow, however, was unclear according to the European Court due to the 'state of the Moldovan legislation'.[77]

The substantive complaint under the criminal limb of Article 6 was that the applicant had not been given enough notice about the appeal in the case against him and that therefore the relevant hearing took place in his absence. The applicant maintained that he had received the summons to appear at the appeal after it had actually taken place, on 4 May 2000. The government maintained that, according to their records, the summons had been issued on 2 May and that the postmarks on the relevant envelope were illegible.[78] The European Court found that the postmark on the envelope containing the summons 'clearly indicated' that it had been posted on 3 May and that, consequently, the applicant did not have prior notice of the hearing.[79] As a result, he was 'simply unable' to organise his defence and there was therefore a violation of Article 6 ECHR.[80]

The first observation from this case is that procedural safeguards may accrue to the exercise of freedom of peaceful assembly even when there are justifiable restrictions placed on it: the *Ziliberberg* case only arose because of the demonstration against the urban transport privileges for students. The second is that the European Court again took an, albeit very minor, swipe at the quality of the legislation in issue.

The pair of Armenian cases dealing with the ill-fated Mothering Sunday demonstration on 7 April 2003, *Galstyan v Armenia* and *Ashughyan v Armenia*, also engaged Article 6 ECHR – although it would seem that the European Court was a little more forgiving in the first of them.

Both involved administrative offences but, again applying *Engel*, the European Court found that the offences were 'criminal' in nature.[81] Both applicants made the serious allegation that there were no independent courts at all in Armenia, because judges were appointed by the Council of Justice presided over by the President of Armenia.[82] The European Court examined

73 *Ziliberberg v Moldova, op. cit. supra* n 54, [28].
74 *Engel v Netherlands* (1976) 1 EHRR 647.
75 *Ziliberberg v Moldova, op. cit. supra* n 54, [35].
76 Ibid., [33–34].
77 Ibid., [34].
78 Ibid., [38].
79 Ibid., [39].
80 Ibid., [41].
81 *Galystan, op. cit. supra* n 38, [55–60]; *Ashughyan, op. cit. supra* n 1, [51].
82 *Galystan, op. cit. supra* n 38, [54]; *Ashughyan, op. cit. supra* n 1, [49].

the system of judicial appointments in Armenia and dismissed these particular complaints in both cases as manifestly ill founded.[83] Both applicants also alleged that there were several other shortcomings in the guarantee of their fair trial rights, including that the trial was unfair because since the 2003 elections police and the courts were 'doing all that was possible to punish the opposition activists in conditions lacking transparency';[84] that documents had been fabricated; that the trials were held late at night and were not 'public'; that there had not been sufficient time to prepare a defence; and that Galystan had been tricked into refusing a lawyer.[85]

The reasoning in *Galystan* was the more detailed. The European Court dismissed all the wider allegations, but found a violation of Article 6(3) taken together with Article 6(1) on the basis that Galystan had been subjected to an expedited process during which he had had 'not longer than a few hours' to prepare his defence and during much of that time he had been in transit.[86]

In *Ashughyan*, the European Court noted that the circumstances of the case were 'practically identical' to those in *Galystan*. However, instead of disaggregating the components of the applicant's complaints and explicitly limiting its findings to the adequacy of time for preparation of the defence, the Court concluded that Ashughyan 'did not have a fair hearing, *in particular* on account of not being afforded adequate time and facilities for the preparation of her defence'.[87]

Taken in conjunction with its findings in relation to Article 11 ECHR itself, these two cases further illustrate the importance of transitional states improving their judicial and administrative arrangements as an adjunct to the development of political rights. Although the wider allegations against the whole of the Armenian judiciary were dismissed, it is notable that when substantially the same facts about the secretive late-night hearings as had been alleged in relation to *Galystan* appeared again in *Ashughyan*, the Court did not take the same step of dismissing them outright. Without necessarily confirming the allegations that the charges were fabricated, and that the absence of lawyers from the process was designed to conceal the fabrication, the European Court left the allegations hanging.

7.2.2.6 *Freedom of peaceful assembly and emergency situations*

The discussion of freedom of peaceful assembly thus far has, like the rest of the book, been focused on the jurisprudence of the European Court itself. To date there have not actually been any judgments or admissibility decisions in

83 *Galystan, op. cit. supra*, n 38, [63]; *Ashughyan, op. cit. supra* n 1, 53.
84 *Galystan, op. cit. supra*, n 38, [71].
85 *Galystan, op. cit. supra* n 38, [54]; *Ashughyan, op. cit. supra* n 1, 49.
86 *Galystan, op. cit. supra* n 38, [87].
87 *Ashughyan, op. cit. supra* n 1, [66].

relation to Article 15 ECHR (on derogations) from the post-communist states. However, there have been two very difficult circumstances arising from assemblies, which have prompted the states in question to issue derogations from the European Convention.

In 2007, after five days of protests calling for the resignation of the Georgian President Mikhail Saakashvili, the President declared a 15-day state of emergency (lifted after eight days). After the Armenian presidential election in 2008 there were 10 days of protests against the result, amid claims that the elections were rigged. The outgoing President, an ally of the purported winner of the election, declared a 20-day state of emergency. At least eight people were killed during efforts to disperse the assembly.[88] In both situations derogations covered states of emergency that banned further assemblies and limited reporting of the incidents to state-run news organisations.[89]

Instead of the 'usual' methods of dealing with unlawful or violent assemblies, which, of course, can be Convention-compliant in accordance with *Ezelin*, these states were seeking to oust the European Court's scrutiny of the relevant (derogable) rights completely. There has been discussion of the relationship between the states of exception claimed in transition and those claimed in 'war or other public emergency'.[90] For now it is important to observe that these two circumstances derive from an arguably distinctly transitional dilemma: the installation of a democratic system and the facilitation of 'democratic turnover' within a widely accepted democratic process. The assemblies that took place in Georgia in 2007 and Armenia in 2008 were not just large assemblies against a particular policy, they were against the president of the state itself – and were bordering on being proto-revolutionary. Indeed, President Saakashvili of Georgia had only come to power himself in 2004 after the so-called Rose Revolution of 2003.[91]

The Council of Europe was so concerned about these derogations that the Parliamentary Assembly commissioned a special report on 'The protection of human rights in emergency situations' by the Committee on Legal Affairs and Human Rights.[92] In addition to setting out further guidance, and recapitulating the relevant European Court jurisprudence, the report observed: '[I]t appears that declarations of a state of emergency are often around the time of elections and *especially in democracies in transition*.'[93]

88 http://news.bbc.co.uk/1/hi/world/europe/7273497.stm (accessed 20.5.2012).

89 See PACE Doc. 11858, 'The protection of human rights in emergency situation', a Report by the Committee on Legal Affairs and Human Rights, available at http://assembly.coe.int/main.asp?Link=/ documents/workingdocs/doc09/edoc11858.htm (accessed 3.4.2012).

90 See F. Ní Aoláin, 'Transitional emergency jurisprudence: derogation and transition', in A. Buyse and M. Hamilton (eds), *Transitional Jurisprudence and the ECHR* (Cambridge: CUP 2011).

91 See http://www.bbc.co.uk/news/world-europe-17303471 (accessed 20.5.2012).

92 PACE Doc. 11858, *op. cit. supra* n 89.

93 Ibid., [61], emphasis added.

7.2.3 *Conclusions on freedom of assembly*

The freedom of assembly cases discussed here have raised some difficult contextual issues closely connected to the transitional experiences of Respondent States. For example, there were significant territorial and ethnic concerns underpinning *Osmani* and *Stankov*. The fact that the protests in *Christian Democratic People's Party v Moldova* were against compulsory teaching of Russian, the main language of the former USSR, and that the spontaneous assembly in *Bukta* related to a cession of territory, are unlikely to be without significance.

Likewise, social issues (including religion, sexuality, the environment, corruption of officials and the rights of students), the discussion of which had been more tightly controlled under the former regimes, generated the cases of *Barankevich*, *Baczkowski*, *Zeleni Balkani*, *Sergey Kutzenov* and *Ziliberberg*, respectively.

There is also a certain flavour of tuition in the cases: even cases that could have been resolved at the admissibility stage (by rejecting that the assembly was peaceful) have proceeded to the merits (e.g. *Osmani*) and, once there, the judgments have given advice on the scope of 'peacefulness' and its relationship to the Convention's protection of assemblies that may 'annoy or offend' – with the European Court, for example, encouraging tolerance of noisy assemblies.[94] Likewise, in *Stankov* and *Christian Democratic People's Party v Moldova*, the European Court has reiterated that allegations of violence must be substantiated. The advice about the general impermissibility of content-based restrictions in the Hyde Park Eurovision case could also be seen in this light.

However, there is a sharp contrast with the freedom of expression cases discussed in Chapter 6 (and with the freedom of association cases to be discussed shortly) in that there were very few examples of either the state citing the transition as a reason for the restriction imposed or of the applicant seeking to place their own situation in a broader transitional context where strict scrutiny of the state would be due. The only clear case of the former was in *Stankov*, although there was an element of it in the European Court's apparently *sua sponte* observation in *Mkrtchyan* that it takes some time for transitional states to arrange their legal systems. However, since the judgment in that case went against the Respondent State, *Mkrtchyan v Armenia* may be closer to those cases in which the applicant has successfully argued that his situation is symptomatic of a wider problem related to the transition itself (in that case a failure to reorganise the legal system sufficiently promptly after the dissolution of the USSR). Even closer would be those cases in which the applicant or the Court identified defects in the content or regular application of the whole regime of relevant law and not just the applicant's treatment under it. The background to the Hyde Park Eurovision case involved allegations of

94 *Ashughyan, op. cit. supra* n 1.

widespread suppression of freedom of expression and assembly and the applicants in *Galystan* and *Ashughyan* made similarly serious allegations against Armenia.

Although, in the last two cases, the allegations were never confirmed, they were certainly not *denied* in *Ashughyan*. This needs to be seen also in the light of the approach to the circumstances giving rise to the (earlier) derogation issued by the President of Armenia, and suggests, along with the 2007 situation in Georgia, a combination of transitional issues that are still relatively novel to the European Court.

7.3 Freedom of association

7.3.1 *'Transitional' arguments by the Respondent State*

In contrast to the cases on freedom of assembly, there have been a considerable number of cases in which the Respondent State has cited the transitional context as a justification for rights-restrictive measures in relation to freedom of association. Indeed, there are enough that, in order to present them and to analyse them from the perspective of transitional relativism, it is possible and necessary to group certain of them together. First of all, we shall examine cases on communist parties, extremism and separatism; then on decontamination of that state apparatus; and, finally, on a claimed special role for religion in transition.

7.3.1.1 Communist parties, extremism and separatism: 'self-defending' democracy

7.3.1.1.1 THE 'CLASSIC' LAW: THE GERMAN POST-WAR BASIC LAW AND 'WEHRHAFTE DEMOKRATIE'

When the notion of self-defending democracy was mentioned in the introduction to the discussion of democratic rights earlier, reference was made to the European Commission's 1957 decision in relation to the dissolution of the German Communist Party. We shall now examine that case alongside several others in which transitional states have attempted to restrict the freedom of association of communist and other extremist parties.

The 1957 admissibility decision in *Germany Communist Party and Others v Germany* is notable for its discussion of the drafting history of Article 17 ECHR. The Commission noted that the preparatory work to that Article had stressed that it was 'necessary to prevent totalitarian currents from exploiting, for their own interests, the principles enunciated by the Convention'. The Commission noted that the same motive appeared to have guided the drafting of Article 21 of the German Basic Law which, embodying the principle of *wehrhafte Demokratie*, allows the Federal Constitutional Court to hold unconstitutional any political parties that 'by reason of their aims or the behaviour of their adherents, seek to undermine or abolish the free democratic basic order or to endanger the existence of the Federal Republic of Germany'. In the case in question the German Federal Constitutional Court had dissolved the German Communist Party on 17 August 1956 on the basis of this provision. The party and its members alleged a violation of Articles 9, 10 and 11 ECHR.

The Commission examined the statements and objectives of the party and found that even if it aimed to gain power through constitutional means its objective, namely the creation of a 'dictatorship of the proletariat', was incompatible with the aims of the Convention. The Commission therefore applied Article 17 ECHR and dismissed the complaint as inadmissible.

Teitel's discussion of 'militant' or 'self-defending democracy' did not engage with the European Commission's decision in this case, but she did discuss Article 21 of the German Basic Law and the earlier domestic judgment on the Communist Party as manifestations of it.[95] The European Court's affirmation of the Federal Constitutional Court's approach, and its likening of Article 21 of the Federal Basic Law to Article 17 ECHR, has opened the door for a range of cases to examine self-defending democracy, which are not confined to the precise question of party dissolution.

For example, in Chapter 5, we encountered the *Glasenapp* and *Vogt* cases on German civil servants' duty of loyalty to the state. The European Court has described this duty as corresponding to the underlying notion of self-defending democracy.[96] Recall that in *Glasenapp*,[97] Germany successfully defended the dismissal of a teacher from her post on the basis that, by not distancing herself from the German Communist Party, she did not possess the qualifications necessary for the post (the party bore the same name as the one dissolved in 1956, but was a different organisation). The case was therefore interpreted as being about *access* to the civil service, which is excluded from the ambit of the European Convention. The European Court thus found that there was no interference with Article 10 ECHR. The case of *Germany Communist Party and Others v Germany* was only cited in *Glasenapp* in order to distinguish between the communist party of which Glasenapp was a member and the one that was dissolved back in 1956.[98] Likewise, there was no discussion of Article 17 ECHR and neither (because there was no 'interference') was there any discussion of 'necessity'.[99] However, the Partly Dissenting Opinion of Judge Speilmann shows that Germany had actually put forward arguments based on self-defending democracy, even though these were not ultimately relevant to the European Court's interpretation of the scope of the case.

95 R. Teitel, *Transitional Justice* (New York: OUP 2000), 177–179.
96 *Vogt v Germany, op. cit. supra* n. 8, [59].
97 *Glasenapp v Germany* (1987) 9 EHRR 25.
98 Ibid., [21].
99 Ibid., [53].

In *Glasenapp*, Judge Spielmann quoted the agent for the German government as having argued that:

> The fall of the Weimar Republic was due among other things to the fact that the State took too little interest in the political views of its civil servants.
>
> [. . .]
>
> [This] was a crucial contributing factor in the repeal of the democratic Weimar Constitution, which had established a State based on the rule of law, and in the emergence of the National Socialist dictatorship.
>
> [. . .]
>
> That is why, in the Federal Republic of Germany, no one can become a civil servant who does not afford a guarantee of constant loyalty to the order established in the Basic Law.

However, Judge Spielmann himself dismissed this as an 'excessively generalised view' of the fall of the Weimar Republic.[100] He likewise dismissed the agent's argument that Germany's bordering on several communist states exposed it to special dangers, observing that several other states also did so and had not taken similar steps.[101] Perhaps the most important part of Judge Spielmann's response to the German arguments was when, in his conclusions, he wondered:

> whether in 1986 – nearly sixty years after the Weimar Republic and more than forty years after the end of the Second World War – the impugned practice of the Federal Republic of Germany really is necessary in order to safeguard democracy.

This is one of the core issues in self-defending democracy: whether it is a fundamental constitutional principle or one that is inherently transitional. Clearly, to Judge Spielmann it was inherently transitional and the time had passed.

In the *Vogt* case, and although the applicant won, at the request of the Respondent State[102] the Grand Chamber of the European Court validated the notion of self-defending democracy as a historical reaction to the experience of the Weimar Republic both in relation to the legitimate aim of the dismissal[103] and its necessity.[104] The Court was critical of the 'absolute' nature of the duty of loyalty, but expressly confined itself to examining *Vogt's* actual dismissal

100 Ibid., Partly Dissenting Opinion of Judge Speilmann, [35].
101 Ibid., [37].
102 *Vogt v Germany, op. cit. supra* n 8, [54].
103 Ibid., [51].
104 Ibid., [59].

rather than legal regime underpinning it.[105] It can be noted that Judge Spielmann was a member of the majority in this case and, in distinction to *Glasenapp*, it was the minority that put the greatest emphasis on self-defending democracy. The Joint Dissenting Opinion of Judges Bernhardt, Gölcüklü, Matscher, Loizou, Mifsud Bonnici, Gotchev, Jungwiert and Kuris argued that having regard to the margin of appreciation doctrine there was no violation of Article 10. They described the antagonism between communism and West Germany and stated that:

> In such a situation and bearing in mind Germany's special history, in particular the destruction of the democratic Constitution of Weimar, the State must be entitled to dismiss civil servants, including school teachers, who are actively engaged in activities on behalf of anti-democratic parties.

This group of judges was, therefore, not only arguing for the continuing validity of self-defending democracy as a Convention-compliant constitutional principle, but also that it should be decisive to the outcome of a German case decided in 1995. For these judges, the key was that there was, by now, a very stable democracy that was worth defending.

The cases thus far in this section have all involved discussion of communism in the context of application of self-defending or militant democracy in Germany. The notion of self-defending democracy has transitional origins, but the European Court continued in its approval of the notion a long time after the transition. Indeed, it could be argued that the principle becomes *more* relevant as there is a greater level of democracy to defend (in the sense that by not doing so, there would be more to lose). The Court's approach to the principle continued to develop in two important Turkish cases, which have had a direct bearing on the jurisprudence concerning the states from central and eastern Europe.

7.3.1.1.2 BUILDING ON THE 'CLASSIC' LAW: EVENTS IN TURKEY

United Communist Party of Turkey v Turkey concerned the dissolution of a communist party before it had even been able to start its activities. Turkey had argued for the application of Article 17,[106] but the European Court distinguished the party in question from the one dissolved in Germany in 1956 because this one had not committed itself to the domination of one social class over the other: in fact, despite its choice of name, it was committed to democracy and pluralism.[107] Nevertheless, the government stressed that after the events of 1990, including the fall of the Berlin Wall, the choice of the name

105 Ibid., [60].
106 *United Communist Party of Turkey v Turkey, op. cit. supra* n 4, [19].
107 Ibid., [54].

'communist' could not be devoid of political meaning.[108] However, there was nothing in the party's constitution or programme of action to suggest that it was attempting to use the Convention to destroy any of the other rights contained in it, so the European Court declined to apply Article 17 and found a violation of Article 11 ECHR.

In terms of the structure of the judgment and its development of the notion of self-defending democracy within the European Court's jurisprudence, it is notable that Article 17 was not treated as an admissibility issue. In the *German Communist Party* case, there was no discussion of necessity in a democratic society or indeed any other elements of Article 11(2) ECHR precisely because on the basis of Article 17 the application was held to be inadmissible. However in *United Communist Party of Turkey*, the Court explained that any restriction on Article 11 would have to be in accordance with Article 11(2) and that:

> *Only when that review is complete* will the Court be in a position to decide, in the light of all the circumstances of the case, whether Article 17 of the Convention should be applied.[109]
>
> [emphasis added]

The judgment is significant because by doing this it paved the way for the European Court to examine in far more detail different types of 'communist' party and to base its conclusions on the actual rather than apparent threat that they might pose to (transitional) democracies in the post-Cold War era.

The most notorious application of self-defending democracy by the European Court came in *Refah Partisi (Welfare Party) and Others v Turkey*.[110] Here the European Court's Grand Chamber declined to find a violation of Article 11 when the Welfare Party, the largest party then in Turkey, was dissolved by the Turkish Constitutional Court on the basis, *inter alia*, that the party intended to replace the democratic order with a system based on sharia law.[111] As Harvey put it: 'Given that the party had over four million members this amounts to the largest single interference with freedom of association in European jurisprudence.'[112]

Without going into the detail of the *Refah Partisi* case, or into the Grand Chamber's concurrence with the Chamber's view that 'sharia is incompatible with the fundamental principles of democracy, as set forth in the Convention',[113] it is worth noting the Court's application of the notion of self-defending democracy. The Court reiterated that Article 17 would only apply after the

108 Ibid., [21].
109 Ibid., [32].
110 *Refah Partisi (Welfare Party) and Others v Turkey* (2003) 37 EHRR 1.
111 Ibid., [40].
112 P. Harvey, 'Militant democracy and the European Convention on Human Rights' (2004) 29(3) *European Law Review* 407, 417.
113 *Refah Partisi, op. cit. supra* n 110, [123].

completion of its analysis based on Article 11(2)[114] and then developed a far more detailed methodology for examining the application of self-defending democracy within the second paragraph of Article 11. The Court confirmed that:

> [A] State cannot be required to wait, before intervening, until a political party has seized power and begun to take concrete steps to implement a policy incompatible with the standards of the Convention and democracy.[115]

It then set out three clear factors that would go to the question of whether the restriction imposed was answering a 'pressing social need'.

> (i) whether there was plausible evidence that the risk to democracy, supposing it had been proved to exist, was sufficiently imminent; (ii) whether the acts and speeches of the leaders and members of the political party concerned were imputable to the party as a whole; and (iii) whether the acts and speeches imputable to the political party formed a whole which gave a clear picture of a model of society conceived and advocated by the party which was incompatible with the concept of a 'democratic society'.

The Court also committed to examining these issues while 'taking into account the historical context in which the dissolution of the party concerned took place' – in this case, the constitutional commitment to secularism.[116] The application of self-defending democracy in *Refah Partisi* is more akin to the later German cases, in which the notion still took on special significance because, in a democracy, there is more to lose.

Armed now with its experiences of post-war Germany and the Turkish cases, the question was whether this would equip the European Court to deal with the issue of communist and other apparently problematic political parties or associations in the transitional states of central and eastern Europe.

7.3.1.1.3 THE POST-COLD WAR ERA

We have seen several transitional arguments regarding freedom of association already, so it is perhaps little surprise that the transitional states from central and eastern Europe have been particularly sensitive about the registration and operation of associations that hark back to the previous era. It is an area in

114 Ibid., [96].
115 Ibid., [102].
116 Ibid., [105].

which the claim for some form of transitional relativism is particularly visible. Indeed, we saw in relation to Article 10 ECHR that in the case of *Vajnai* even the display of the five-pointed red star at a lawful demonstration had been deemed worthy of restriction by the Hungarian authorities because of the offence that it might have caused to victims of communism (although the European Court found that the restriction was unjustified).[117]

The case of *Partidul Comunistilor (Nepeceristi) and Ungureanu v Romania*[118] concerned the final refusal by the Romanian authorities (including the courts) in 1996 to allow the registration of a new communist party: the PCN. The party's constitution committed it to democracy and political pluralism and clarified that it was in no way a successor to the former Romanian Communist Party. The second applicant was the PCN's chairman, and after the refusal he continued to make very public statements about his commitment to communism and his concerns about the post-1989 political settlement in Romania.[119] The European Court declined to take these particular comments into account in its reasoning, since they were made some years after the initial refusal about which the applicants complained.[120]

The European Court said that it could not 'accept the government's argument that Romania cannot allow the emergence of a new communist party to form the subject of a democratic debate'. It went on to state that it was:

> prepared to take into account the historical background to cases before it, in this instance Romania's experience of totalitarian communism prior to 1989. However, it observes that that context cannot by itself justify the need for the interference, especially as communist parties adhering to Marxist ideology exist in a number of countries that are signatories to the Convention.[121]

The European Court could see no calls for violence or anti-democratic statements in the party's proposed constitution[122] and so there was no 'pressing social need' (in relation to Article 11(2)), no 'imminent risk to democracy' (in the *Refah Partisi* sense)[123] and no other reason to bring Article 17 ECHR into play.[124]

This is an unusually frank – and clearly identifiable – exchange between the European Court and the Respondent State on how a democracy might defend itself from anti-democratic forces in a transitional context. The judgment of

117 *Vajani v Hungary* (2010) 50 EHRR 44, discussed in Chapter 7.
118 *Partidul Comunistilor (Nepeceristi) and Ungureanu v Romania* [2005] ECHR 58.
119 Ibid., [17–22].
120 Ibid., [52].
121 Ibid., [58].
122 Ibid., [54].
123 Ibid., [58].
124 Ibid., [59].

the European Court applied the reasoning concerning the dissolution of the party in *Refah Partisi*, but noted that in this case action had been taken before the PCN's activities had even begun.[125]

Very similar issues were presented by *Tsonev v Bulgaria*,[126] which also concerned the refusal to register a new communist party, but the exchange between the Respondent State and the European Court was less frank. The domestic Supreme Court, which had upheld the refusal, noted in its judgment that:

> The name 'Communist Party of Bulgaria' uses the ideological term 'communist', which term, viewed in a historical context, resembles a party from the not so distant past.[127]

However, the government did not build on the historical context at the European Court and neither did it build a strong argument on the basis of self-defending democracy.

The European Court interpreted Article 11 in the light of Article 10[128] and noted that the restriction imposed was at least in part due to the content of the party's views and statements.[129] However, the principal reason for failing to register the party was about the technicalities of the registration process, including that the name was too similar (indeed identical) to another, rather than that the aims of the party were particularly deleterious to democracy.[130] These arguments were dismissed.

The Bulgarian government also claimed that the refusal to register was supported, *inter alia*, by a constitutional prohibition on organisations whose 'activity is directed against the sovereignty [or] the territorial integrity of the country and the unity of the nation, towards the incitement of racial, national, ethnical or religious enmity . . . as well as organisations which seek to achieve their goals through violence'.[131] This Bulgarian constitutional provision is very similar to that at issue in the 1957 case on the German Communist Party, which the European Court had likened to Article 17 ECHR. However, citing the *United Communist Party of Turkey* case and not the *German Communist Party* case, the European Court examined the documents pertaining to the party and found that there was no commitment to the domination of one social class over another (for example via a 'dictatorship of the proletariat') or any 'real threat'

125 Ibid., [57], [60].
126 *Tsonev v Bulgaria* (2008) 46 EHRR 8.
127 Quoted in ibid., [24].
128 Ibid., [48].
129 Ibid., [49].
130 Ibid., [55–57].
131 Article 44(2) of the Bulgarian Constitution, cited in *Tsonev* at [59]. The Bulgarian Political Parties Act of 1990 reinforces this element of the constitution: see *Tsonev*, *op. cit. supra* n 126, also at [59].

to the Bulgarian society or state.[132] There was no intention to use violence[133] and, therefore, no reason to bring the notion of self-defending democracy into play as a means of legitimating the refusal. *Refah Partisi* was cited in the context of checking the contents of the party's political programme against the actions of its members, but the European Court observed that since the party had been prohibited from the outset there were no 'actions' to check.[134] There was, therefore, a violation of Article 11 ECHR.

It was the applicants who perhaps made more of the transitional context, arguing that the circumstances of the case were indicative of a general lack of political pluralism in Bulgaria. To this extent it is reminiscent of those free expression cases discussed in Chapter 6, in which the applicant sought to situate their case in the wider transitional context and thus gain more in-depth scrutiny by the European Court.

Finally, in this section, and by way of contrast to the cases on contemporary communism, we turn to case concerning the refusal to register a different type of allegedly extremist association: *W.P. and Others v Poland*.[135] The European Court found a violation of the Convention in this case, so it provides valuable evidence for the creation of a 'control group' against which to judge the cases on contemporary communism.

The applicants in *W.P. and Others v Poland* were by occupation a police officer, a farmer, a police officer, a tailor, a teacher and a pensioner. They had applied unsuccessfully to register three different associations, each of which was rather against the reforms undertaken in Poland since 1989 and which, in particular, claimed that former and present functionaries of the Ministry of Internal Affairs were being subject to various forms of persecution and discrimination. Initially, it might have been possible to see the applicant's concerns against the backdrop of lustration in Poland, but as each refusal was issued the nature of the next proposed association became more disturbing.

The first proposed association was the 'Association of Persecuted Functionaries of the Ministry of Internal Affairs'. The registration of this association was refused on the basis that, *inter alia*, it defamed a public institution. The second proposed association was the 'National and Patriotic Association of Persecuted Police Officers and Teachers'. The registration was again refused, but this time the applicants failed to attend the regional court's hearing stating that they could not afford to attend due to 'Jewish and Bolshevik reforms'. The third and final proposed association was to be called the 'National and Patriotic Association of Polish Victims of Bolshevism and Zionism'. Among its aims were:

132 *Tsonev, op. cit. supra* n 126, [59].
133 Ibid.
134 Ibid., [60].
135 *W.P. and Others v Poland* (dec.), App no 42264/98 (ECtHR, 2 September 2004).

> Taking action aimed at equality between ethnic Poles and citizens of Jewish origin by striving to abolish the privileges of ethnic Jews and by striving to end the persecution of ethnic Poles.

And:

> Taking action aimed at prosecuting and making financially liable tormentors and criminals (including tormentors and criminals sitting behind official desks and tormentors and criminals wearing the gown of a judge or prosecutor) responsible for persecution, repression, harassment and discrimination.

Clearly, by this stage, the application for registration was itself a protest against the previous refusals, but the descent into extremism disconnects the protest from any of the human rights-based opposition to transitional reforms, such as we saw in relation to restitution or lustration itself in Chapters 4 and 5.

The applicants relied on Article 6 ECHR, as well as Article 11 both alone and taken in conjunction with Article 14 ECHR. In relation to the latter, they argued: '"the judiciary of the so-called Third Republic of Poland controlled by Jewish interests" prohibited the formation of associations by ethnic Poles.'

The European Court's approach to the case was to dismiss it at the admissibility stage: the first refusal was necessary in a democratic society; the applicants had not exhausted domestic remedies in relation to the second refusal; and the allegation regarding the final registration (including the complaint citing Article 14 ECHR) was dismissed by reference to Article 17 ECHR. The Respondent State did not need to emphasise the transitional context to strengthen its argument: the jurisprudence of the European Court in relation to Article 17 ECHR has demonstrated that anti-Semitism can never benefit from protection under the Convention.[136]

W.P. and Others v Poland can be contrasted with the cases on the refusal to register communist political parties because, in those cases, Article 17 was not decisive: in *Partidul Comunistilor (Nepeceristi) and Ungureanu v Romania*, the European Court explicitly rejected any need to apply Article 17 and the provision was not mentioned at all in *Tsonev v Bulgaria*. Although the transitional states have made arguments that communist parties, and their symbols, are particularly problematic in their transitional context, it remains the case that, aside from the 1957 admissibility decision on the German Communist Party, there are very few examples of Article 17 being used successfully against them. In contrast to the cases about the far right, Harvey has observed that the European Court 'has been much more ambivalent in its attitude to anti-democratic actors coming from the other end of the political spectrum'.[137]

136 Note the discussion of 'gatekeeping' provisions of the Convention in Part 2.

137 Harvey, *op. cit. supra* 112, 414.

7.3.1.1.4 SELF-DEFENDING DEMOCRACY: ETHNIC AND NATIONAL TENSIONS IN TRANSITION

Even *without* advocating separatism on ethnic grounds the actions of some minorities have caused nervousness among the authorities of the post-communist states. The case of *Gorzelik and Others v Poland*[138] was decided by the Grand Chamber in 2004. The case dealt with the applicants' allegation that their rights under Article 11 were violated when the government refused to allow the registration of their association, the 'Union of People of Silesian Nationality'. The stated aim of the Union was 'the awakening and strengthening of the national consciousness of Silesians'. The Polish authorities disputed that there was such a thing as a 'Silesian nationality'. However, rather than invoking any arguments based on self-defending democracy, the key argument was that the association had an undisclosed aim to put forward candidates for elections and that the reference to a 'Silesian nationality' was inserted in order to benefit from certain electoral laws that benefited organisations of national minorities. Since the association could have dispelled these suspicions with a modest alteration to its name and memorandum of association the European Court found no violation of Article 11.

We saw in relation to freedom of assembly that where ethnic or national groups really do advocate separatism there have been difficult discussions about whether assemblies designed to promote or promulgate such aims could be 'peaceful' for the purposes of freedom of assembly as guaranteed by Article 11. Chief among these cases was *Stankov and the United Macedonian Organisation Ilinden v Bulgaria*, in which the European Court found a violation of Article 11.[139]

The right to freedom of association does not have the prerequisite condition of 'peacefulness', but there have been difficult discussions about what constitutes 'violence' for the purposes of triggering reliance on self-defending democracy as a rationalisation for dissolving (or failing to register) associations and political parties. For example, could a particular viewpoint be inherently violent were it reprehensible enough? This raises the question of whether the transitional context would require a redefinition of the concept of 'violence' in the Convention. The relationship, indeed overlap, between 'peaceful' or 'non-violent' as gatekeeping concepts in the context of freedom of assembly and association respectively is best illustrated by a series of freedom of association cases that deal with the same movement at issue in the *Stankov* case, all of which concern the underlying tensions about the existence or otherwise of a Macedonian ethnicity.

7.3.1.1.4.1 Macedonians in Bulgaria The *Stankov* case actually formed one of several relating to particular alleged interferences by the Bulgarian

138 *Gorzelik and others v Poland* (2005) 40 EHRR 4.
139 *Stankov and the United Macedonian Organisation Ilinden v Bulgaria, op. cit. supra* n 12.

authorities with the rights of the 'United Macedonian Organisation Ilinden' (UMO Ilinden). There have been cases concerning each of the decisions of the authorities to refuse registration of the association, which were taken in 1990–1991 (the complaint about which was declared inadmissible *ratione temporis*),[140] 1998–1999[141] and 2002–2004.[142] There have also been cases on the dissolution and attempted re-registration of a related political party. Recall that, in the *Stankov* case, the Bulgarian government had argued that the association was continuing a communist era aim to promote, or even enforce, the acceptance of Macedonian ethnicity within Pirin Macedonia.[143]

Turning first to the cases about the association rather than the political party, both of the admissible applications disclosed violations of the Convention. Judge Botoucharova of Bulgaria dissented in relation to the 1998–1999 refusal, while the judgment in relation to the 2002–2004 refusal was unanimous (Judge Kalaydjieva had by this time succeeded Judge Botoucharova as the Bulgarian judge).

For our purposes, the crucial part of the two refusal-to-register cases concerning the association decided on the merits, is the Bulgarian authorities' suspicion that UMO Ilinden's real goal was to seek the secession of Pirin Macedonia – and that it might use violence to achieve this aim. In relation to the 1998–1999 refusal, which was examined in the case of *United Macedonian Organisation Ilinden and Others v Bulgaria*, the Blagoevgrad (being another name for Pirin Macedonia) Regional Court had found that the applicants intended to conduct a national liberation struggle and that 'there was certain doubt as to whether this aim would be pursued by peaceful means'.[144] The European Court interpreted the state's refusal to register the association as being 'at least in part' in relation to its views and statements.[145]

As regards the alleged dangers stemming from UMO Ilinden's goals and declarations, the European Court referred back to its discussions in *Stankov*. The Court reiterated that the mere fact of campaigning for secession does not justify in itself a restriction on Article 11.[146] Moreover, and despite the findings of the domestic court (but following its own reasoning in *Stankov*), the European Court could still find no evidence that the association had violent intentions. In the light of the seriousness of the interference, the European Court found by six votes to one that there was therefore a violation of

140 *Stankov, Trayanov, Stoychev, the United Macedonian Organisation Ilinden, Mechkarov and Others v Bulgaria* (dec.), App nos. 29221/95, 29222/95, 29223/95, 29225/95 and 29226/95 (ECommHR, 21 October 1996).

141 *United Macedonian Organisation Ilinden and Others v Bulgaria*, App no 59491/00 (ECtHR, 19 January 2006.

142 *United Macedonian Organisation Ilinden and Others v Bulgaria (No. 2), op. cit. supra* n 27.

143 See *Stankov, op. cit. supra* n 12, [47].

144 *United Macedonian Organisation Ilinden and Others v Bulgaria, op. cit. supra* n 141, [49].

145 Ibid., [59].

146 Ibid., [76].

Article 11. The case is consistent with the European Court's earlier reasoning in *Tsonev v Bulgaria*, to the extent that the feared 'violence' would be interpreted as something more than words and that therefore as a reason for restriction there must be evidence that it would take place.

Since there was no evidence of violence, the judgment of the majority said very little about the local context, self-defending democracy or transitional justice. The second case on UMO Ilinden, *United Macedonian Organisation Ilinden and Others v Bulgaria (No. 2)*, did little to add to this, save to say that the earlier one had found that the allegations that the association had separatist ideas capable of engendering 'confrontational' attitudes and based on an historical interpretation considered 'absurd' by the authorities and the majority of the population were, 'clearly insufficient'.[147] This phrase is actually absent from the first judgment itself, so it would seem that the European Court gained in confidence by the time that it summarised its earlier work.

The dissenting opinion in the first of the cases, by Judge Botoucharova, however, had equally clearly stated that a different conclusion would have been reached in the case 'if due weight had been given to the particular circumstances'. She argued that the findings of the domestic courts regarding the threat of violence were not unreasonable and said that Ilinden's articles of association 'astound with the harshness of the language used'. Invoking the margin of appreciation doctrine, Judge Botoucharova also stressed that: 'Due weight should also be given to the local sensitivities which exist in the Pirin region and the resulting need for heightened vigilance of the authorities.' Judge Botoucharova did not, however, specifically allude to the apparent thematic consensus between the policies of the communist authorities and those of the UMO Ilinden.

Judge Botoucharova's dissent is, at first glance, similar in theme to the joint dissent by Judges Lorenzen, Tulkens, Zagrebelsky, Fura-Sandström and Popović in *Korbely v Hungary*, in which they criticised the majority for contradicting the domestic findings of fact in that case (concerning the attempted prosecution of a military officer for his part in suppressing the 1956 uprising).[148] However, the contradicted findings of the Bulgarian courts in *UMO Ilinden (No. 1)* were not so much that there was an evidential base for the allegation of violent intentions, but rather that, taking into account the local context, 'violence' should be defined more broadly. Put like this, the judgment of the majority of the European Court in *UMO Ilinden (No. 1)* can be seen as a rejection of a transitionally relativistic claim for a different interpretation of a Convention principle.

The cases on the related political party, the 'United Macedonian Organisation Ilinden – Party for Economic Development and Integration of the Population' (referred to subsequently as 'PIRIN' to distinguish it from

147 *United Macedonian Organisation Ilinden and Others v Bulgaria (No. 2)*, *op. cit. supra* n 27, [36].
148 *Korbely v Hungary* [2008] ECHR 848; see the discussion in Chapter 2.

UMO Ilinden), follow a similar pattern to the majority in *UMO Ilinden (No. 1)*, although the last (for now) of them managed to criticise but disentangle the Bulgarian authorities' generally hostile attitude to the party from the precise complaint it was deciding, and found for Bulgaria. *En route* to this conclusion the European Court began to grapple with the obvious systemic issues revealed by this series of cases and the relationship between them and the Council of Europe's wider efforts at supporting democratic transition.

The first of the cases concerning PIRIN was about its dissolution, and the second was about several failed attempts to have it re-registered. The first unanimously followed the reasoning in *Stankov* quite closely and found a violation of Article 11. In other words, there was no basis on which to have regard to the notion of self-defending democracy, because there was no evidence that the party would resort to violence even though its views were deemed controversial. Again, the notion of 'violence' remained consistent with the earlier jurisprudence. Judge Botoucharova added a carefully worded concurring opinion, showing how the domestic Constitutional Court could have reasoned differently and thus could have left the European Court no option but to agree with the dissolution and thereby to decide the case differently.

In the second case, *UMO Ilinden – PIRIN and others v Bulgaria (No. 2)*,[149] and in which the domestic authorities may have heeded Judge Botoucharova's advice in their reasoning to refuse re-registration of the party, the European Court's statements about the relationship between the broader issues of democratic consolidation and narrower issues of the cases it has to decide are at their most revealing.

The European Court reaffirmed that Contracting Parties may impose proportionate legal formalities on the registration of organisations, but that 'such requirements should not be used to hinder the freedom of association of groups disliked by the authorities or advocating ideas that the authorities would like to suppress.'[150] The European Court went on to examine the precise basis on which the Supreme Court of Cassation had upheld two refusals to register the party, noting that several of the arguments put forward by the authorities were actually dismissed by the Supreme Court.

The European Court noted that the Supreme Court's judgments were 'set against the backdrop of the persistent efforts of the local authorities in the Pirin region to hinder the holding of rallies by the party and by that association'[151] and noted that several 'official figures' were reluctant to see the party re-registered.[152] Indeed, of the generally oppressive behaviour of the police towards the party, the European Court observed that: 'In a democratic society,

149 *UMO Ilinden – PIRIN and others v Bulgaria (No. 2)* [2011] ECHR 1714.
150 Ibid., [83].
151 Ibid., [86].
152 Ibid., [87].

the use by the authorities of such tactics is rather disquieting and worryingly reminiscent of past infamous persecutions.'[153]

However, and despite this, the relevant judgments of the Supreme Court of Cassation were found to be about important but technical deficiencies in the party's formation process; were not on account of the party's points of view; and could be distinguished from any attempt at hindering the execution of the European Court's earlier judgment in the dissolution case.

When all these cases are taken together, we can see that Bulgaria was gradually coaxed away from making unsustainable arguments based on a redefinition of violence as a trigger for self-defending democracy not only in relation to communism, as in *Tsonev*, but also in the face of secession. However, it is apparent from the facts of the cases that Bulgaria maintained in practice a fairly aggressive policing approach to people supporting UMO Ilinden and PIRIN and eventually found a Convention-compliant way of refusing to re-register PIRIN as a political party. Whether the European Court was able to debate the applicability of the jurisprudence on 'violence' in the context of self-defending democracy as a way of 'tutoring' Bulgaria into Convention compliance, or whether Bulgaria simply got better at narrowing and justifying its reasons for restricting freedom of association, can be open to interpretation. The fact that the European Court was moved to express its disquietude about the wider context of the second PIRIN case suggests that although it found for the Respondent State on the precise legal question at issue, it was by no means satisfied with the approach to freedom of association in Bulgaria.

7.3.1.1.4.2 Bulgarians in Macedonia In this discussion of self-defending democracy and secession in Bulgaria and Macedonia, it would be remiss not to briefly discuss the situation in Macedonia itself. Recall that in the cases discussed earlier, the Bulgarian authorities had begun from the premise that the idea of 'Macedonia' itself was a communist creation. Such views have, unsurprisingly, been greeted with hostility in Macedonia.

In *Association of Citizens Radko v Macedonia*,[154] Bulgaria intervened in support of a dissolved association which, although on the face of it was aimed at 'affirming the Macedonian cultural space, establishing traditional ethical and human values, affirmed in the ideas of the Macedonian Liberation Movement',[155] in fact was committed to, 'the revolutionary and cultural struggle of *the Bulgarians from Macedonia*'.[156] Indeed, despite being a 'Macedonian' movement, the association was actually committed to following the teaching of Ivan Mihajlov, known as 'Radko' – and after whom the association was named – who had taught that Macedonian ethnicity never actually existed and that the

153 Ibid., [88].
154 *Association of Citizens Radko v Macedonia* (2009) 49 EHRR 21.
155 Ibid., [15].
156 Ibid., [16], emphasis added.

recognition of Macedonian ethnicity 'was the biggest crime committed by the Bolshevik headquarters during its existence'.[157]

The Macedonian Constitutional Court explained that according to the teachings of Ivan Mihajlov:

> the process of de-Bulgarisation of Macedonia, which was violently carried out after the Second World War, was a [form of] slavery executed by the Serb-communist regime and such Serb-communist doctrine continued to be the official one of the State after it became independent in 1991.[158]

The association was dissolved on the basis that it was unconstitutional, because its articles and programme 'were directed towards violent destruction of the constitutional order of the Republic of Macedonia and incitement to national or religious hatred or intolerance'.[159]

At the European Court, the Macedonian government argued explicitly that the association's dissolution 'should be assessed in the light of the political circumstances of the former Yugoslav Republic of Macedonia.'[160] Following the position taken by some of the media in protest at the formation of the association,[161] the government also argued that Mihajlov had collaborated with the Nazis and was 'considered as a person who used terrorist methods to impose the fascist idea of denunciation of the Macedonian people's identity'. The government therefore argued that the case fell within its margin of appreciation[162] and should also be considered in the light of Article 17 ECHR.[163]

The European Court deemed the aims of the association case more serious than those discussed in *Stankov*, because they were not just about promoting the interests of a particular minority but about calling into question the national identity of certain other people.[164] The European Court accepted that naming the organisation 'Radko' would arouse hostile reactions from some people, but that a name in itself could not constitute a 'present and imminent threat to public order'. That is to say, the nevertheless offensive name on its own was not sufficient evidence of violence or the rejection of democratic principles to establish the preconditions for triggering self-defending democracy. Although the European Court reaffirmed that its approach in *Refah Partisi* remained valid, the association here was penalised purely on grounds related to freedom of expression, rather than any real threat to democracy. There was, therefore, a violation of Article 11.

157 Ibid., [27], citing the Macedonian Constitutional Court.
158 Ibid., [27] – although it would seem that Mihajlov died in 1990.
159 Ibid., [24].
160 Ibid., [47].
161 See ibid., [19].
162 Ibid., [48].
163 Ibid., [49].
164 Ibid., [70].

It is perhaps unsurprising that Judge Trajkovska of Macedonia 'deeply disagreed' with the majority. As well as arguing that domestic remedies had not been exhausted in the case, Judge Trajkovska stressed that the aims of the association could be classified as 'hate speech' and that denying the existence of the Macedonian nation 'was a serious and historically used ground for violence and national intolerance'. In other words, like the domestic Constitutional Court, she argued that the aims could not only lead to violence but, being hate speech, were 'violent' in themselves. The European Court has, of course, interpreted the notion of violence more narrowly than this and in this case again declined to broaden its definition – but the point remains that the majority in the European Court chose to discount a particularly strong domestic judicial finding on a question of national, indeed existential, importance.

7.3.1.1.5 REFLECTIONS ON COMMUNIST PARTIES, EXTREMISM AND SEPARATISM: 'SELF-DEFENDING' DEMOCRACY

The cases discussed in this subsection have raised some extremely serious issues for the states in question, centring on a perceived need to protect the state's democracy from an existential threat. The European Court's early approach in the German cases was not only to recognise that the notion of self-defending democracy could be accommodated within the reasoning of the European Court, but that its application in certain circumstances could justify restrictions on freedom of association (in *Germany Communist Party and Others v Germany* or *Glasenapp*, for example).

This approach was most visible in the *Refah Partisi* case, by which time the European Court had confirmed that the application of self-defending democracy within its reasoning went to the merits of the case, rather than exclusively its admissibility.

Although several of the newer Contracting Parties attempted to rely on the notion of self-defending democracy, the European Court did not use it as a basis to relax its position on what constitutes evidence of violence for the purposes of dissolving or failing to register associations. The Court has therefore resisted calls for transitional relativism in this context.

7.3.1.2 Decontaminating the state apparatus

The cases in the previous section all concerned the argument that in order to protect the future existence of the state, some compromises about the exercise of democratic rights would be needed. The states were not particularly successful in this argument. In this section, we shall examine similar, but smaller scale, democratic compromises designed not just to protect the state from existential threats, but also to decontaminate its apparatus after communist totalitarianism. The limitations on freedom of association discussed here, therefore, were imposed with a similar aim in mind to the statutory lustration process discussed in Chapter 5.

We first examined the 1999 case of *Rekvényi v Hungary* in relation to Article 10 ECHR in Chapter 6.[165] The facts were that the applicant, a police officer, complained that a Hungarian law prohibiting police officers from engaging in political activity unduly restricted his rights to free expression and association under Articles 10 and 11 of the ECHR.[166] The Hungarian government put great weight on the context and successfully argued that the restrictions on Rekvenyi's free expression were necessary in a democratic society.

The legal analysis under Article 11 was slightly different. In addition to the regular qualifications, comparable to those in the second paragraphs of Articles 8 to 10 ECHR, a unique second sentence in Article 11(2) provides that Article 11: '[S]hall not prevent the imposition of lawful restrictions on the exercise of these rights by members of the armed forces, of the police or of the administration of the State.'

Both the parties to the Rekvenyi case accepted that there was an interference with Article 11[167] and thus the discussion centred on whether the restriction was 'lawful' in the sense used in the second sentence of Article 11(2). This would require not only compliance with domestic law, but also the qualities of foreseeability and an absence of arbitrariness.[168]

The applicant conceded that the final sentence of Article 11(2) does not refer to 'necessity' as such, but argued that *any* valid interference with his rights would still have to be necessary in a democratic society. In this regard, he explicitly cautioned the European Court against showing any leniency to Hungary on account of its only 'recently' having become 'a pluralistic democracy and member of the Council of Europe'.[169] Parallels can therefore be drawn between these arguments and those discussed in Chapter 6, where certain applicants stressed that their case should be seen in the light of the transition as a whole.[170]

The government argued that the wish to depoliticise the police could not be seen as arbitrary so as to render the restriction unlawful.[171] Moreover, they reiterated the transitional argument made in relation to Article 10, maintaining that:

> the prohibition on party membership on the part of police officers had been intended to contribute to the elimination of any direct party

165 *Rekvényi v Hungary, op. cit. supra* n 21.

166 Ibid. The Court held by 16 votes to 1 that there had been no violation of Article 11. It held unanimously that there was no violation of Article 14, on which the applicants had also sought to rely in conjunction with Article 11 (but not Article 10).

167 Ibid., [52].

168 See the Court's summary at ibid., [59].

169 Ibid., [54].

170 See, e.g., *Dalban v Romania* (2001) 31 EHRR 39.

171 *Rekvényi v Hungary, op. cit. supra* n 21, [56].

> political influence on the police by severing the institutional links which had previously existed between the armed forces and the police on the one hand and political circles on the other.[172]

The European Court agreed that the restriction was justified in accordance with the final sentence of Article 11(2) and that, even if the first sentence were applicable, then following its reasoning on Article 10 the conditions specified therein would also have been met[173] (and recall that the European Court had validated the 'legitimate aim' in the transitional context by reference to the *Vogt* case's invocation of '*wehrhafte Demokratie*').[174] The Court dismissed an ancillary argument of discrimination based on Article 14 on this basis also.[175]

The findings in relation to Articles 10 and 14 ECHR were made unanimously in *Rekvenyi*, but Judge Fischbach dissented in relation to Article 11. He argued for greater emphasis to be placed on 'necessity' even in the application of the final sentence of Article 11(2). His comments in this regard demonstrate a difference of opinion in how best to regulate democratic rights in transitional states. Judge Fischbach considered that:

> [T]he unhappy experiences suffered under the communist regime ought to encourage political leaders to advocate a fresh approach so that the democratic process can be consolidated and the future prepared for in a spirit of open-mindedness and tolerance.
>
> As the police are now no longer at the service of the communist party, but of democracy, it is essential that change be accompanied by an approach fostering awareness of democratic pluralism through divergent political views that fuel debate over ideas.

Instead of accepting the transitional context as an underlying justification for the restriction, according to Judge Fischbach, the transitional context would instead tend towards *stricter* scrutiny of restrictions on Article 11, as part of the process of encouraging public debate. However, it is worth recalling that when we discussed the application of Article 10 in this case, we observed that the majority in the European Court accepted transitional arguments both in relation to the legitimacy of the aim pursued by the restriction *and* in relation to its necessity.[176] This is in stark contrast to Judge Fischbach's arguments for stricter scrutiny and marks the case as one of most strongly transitionally relativistic ones discussed in this book.

172 Ibid., [56].
173 Ibid., [60–62].
174 See ibid., 61, on freedom of association, referring back to [41] on freedom expression, where *Vogt* was cited.
175 Ibid., [68].
176 Ibid., [41].

In his examination of self-defending, or militant, democracy Harvey described the *Rekvényi* case as demonstrating that the European Court was returning to a 'more militant' stance after the 'progressive attitude to anti-democratic actors' seen in *Vogt*.[177] In other words, it was more ready to allow rights-restrictive measures that could fall within the self-defending democracy paradigm. The case can certainly be placed on a continuum that contains the cases explicitly on self-defending democracy, but *Rekvényi* did not actually concern anti-democratic actors at all: the impugned constitutional restrictions on the political activity of police officers applied whatever political point of view was at issue.

In this sense, the European Court's approach in *Rekvenyi* was particularly lenient, especially given that there was no basis on which Article 17 could have been conceivably applied to the case. However, and as Harvey also identified, the case must be viewed in its transitional context – at which point the European Court's approach can be seen as performing a 'tutelary' function to the transitional Respondent State.[178] This is not an inevitable or necessary development of the earlier jurisprudence on self-defending democracy (such as the 1957 case on the German Communist Party). The logic of the European Court's reasoning in *Germany Communist Party and Others v Germany* was that history had demonstrated that a democracy can quickly be dismantled and that democratic states should therefore be able to defend themselves. The application of this logic to *transitional* democracies is quite different. It is not so much 'self-defending democracy' as 'self-consolidating democracy'. The emergence of this approach is also clear in relation to the cases on Article 3, Protocol 1, discussed in Chapter 8.

7.3.1.3 Religion as a stabilising factor

In both *Metropolitan Church of Bessarabia v Moldova* and *Holy Synod of the Bulgarian Orthodox Church (Metropolitan Inokentiy) and Others v Bulgaria*, the European Court again heard arguments that the transitional context underpinned both the aim of the impugned interference and its necessity. Both cases concerned alleged violations of Article 9 ECHR interpreted in the light of Article 11.[179]

In *Metropolitan Church of Bessarabia v Moldova*, the Moldovan government argued that their refusal to register a religious association that they deemed a schismatic group within the Church of Moldova was justified because Moldova 'had few strengths it could depend on to ensure its continued existence, but

177 Harvey, *op. cit. supra* 112, 415.

178 Ibid.

179 *Metropolitan Church of Bessarabia v Moldova* (2002) 35 EHRR 13, 118; *Holy Synod of the Bulgarian Orthodox Church (Metropolitan Inokentiy) and Others v Bulgaria* [2010] ECHR 1293, [103].

one factor conducive to stability was religion'.[180] On this basis, the government argued, and the Court accepted, that 'having regard to the circumstances of the case' the restriction pursued the legitimate aim of protecting public order and public safety.[181] In other words, the transitional context clearly contributed to the translation of the restriction's purpose into a 'legitimate aim' in the Convention sense.

The European Court of Human Rights then turned to the question of necessity and examined the Respondent State's arguments that the measure was necessary in order to uphold Moldovan law and Moldovan constitutional principles; to prevent a threat to territorial integrity; and to protect social and peace and understanding between believers.[182] The European Court did not engage any further with the issue of whether the transitional context amplified or even impacted at all on these arguments and found unanimously a violation of Article 9 ECHR.

Bulgaria made similar arguments about the special role of religion during democratic transition in the January 2009 case of *Holy Synod of the Bulgarian Orthodox Church (Metropolitan Inokentiy) and Others v Bulgaria*.[183] The case concerned a dispute arising from the first democratic Bulgarian government's attempts to replace the patriarch imposed during the communist era (Patriarch Maxim) and the subsequent government's decision to reinstate him in order to end the ensuing confusion within the Bulgarian Orthodox Church. Noting recent history, the European Court observed that:

> Religious freedoms were reduced to a minimum during the communist period and the leaderships of religious communities, including the Bulgarian Orthodox Church, were nominated and controlled by the Communist Party and the State authorities.

The government went on to argue that, 'the unity of the Bulgarian Orthodox Church was an important national goal of historical significance, with ramifications affecting the very fabric of the Bulgarian nation and its cultural identity' and therefore their reinstatement of Patriarch Maxim was necessary and proportionate.[184]

The European Court again accepted that the transitional context was relevant both to the 'legitimacy' of the aim and to the 'necessity' of the measure.[185] However, it failed to distinguish exactly which legitimate aim or aims were at

180 *Metropolitan Church of Bessarabia v Moldova*, [111].
181 Ibid., [113].
182 Ibid., [123–127].
183 *Holy Synod of the Bulgarian Orthodox Church (Metropolitan Inokentiy) and Others v Bulgaria* (2010), *op. cit. supra* n 179.
184 Ibid., [143].
185 Ibid., [145].

stake or to separate their identification from answering the questions of necessity and proportionality.[186] The Court found that:

> [Taking] into account the margin of appreciation [. . .] the Bulgarian authorities had legitimate reasons to consider some form of action with the aim of helping to overcome the conflict in the Church, if possible, or limiting its negative effect on public order and legal certainty.[187]

This is intriguing at a doctrinal level because the margin of appreciation is normally said to attach to the question of whether a restriction is 'necessary', rather than 'legitimate'. Moreover, in earlier non-transitional cases, the Court had explained that the width of the margin of appreciation in each case will relate to the legitimate aim put forward by the state.[188] If the Court is to apply the margin of appreciation doctrine coherently, it must therefore always first identify the aim at stake.

It is also worth recalling that the legitimate aims for restricting Article 11 have previously been held to have been listed exhaustively in Article 11(2). Thus, when Greece attempted to put forward that a particular interference was pursuing the aim of 'upholding [. . .] Greece's cultural traditions and historical and cultural symbols', the European Court was not persuaded that such an aim was 'legitimate' in the Convention sense.[189] The exceptions to freedom of association 'must be narrowly interpreted, such that the enumeration of them is strictly exhaustive and the definition of them necessarily restrictive', it continued.[190]

In relation to the ultimate question of whether the restrictions in *Holy Synod of the Bulgarian Orthodox Church (Metropolitan Inokentiy) and Others v Bulgaria* could be deemed 'necessary', the Court did not invoke the margin of appreciation at all, and simply determined that:

> [The] legitimate aim of remedying the injustices inflicted by the unlawful acts of 1992 and the following years, could not warrant the use of State power, in 2003, 2004 and afterwards, to take sweeping measures, imposing a return to the *status quo ante* against the will of a part of the religious community.[191]

186 Ibid., [159].

187 Ibid., [131].

188 See, e.g., *Sunday Times v UK* (1979) EHRR 245, [59], in which the European Court compared the aims of 'maintaining the authority and impartiality of the judiciary' and 'the protection of health or morals', concluding that there would be a narrower margin of appreciation in relation to the former than the latter.

189 *Sidiropoulos and Others v Greece* (1999) 27 EHRR 633, [38].

190 Ibid.

191 *Holy Synod of the Bulgarian Orthodox Church (Metropolitan Inokentiy) and Others v Bulgaria, op. cit. supra* n 183, [138].

In this sentence, the European Court thus confirmed that remedying certain historical injustice was a 'legitimate aim', notwithstanding that no reference to such an aim is actually made in Article 11(2).

Both *Metropolitan Church of Bessarabia* and *Holy Synod of the Bulgarian Orthodox Church* raise issues about state neutrality in religious matters that had arisen in non-transitional cases as well.[192] The European Court has consistently held that measures favouring a particular leader of a divided religious community or seeking to force the community to place itself, against its will, under a single leadership, would constitute a violation of Article 9.[193] It would appear that this approach remains valid in transitional states, whether the transitional context is stressed (as in *Metropolitan Church of Bessarabia* and *Holy Synod of the Bulgarian Orthodox Church*) or not (as in, for example, *Hasan and Chaush v Bulgaria* or *Supreme Holy Council of the Muslim Community v Bulgaria*).

The most novel element of both *Metropolitan Church of Bessarabia* and *Holy Synod of the Bulgarian Orthodox Church* is the argument that stability within religious organisations is of sufficient importance in transitional states that it could serve to justify restrictions on religious associations. This is rather different to the arguments clearly based on self-defending democracy and democratic compromises validated in, for example, *Refeh Partisi v Turkey* or even in *Rekvényi v Hungary*. It presents a distinct, and contestable, view of the role of religion in transition. Indeed, nowhere in the catalogue of common transitional policies encountered in Chapters 2 to 4 of this book did we come across any transitional arguments in favour of abandoning state neutrality in religious matters. It is all the more striking, therefore, that the European Court seemed to allow some transitional relativism into its interpretation of Article 11 to acknowledge the 'legitimacy' of such an approach (although the effects of this approval were mitigated by the findings on 'necessity').

7.4 Freedom of association: 'echoes' of totalitarianism and systemic problems

We saw that in the various cases on UMO Ilinden, the European Court eventually expressed concern that the Bulgarian authorities' approach to association and its supporters was becoming 'worryingly reminiscent of past infamous persecutions'.[194]

The cases on self-defending democracy showed us that in terms of the reception of Convention standards, there has been some resistance to the idea that contemporary communist or secessionist parties can *ever* be valid, peaceful,

192 For example, in *Hasan and Chaush v Bulgaria* (2002) 34 EHRR 55.

193 *Serif v Greece* (2001) 31 EHRR 20, [52]; *Hasan and Chaush v Bulgaria*, ibid., [78]; *Metropolitan Church of Bessarabia v Moldova, op. cit. supra* n 179, [117]; *Holy Synod of the Bulgarian Orthodox Church (Metropolitan Inokentiy) and Others v Bulgaria, op. cit. supra* n 179, [120].

194 *UMO Ilinden – PIRIN and others v Bulgaria (No. 2), op. cit. supra* n 149, [88].

democratic actors. The European Court has been generally reluctant to dismiss these cases at the admissibility stage, thus guaranteeing that states have been forced to articulate their 'relevant and sufficient' reasons for the restrictions. On occasion, they have been successful, such as in *PIRIN (No. 2)* and *Rekvényi*. Nevertheless, it is clear that the European Court had to deal with some broad conceptual incongruities between its existing jurisprudence and the way that the newer Contracting Parties thought it would apply to them.

It is notable, therefore, that the various judgments on UMO Ilinden eventually contained detailed discussion of the efforts of the Committee of Ministers and the guidance of the Venice Commission, as well as the new provisions on the execution of judgments in systemic cases.

In a sense, therefore, all the cases discussed here, in which the Respondent State cited distinctively transitional motives for restricting freedom of association, have revealed systemic problems with the understanding of Convention concepts. However, in the other chapters of this book we have examined somewhat narrower systemic problems, concerning, for example, the legal regulation of procedural safeguards within national legislative frameworks on freedom of assembly.

The Court has likewise given general guidance on the Convention compliance of legal requirements for the registration of associations. In *Tebieti Mühafize Cemiyyeti and Israfilov v Azerbaijan*, the European Court was critical of a regime in which the only sanction for breach of an association's internal management rules (such as a rule requiring a regular general assembly of its members) was dissolution, even though it said it 'did not see a problem' with there being some formal legal requirements for lawful corporate legal forms.[195] Recall also the warning in *PIRIN (No. 2)* that: '[S]uch requirements should not be used to hinder the freedom of association of groups disliked by the authorities or advocating ideas that the authorities would like to suppress.'[196]

It is not only associations with a political objective that have vexed the transitional states. In a series of cases concerning Russia's reforms of religious associations, the European Court has reiterated that Article 11 is not just for political parties: '[A]ssociations formed for other purposes, including those proclaiming or teaching religion, are also important to the proper functioning of democracy.'[197]

It is in this context that a systemic problem with the regulation of religious associations in Moscow has been discussed.

As noted earlier, religion was suppressed under communism. When Russia passed liberalising laws in 1990, it was welcomed by the Council of Europe. However, in 1997 a new, more restrictive law was introduced. It has been

195 *Tebieti Mühafize Cemiyyeti and Israfilov v Azerbaijan* [2009] ECHR 1473, [72].
196 *UMO Ilinden – PIRIN and others v Bulgaria (No. 2), op. cit. supra* n 149, [83].
197 *Moscow Branch of the Salvation Army v Russia* (2007) 44 EHRR 46, [61].

accused of favouring Orthodox Christianity at the expense of other religions,[198] but its clearest practical effect was to require all religious associations to re-register with the state by 31 December 2000 or face dissolution. Three associations based in Moscow were refused re-registration, generating three separate judgments: *Moscow Branch of the Salvation Army v Russia* in 2006, *Church of Scientology Moscow v Russia* in 2007 and *Jehovah's Witnesses of Moscow and Others v Russia* in 2010.

None of the cases raises transitional issues explicitly, but they represent a systemic problem within a state that emerged from the post-1989 changes but has not necessarily completed the transition to democracy.[199] Presumably Peter Leuprecht would not be surprised.[200] However, the real problem in these particular cases was with the Moscow authorities, rather than with Russia as a whole. In the Salvation Army case it was notable that in other regions, and at the federal level, the association had been re-re-registered. The European Court thus went so far as to state that the Moscow authorities '*did not act in good faith* and neglected their duty of neutrality and impartiality *vis-à-vis* the applicant's religious community'.[201] It is also worth noting that one of the several objections against the re-registration of the Jehovah's Witnesses of Moscow was the allegation that they had a 'disrespectful attitude to state symbols'.

While these cases have not raised particularly explicit transitional arguments, it is clear that they took place against the backdrop of democratic consolidation. The more worrying aspect of the three Moscow cases is that they may represent an instance, not so much of 'echoes of communism' *during* transition, but of outright regression. If the transition to democracy is no longer an aim, then it is unsurprising that states would not raise explicitly 'transitional' arguments in their defence.

7.4.1 Conclusions on freedom of association

In this part of Chapter 7, we first of all identified three particularly visible circumstances in which states have put forward distinctively transitional arguments to justify purported restrictions on freedom of association, ranging from concerns about extremist parties to decontaminating the state and a perceived special role for religion in transition.

The European Court has contemplated the application of its reasoning about self-defending democracy in the cases on contemporary communism, extremism and secession, but has rarely accepted the transitional arguments made by the Respondent States (although frequently the 'national' judge dissented in these cases).

198 Ibid., [47].
199 See Harvey, *op. cit. supra* 112, 410–411.
200 Note the discussion of Leuprecht's resignation in Chapter 1.
201 *Moscow Branch of the Salvation Army v Russia* (2007) 44 EHRR 46, [97] emphasis added.

This quite defensible lack of flexibility is what makes the judgment in *Rekvenyi* all the more notable, where both in relation to the 'legitimate aim' and the 'necessity' of the measure the European Court conceded a level of transitional relativism, via the invocation of what can only be described as 'self-consolidating' democracy. Likewise, the validation that infringing state neutrality in religious matters can be a 'legitimate aim' during transition is particularly generous.

8 Free elections

8.1 Introduction

In Chapter 5, we discussed the relationship between lustration and the wider notion of decommunisation. The latter can include not only attempts to clarify the events of the past, but also prospective restrictions on the political activity of certain classes on people. According to the guidance from the Council of Europe lustration, by contrast, should not apply to elected office.[1] The distinction is not easy to maintain and we saw that the leading *Vogt* case and recent *Ādamsons* case discussed the concepts together.[2] Likewise, even the 'pure' lustration case of *Chodynicki v Poland* certainly had democratic implications, because of the effects of the lustration process on the applicant's ability to remain an MP.

The cases discussed here raise the question of democratic rights explicitly, in particular through the discussion of Article 3, Protocol 1. By signing Protocol 1, states undertake:

> to hold free elections at reasonable intervals by secret ballot, under conditions which will ensure the free expression of the opinion of the people in the choice of the legislature.

The right to free elections is thus expressed loosely and without the characteristic qualifying paragraph that accompanies, for example, Articles 8 to 11 of the ECHR. *Mathieu-Mohin and Clerfayt v Belgium* was the first case on Article 3, Protocol 1, and in it the Court developed various sub-principles, such as the right to stand for election, but also recognised that the right is not absolute: it is subject to 'implied limitations'.[3] Crucially, even in *Mathieu-Mohin and Clerfayt*, the European Court accepted that:

1 Pace Resolution 1096 (1996), Explanatory Memorandum, Council of Europe Doc. 7568, report of the Committee on Legal Affairs and Human Rights, 16(e) and 46(e).

2 *Vogt v Germany* (1996) 21 EHRR 205; *Ādamsons v Latvia*, App no 3669/03, (ECtHR, 24 June 2008) (available only in French).

3 *Mathieu-Mohin & Clerfayt v Belgium* (1988) 10 EHRR 1.

> any electoral system must be assessed in the light of the political evolution of the country concerned; features that would be unacceptable in the context of one system may accordingly be justified in the context of another.[4]

This approach has come to be highly significant in relation to the accommodation of difficult issues arising from the transitional states. The cases discussed in this chapter build on the foundations of the early cases on self-defending democracy (in its narrow sense of restricting particular political parties), but also tap into the wider issues of transition acknowledged explicitly in *Rekvényi v Hungary*.[5]

8.2 'Transitional' arguments by the Respondent State

One of the clearest examples of transitional relativism is given by the 2006 Grand Chamber judgment in the case of *Ždanoka v Latvia*.[6] The Grand Chamber contradicted a Chamber judgment of the First Section, and found no violation in relation to certain restrictions placed on a former communist. However, it cautioned that were it to be presented with a similar case in the future it might not come to the same conclusion. We shall examine *Ždanoka* first and then contrast it with two cases in which the European Court has applied its reasoning on the relationship of the passage of time to restrictions imposed on transitional grounds, but has come to a rather different conclusion.

In *Ždanoka*, the Grand Chamber upheld a restriction on the political activities of a member of the Communist Party of Latvia, in order to defend Latvia against the resurgence of communism during the transitional phase. The parallels with the discussion of self-defending and 'self-consolidating' democracy in Chapter 7 are clear from the outset.

The applicant in *Ždanoka* was prohibited from standing for election to the Latvian national parliament in 2002, as a result of her active participation in the Communist Party of Latvia after 13 January 1991 (the date on which they had launched an attempted coup).[7] Despite citing *Refah Partisi* and confirming 'the legitimacy of the concept of a "democracy capable of defending itself"',[8] the substance of the judgment owes a lot more to the Court's appraisal of the transitional context.[9]

The Chamber had examined the Municipal Elections Act, which prohibited people who had participated in the communist party after 13 January 1991 from standing for office and decided the case by five votes to two in

4 Ibid., [54].
5 *Rekvényi v Hungary* (1997) 23 EHRR CD63.
6 *Ždanoka v Latvia* (GC) [2006] ECHR 231.
7 Ibid., [22].
8 Ibid., [100].
9 Ibid., [133–135].

favour of a violation of Article 11 and Article 3, Protocol 1. In relation to the latter, the Chamber did 'not exclude the possibility' that this type of restriction would have been Convention-compliant in the 'first years' of Latvian independence.[10] However, time had passed and so the Chamber found it decisive in relation to Article 3, Protocol 1, that the Latvian authorities had provided no evidence that the applicant herself had done anything that was capable of endangering the Latvian state, its national security or its democratic order.[11] Likewise, in relation to Article 11 ECHR, the Chamber could see no evidence that the applicant was engaged in activity such as would necessitate the engagement of Article 17 and so found a violation of Article 11.

The judgment provoked some revealingly strong dissent. Judge Bonello cautioned against promoting compliance with human rights norms:

> even in defiance of historical realities, the weakness of emergent and fragile pluralisms and the contradictions faced by a democracy called to contain democratically those who consider democracy, at best, expendable and, at worst, wholly detrimental.[12]

He described the 'horrific and blood-splattered coup' of 1991 and criticised those who 'vote Communist and dream Neanderthal'.[13] Judge Bonello then called for the 'maximum of judicial restraint' in this case and a wide margin of appreciation. On the issue of timing he argued:

> I fail to see how an international Court is better placed to impose its own value judgements on such evanescent and ephemeral issues as to exactly when a state of emergency or transition is over.[14]

Judge Levits likewise argued for a wide margin of appreciation[15] and in a long and scholarly dissent drew inspiration from key academic literature and international experiences of transitional justice in South Africa amongst other places.

Nevertheless, and although Judge Levits made reference to successor trials, truth commissions and lustration, he did not invoke the language of 'transitional justice' at all, instead using the post-war German terminology of *Vergangenheits-bewältigung*: 'coping' or 'coming to terms with' the past. He argued that these issues were deeply political, but that restrictions on human

10 *Ždanoka v Latvia* (Chamber) [2004] ECHR 268, [92].
11 Ibid., [98]
12 Ibid., Dissenting Opinion of Judge Bonello Dissent, [2.2].
13 Ibid., [2.5].
14 Ibid., [3.3].
15 *Ždanoka v Latvia* (Chamber) [2004], *op. cit. supra* n 10, Dissenting Opinion of Judge Levits, [3] and [50].

rights aimed at *Vergangenheits-bewältigung* would be covered by the European Court's recognition of 'self-defending democracy'.[16]

The argument of Judge Levits can, therefore, be summarised as stressing the consolidating, transitional, element to the German approach to *wehrhafte Demokratie*, rather than stressing the purely protective element. It is this that allows self-defending democracy to morph into self-consolidating democracy.

The effect of these two dissenting opinions to the Chamber judgment was significant. When the case reached the Grand Chamber it reasoned that:

> While such a measure may scarcely be considered acceptable in the context of one political system, for example in a country *which has an established framework of democratic institutions going back many decades or centuries*, it may nonetheless be considered acceptable in Latvia in view of the historico-political context which led to its adoption and given the threat to the new democratic order posed by the resurgence of ideas which, if allowed to gain ground, might appear capable of restoring the former regime. [emphasis added]

On the passage of time, the Grand Chamber drew on *Rekvényi v Hungary*[17] and noted that, in that case, the exclusion of police officers from political activities had become effective some four years after the transition. The Grand Chamber continued that it was:

> not surprising that a newly established democratic legislature should need time for reflection in a period of political turmoil to enable it to consider what measures were required to sustain its achievements.

This approach to legislative reform is another complete contrast to the early case of *Guincho v Portugal*, but sits more comfortably alongside the 2007 *Mkrtchyan v Armenia* case (in which it was conceded that it may take some time for a country to establish its legislative framework 'in a transition period').[18] However, recall that in *Mkrtchyan*, the European Court found *against* Armenia because there had been a delay of 13 years. In *Ždanoka*, the European Court adverted to the importance of the passage of time and cautioned that:

> [E]ven if today Latvia cannot be considered to have overstepped its wide margin of appreciation under Article 3 of Protocol No. 1, it is nevertheless the case that the Latvian parliament must keep the statutory restriction under constant review, with a view to bringing it to an early end.

16 Ibid., [33].
17 *Rekvényi v Hungary, op. cit. supra* n 5.
18 *Mkrtchyan v Armenia*, (2009) 49 EHRR 16.

> Such a conclusion seems all the more justified in view of the greater stability which Latvia now enjoys, inter alia, by reason of its full European integration. Hence, the failure by the Latvian legislature to take active steps in this connection may result in a different finding by the Court.[19]

This is a more equivocal approach than that taken in the Chamber: the Grand Chamber did not claim the power to conclude that the transition was over and did not even state conclusively that it was ongoing. To this extent the Grand Chamber therefore seems to have been particularly influenced by Judge Bonello's dissent. Nevertheless, the issue of timing must be taken as having been decisive in the sense that, but for the conditions in Latvia 'today', there would have been a violation of the Convention.

The threat to democracy in *Ždanoka* was of a very different scale to that in *Refah Partisi*: the election of one person as opposed to the election of a government (indeed the Dissenting Opinion of Judge Rozakis made precisely this point). The Court seems to have implied that it would deem there to be an 'imminent threat' to democracy[20] at a lower threshold during the transitional period. However, since *Refah Partisi* was not a transitional case, the reference to the paradigm of self-defending democracy arguably minimises the impression that the Court was delivering *exclusively* 'transitional' justice (unless it is assumed that *all* valid references to self-defending democracy are inherently transitional). The approach in *Ždanoka* stretched the self-defending democracy paradigm so far that, taken together with *Rekvenyi*, it might fairly be concluded with much more certainty that the European Court now recognises a paradigm of 'self-consolidating' democracy.

Needless to say, there was strong dissent in the Grand Chamber as well, where the case was decided by 13 votes to 4[21] and with a Party Dissenting Opinion by Judge Wildhaber (then President); a Partly Dissenting Opinion by Judges Spielmann and Jaeger; the Dissenting Opinion of Judge Rozakis mentioned earlier; a Dissenting Opinion by Judge Zupančič; and a Joint Dissenting Opinion by Judges Mijović and Gyulumyan.

The most challenging of these dissenting opinions was that by Judge Zupančič, who pointed out that the background was that it would have been predominantly the 30 per cent Russian-speaking minority who would have voted for the applicant. He noted the wider issue of members of previous totalitarian regimes taking advantage of human rights law: 'They barefacedly claim the very human rights which they spent their life denying to others, nay, often cold-bloodedly violating them in the most brutal fashion.'

19 *Ždanoka v Latvia* (GC), *op. cit. supra* n 6, [135].

20 That is, applying *Refah Partisi (the Welfare Party) and Others v Turkey* (2003) 37 EHRR 1, [104].

21 The finding was that there was no violation of Article 3, Protocol 1, and by the same pattern of votes that no separate issue arose under Article 11.

Judge Zupančič made reference to *Streletz, Kessler and Krenz*, discussed in Chapter 2, as a case involving such people. However, he confirmed the analysis presented in Chapter 2 by de-emphasising the exceptionality of the European Court's reasoning – in essence, denying that by validating the applicants' prosecutions the European Court was delivering transitional justice. He referred to his own Concurring Opinion in *Streletz, Kessler and Krenz* as authority for the proposition that the European Court had not approved the exceptional, transitional, retroactive application of criminal law, but had based its reasoning on an earlier inexcusable mistake of law (i.e. not prosecuting the applicants under East German law at the time). The validation of the Latvian electoral law in *Ždanoka* could not be normalised in this way: to do so would, he argued, amount to correcting historical wrongs. Indeed he went so far as to imply that, by allowing the restriction on the applicant's rights in this case, it might even suggest that the 30 per cent Russian-speaking minority in Latvia were present illegally. Judge Zupančič would, therefore, be unconvinced that the Grand Chamber had successfully avoided the impression that it was delivering *exclusively* 'transitional' justice.

8.2.1 The legacy of Ždanoka*: 'self-consolidating' democracies, transitional relativism and the question of timing*

The case of *Ādamsons v Latvia*, decided in 2008, is very nearly a sequel to *Ždanoka*, since it also concerns the application of the Latvian Parliamentary Elections Act to exclude someone from the electoral process due to their involvement with the prior regime. However, like all of the cases subsequent to *Ždanoka* that have discussed the proximity of restrictive measures to the transition and that have concerned both notable individuals and systemic discrimination (discussed in the next section), the European Court has found a violation of the European Convention.

In *Ādamsons v Latvia*,[22] the applicant was disqualified from standing for election due to his previous service in the KGB Border Guard Forces, which were separate from but subordinate to the KGB. He was also removed from the electoral list of the party of which he was a member. He complained about this situation under Article 3, Protocol 1.

The Court gave a detailed summary of its Grand Chamber judgment in *Ždanoka*, including the usual statement that cases on Article 1, Protocol 3, were about proportionality and the avoidance of inhibiting the free expression of public opinion,[23] but actually approached the case as if it were about lustration.[24] The Court would examine the legality of the measure (comparable to

22 *Ādamsons v Latvia*, App no 3669/03, (ECtHR, 24 June 2008) (available only in French).
23 Ibid., [111].
24 Ibid., [116].

whether the restriction was 'prescribed by law'); whether it pursued a legitimate aim; and whether it was proportionate. It is notable that in the summary of lustration cases in *Ādamsons*, the European Court stated that:

> national authorities must keep in mind that the lustration measures are, by their nature temporary, the objective necessity of a restriction of individual rights resulting from this procedure decreases with time.[25]

This is intriguing because the European Court never actually said that this would be decisive in any of the previous cases on lustration (in *Sidabras and Džiautas v Lithuania* it had merely described the belated nature of the impugned restriction as relevant to the question of proportionality but 'not in itself decisive'[26]: see the discussion in Chapter 5). Moreover, the *Ādamsons* case is not strictly about lustration (in the sense of the 'removal of individuals responsible for abuses, especially from police, prison services, the army and the judiciary'),[27] but rather about the content of the right to free elections in transitional democracies.

As to the application of these tests, the European Court first noted that the provision under which Ādamsons had been prevented from standing for election was slightly different to the one at stake in *Ždanoka*. Ādamsons was subject to a restriction aimed specifically at 'former KGB *agents*', but he argued that as a KGB *border guard* this should not apply to him. In the *Ādamsons* view, therefore, the test of 'legality' was not met. Nevertheless, the European Court found that the domestic interpretation of the provision in Ādamsons' case was not arbitrary.

The issue of self-defending (or self-consolidating) democracy was recast as going to the question of whether the restriction pursued a legitimate aim. The European Court noted Latvia's experience under Soviet rule and found it 'understandable' that the state was now founded on the belief that it must be a democracy capable of defending itself.[28] With this in mind, the restriction was found to be pursuing a goal that was consistent with the objectives of the Convention.[29] There was, therefore, an element of transitional relativism on the legitimate aim, just as we saw in relation to the claimed transitional need to depoliticise the police, and to abandon state neutrality in religious affairs in Chapter 7.

As to proportionality, the European Court found that *Ādamsons* was 'fundamentally different' to *Ždanoka* because of the wide range of people to which

25 Ibid.

26 *Sidabras and Džiautas v Lithuania* (2004) 42 EHRR 104, [60].

27 UN Secretary General, 'The Rule of Law and Transitional Justice in Conflict and Post-Conflict Societies', UN Security Council, S/2004/616, 3 August 2004, 18; discussed in Chapter 5.

28 *Ādamsons v Latvia, op. cit. supra* n 22, [120].

29 Ibid., [120].

the impugned restriction could apply.[30] Since the group was so wide there would have to be some degree of individualisation and:

> In the eyes of the Court, the need for such individualization is becoming increasingly important with the passage of time, since the distance from the time when the actions at issue are alleged to have occurred.

The Court went on to find that there was no evidence of the applicant's being involved in anti-democratic activities[31] (indeed he had had an illustrious military and political career in 'restored' Latvia).[32] Although it was still clear that even nascent democracies in need of consolidation could rely on the notion of self-defending democracy in principle, there was still a violation of the Convention.

The Concurring Opinion of Judge Garlicki, joined by Judges Zupančič and Gyulumyan, would have preferred the violation to have been found purely on the basis of the quality of the law, since to do so would have avoided the discussion of proportionality, the passage of time and the completion of the transition: 'We are experts in law and legality, but not in politics and history, and we should we venture into these two areas when it proves absolutely necessary.'

The Dissenting Opinion of Judge Fura-Sandström, by contrast, argued that the applicant had acted in bad faith by supporting his bid for election by contending that he had not been an agent of the KGB (and was not subject therefore to the prohibition in the Parliamentary Elections Act). As to timing, and whether the transition was complete, she was more equivocal but stated: 'What I do know, however, is that it is certainly not an international court such as ours to judge.'

Much like in the *Vajnai* case on communist symbols, the force of the majority's argument was that the legislation in *Ādamsons* was overbroad and not sufficiently well formulated.[33] However, their reasoning suggested that there might have been more generosity on this point earlier in the transition. This builds on the question of timing raised in the caveat to *Ždanoka*, but does not go quite so far as to make the issue of timing conclusive: in essence, there was a balance between precision and proximity to the start of the transition. The same observation was made about the 'pure' lustration case of *Sidabras and Džiautas v Lithuania*, in which the European Court implied that a broader lustration measure might have been Convention-compliant had it been introduced earlier.[34]

30 Ibid., [124].
31 Ibid., [128].
32 Ibid., [129].
33 See M. Varju, 'Transition as a concept of European human rights law' (2009) *EHRLR* 170, 175.
34 *Sidabras and Džiautas v Lithuania, op. cit. supra* n 26; discussed in Chapter 5.

It cannot be said, however, that the question of timing was decisive in this case. Since it is very arguable that the provision was not particularly precise, then Judge Fura-Sandström's concern that the majority had come to its conclusions essentially by way of declaring the transition complete can be met.

In *Paksas v Lithuania*,[35] the Grand Chamber again dodged the issue of conclusively determining whether the transition was complete. The case is highly significant since it concerned electoral restrictions imposed on the former Prime Minister and President of Lithuania after impeachment proceedings against him removed him from office.

The government made specific reference to the previous jurisprudence on the protection of democracy and argued that Paksas was attempting to use the Convention machinery to 'gain political revenge'.[36] The European Court declined to take this as a basis for declaring the application inadmissible on the application of Article 17.[37]

It was therefore necessary to examine the merits. The government argued that impeachable conduct by someone so prominent undermined people's trust in state institutions and posed a 'serious and imminent threat to democracy' and the constitutional order. Citing *Ždanoka* and relying on the notion of self-defending democracy, the government stressed the need to take into account the Lithuanian political context, including that it did not have a long-standing democratic tradition. They claimed a wide margin of appreciation on the prohibition of such people standing for election.[38] The Partly Dissenting Opinion of Judge Costa, joined by Judges Tsotsoria and Baka, likewise advocated restraint in the supervision of the 'delicate field' of electoral law.[39]

The European Court again checked the measure's legality, aim and proportionality.[40] As to the last, it recast the judgment in *Ždanoka* as not being about whether the Latvian transition was or was not complete, but whether the rights-restrictive domestic law had a sunset clause. In truth, *Ždanoka* had merely 'attached weight' to the possibility of parliamentary periodic review of the measure (most recently in 2004) and 'noted that' the domestic Constitutional Court had recommended back in 2000 that the parliament should establish a time limit on the restriction.[41] Surely, since the 2004 review had chosen *not* to add a time limit to the Latvian restriction, the Court's reliance in *Paksas* on *Ždanoka* as authority for the centrality of sunset clauses was a little disingenuous.

35 *Paksas v Lithuania* [2011] ECHR 1.
36 Ibid., [85].
37 Ibid., [89].
38 Ibid., [92].
39 Ibid., Partly Dissenting Opinion of Judge Costa joined by Judges Tsotsoria and Baka, [12].
40 *Paksas v Lithuania, op. cit. supra* n 35, [97].
41 *Ždanoka v Latvia* (GC), *op. cit. supra* n 6, [134–135].

Nevertheless, just as in *Ādamsons*, where the European Court had stressed that the case was 'fundamentally different' to *Ždanoka*, this time it noted that the circumstances of the case, 'differ[ed] greatly'.[42] The European Court did not disagree with the importance of taking into account the evolution of the local and political context[43] and thus confirmed again that transitional or nascent democracies could still have recourse to self-defending democracy during their democratic consolidation, but observed that (apparently unlike in *Ždanoka*): '[N]ot only is the restriction in issue not subject to any time-limit, but the rule on which it is based is set in constitutional stone.'[44]

'Decisive weight' should be given to the existence of time limits to, or reviews of, the measure, because the initial justification for the restriction may subside with the passing of time.[45] In addition, and not as a decisive factor, the European Court criticised the 'striking rapidity' of the legislative process that led to the introduction of the restrictive measure because it gave the impression that the process was triggered specifically to prevent the applicant running for election.[46] Taking all this together, the Grand Chamber found a violation of Article 3, Protocol 1, by 14 votes to 3.

Just as in *Ādamsons*, there was an attempt to show that the transitional question was not alone decisive: here, it was not the quality of the law that contributed to the Court's findings, but the 'striking rapidity' of the legislative process creating it. Moreover, on the timing of the measure the European Court moved *away* from giving the impression that it would, or could, decide whether the transition was complete and *towards* ensuring that there was a domestic mechanism for doing this. This is actually a very important and useful step, which complies with the principle of subsidiarity. However, to suggest that this had been its approach all along is rather creative.

8.3 Free elections: 'echoes' of totalitarianism and systemic problems

The question of whether there exists a Convention principle of self-consolidating democracy and what relationship it might have to the timing of restrictions imposed in its name carries through in to cases that have raised broader systemic problems.

The European Court has examined electoral legislation on candidates' knowledge of the state's official language; required period residency in the relevant state; renunciation of a formal role in religion; and, most controversially, ethnicity and nationality. All of these have raised issues about the

42 *Paksas v Lithuania, op. cit. supra* n 35, [107].
43 Ibid., [104].
44 Ibid., [110].
45 Ibid., [109].
46 Ibid., [111].

extent to which the provision in question can be supported by notions of loyalty to the state. There is a subtle difference, therefore, between these cases and those in which the restriction was imposed due to an individual's perceived lack of loyalty to the democratic process itself. These cases do not so much involve allegations that certain people pose a particular threat to the nascent democracy, but rather that, in order to consolidate democracy, restrictions on certain classes of people are necessary.

The cases on ethnicity and nationality are the most revealing, but we shall briefly sketch a few others to demonstrate the wider systemic issue of loyalty. Recall that the concept of 'loyalty' ran behind the cases on lustration as well, for example in *Sidabras and Džiautas v Lithuania*,[47] discussed in Chapter 5.

8.3.1 Loyalty and fitness to stand for election

In the 2002 case of *Podkolzina v Latvia*,[48] the applicant complained that the removal of her name from the list of candidates at a general election because she had insufficient knowledge of Latvian (the official language in Latvia) constituted a breach of the right to stand as a candidate in an election.[49] The European Court found that, having regard to the margin of appreciation, requiring a candidate for election to the national parliament to have sufficient knowledge of the official language pursued a legitimate aim.[50] It is worth noting again that in this case the European Court invoked the margin of appreciation in relation to the legitimate aim of the measure and not just its necessity. However, the applicant actually had the requisite level of Latvian provided for by law,[51] but was subjected to a further test which the European Court doubted had a viable legal basis.[52] The test was administered by a single civil servant and the European Court found that the whole process was therefore incompatible with the level of procedural fairness and legal certainty required by the Convention.[53] Moreover, and with some 'echoes' of communism, it further transpired that during the additional examination the questions had focused on the reasons for the applicant's political orientation.[54] The issue of loyalty arises because the applicant had stressed that Latvian was not the first language of the members of the Russian-speaking minority, which accounted for almost 40 per cent of the population of Latvia and of which she was a member.[55] In other words, and just as in *Ždanoka* (decided four years

47 *Sidabras and Džiautas v Lithuania, op. cit. supra* n 26.
48 *Podkolzina v Latvia* [2002] ECHR 405.
49 Ibid., [33].
50 Ibid., [34].
51 Ibid., [36].
52 Ibid., [35].
53 Ibid., [36].
54 Ibid.
55 Ibid., [30].

later), the case involved post-USSR actions having an effect on the Russian-speaking minority in Latvia.

Melnychenko v Ukraine[56] is a legally more straightforward case, but it is worth noting that the applicant was an extremely well-known figure and that the circumstances almost defy belief. Mykola Melnychenko was a former presidential bodyguard to President Leonid Kuchma and he had gained notoriety by releasing secretly recorded tapes that apparently implicated Kuchma in the murder of journalist Georgiy Gongadze.[57] President from 2005 to 2010, Viktor Yushchenko (an apparent victim of attempted assassination by poisoning in 2004)[58] seemingly made finding the killers a top priority.[59] Aleksander Litvinenko, a former FSB agent who had gained asylum in the UK, claimed that the bugging operation was authorised by the then Ukranian Security Council Chief, Yevhen Marchuk.[60] Litvinenko was himself then murdered by poisoning in London in 2006.[61]

The European Convention case concerned Melnychenko's attempts to be added to a party list in order to stand for election to the Verkhovna Rada (parliament) in 2002.[62] By this time the applicant was living in the USA as a refugee.[63] Electoral law required that, in order to be eligible for election in Ukraine, candidates would have to have resided there for the preceding five years. The *propiska*-registered address contained in the candidate's internal passport would be decisive. Although he was by now living as a refugee in the USA, Melnychenko's *propiska* address, which he supplied, was still in Kiev. Nevertheless, the Central Election Commission rejected the application on the basis that the statement it contained about his place of residency during the last five years was untruthful.[64] The European Court found that since Melnychenko's *propiska* address was still in Kiev, the subsequent refusal to register him was arbitrary and unnecessary and it violated his rights under Article 3 of Protocol 1.[65] The underlying issues were about verifying the suitability of candidates for election and the European Court did not discount the idea of a five-year residency rule outright, but it clearly decided the case on formal rule of law grounds.

56 *Melnychenko v Ukraine* [2004] ECHR 528.
57 See, e.g., BBC, 'Notorious Murder Grips Ukraine' (1.4.2005), http://news.bbc.co.uk/1/hi/world/ europe/4402129.stm (accessed 11.5.2012).
58 BBC, 'Ukraine's Yushchenko in hospital' (10.12.2004), http://news.bbc.co.uk/1/hi/world/europe/ 4087253.stm (accessed 11.5.2012).
59 BBC, 'Notorious Murder Grips Ukraine', *op. cit. supra* n 57.
60 BBC, 'Notorious Murder Grips Ukraine', *op. cit. supra* n 57.
61 See BBC, 'Obituary: Alexander Litvinenko' (24.11.2006), http://news.bbc.co.uk/1/hi/uk/6163502.stm (accessed 11.5.2012).
62 *Melnychenko v Ukraine, op. cit. supra* n 56, [17].
63 Ibid., [7].
64 Ibid., [21].
65 Ibid., [67].

A similar issue arose in *Seyidzade v Azerbaijan*,[66] in which the European Court found unanimously that a prohibition on anyone engaged in 'professional religious activity' from standing for election to the Milli Majlis (parliament) was 'too wide and imprecise' to guard against impairment of the very essence of Article 3, Protocol 1.[67] Although it was an unanimous judgment, the Concurring Opinion of Judge Malinverni, joined by Judges Vajić and Kovler, identified one of the key methodological problems in judging (and indeed analysing) cases like this. They argued that:

> It is [. . .] not the legislation as such which should be criticised in the present case but the way in which it was applied by the courts. The fault lay not with the legislature, but with the courts and with them alone.

Thus they might contest that this case, in fact, was part of a systemic problem concerning the legal regulation of elections. However, nobody contested the conclusion as whole.

This is interesting because of certain parallels with the hugely important *Refah Partisi* case, on which the leading transitional electoral rights case of *Ždanoka* was founded. Recall that, in *Refah Partisi*, the dissolution of an Islamic political party was considered in the light of Turkey's commitment to secularism.[68] In *Seyidzade*, the Azerbaijani Constitutional Court had stressed that, according to the Constitution, Azerbaijan was also a secular republic.[69] It would seem that neither this nor any transitional considerations engendered any particular sympathy from the European Court.

8.3.2 Ethnicity and nationality-based restrictions: the question of timing revisited

We saw that after the *Ždanoka* case, in which the European Court appeared to recognise an element of transitional relativism, applicants, Respondent States and individual judges all expressed different views on whether particular transitions were complete or whether it was in the power of the European Court at all to make such an assessment.

This question of timing has carried over into cases that have raised arguably more systemic problems with the regulation of free elections. There have been some extremely difficult cases in which, apparently for reasons intimately connected to the transition, restrictions were placed on the eligibility of candidates to stand for election and which were based on ethnicity and nationality.

66 *Seyidzade v Azerbaijan* [2009] ECHR 1983.
67 Ibid., [39].
68 *Refah Partisi, op. cit. supra* n 20, [67].
69 *Seyidzade v Azerbaijan, op. cit. supra* n 66, [15].

The most divisive of these was the 2009 Grand Chamber judgment in *Sejdić and Finci v Bosnia and Herzegovina*.[70] It concerned the Constitution of Bosnia and Herzegovina, which was created by the Framework Agreement for Peace in Bosnia and Herzegovina (better known as the Dayton Peace Agreement) in 1995.[71] In order to stand for election to the House of Peoples or to the post of President, the Constitution required that candidates declared affiliation with one of the 'constituent' peoples of Bosnia and Herzegovina, namely Bosniacs, Croats and Serbs. The applicants in the case were of Roma and Jewish origin and did not want to make this declaration.[72] The government relied on the *Ždanoka* case to justify a wide margin of appreciation in relation to the exclusions.[73]

As regards the House of Peoples, the European Court examined Article 14 taken in conjunction with Article 3, Protocol 1. The Court accepted that given the terrible conflict in the former Yugoslavia the exclusion reflected one of the general objectives of the Convention, specified in its preamble: the restoration of peace.[74] However, it declined actually to make a firm finding on this point since it considered that the restriction was in any event disproportionate.

The European Court noted positive developments in Bosnia and Herzegovina since 1995[75] and that other power-sharing mechanisms did not exclude whole communities in the same way.[76] The European Court also stressed that Bosnia and Herzegovina had 'voluntarily agreed' to meet the standards of the Convention and its protocols by ratifying them after joining the Council of Europe in 2002.[77] This echoes the very firm stance taken against Portugal in the *Guincho* case,[78] first discussed in Chapter 1, where the European Court declined to take into account the transitional context of the case because by virtue of Article 1 ECHR Portugal had unequivocally guaranteed to 'secure to everyone' the rights in the Convention.[79] The adoption of this stance led the European Court to conclude that there was no objective and reasonable justification for the evident discrimination.[80]

The question of election to the Presidency resulted in the European Court's first judgment on Protocol 12 to the ECHR: the freestanding prohibition on discrimination. However, the European Court merely confirmed that the

70 *Sejdić and Finci v Bosnia and Herzegovina* [2009] ECHR 2122.
71 Ibid., [6].
72 Ibid., [45].
73 Ibid., [34] (the government actually used the term 'considerable latitude' rather than margin of appreciation).
74 Ibid., [45].
75 Ibid., [47].
76 Ibid., [48].
77 Ibid., [49].
78 *Guincho v Portugal* (1985) 7 EHRR 223.
79 Ibid., [38].
80 *Sejdić and Finci v Bosnia and Herzegovina, op. cit. supra* n 70, [50].

concepts of discrimination in Article 14 and Protocol 12, Article 1, were identical[81] and concluded that, for the reasons given in relation to the House of Peoples, there was a violation of Article 1, Protocol 12, in relation to the presidency.[82]

The reasoning in the majority judgment could be described as taciturn at best. In relation to the House of Representative and Article 14, there was a majority of 14 to 3 in favour of a violation. In relation to Protocol 12, Article 1, and the presidency, the majority grew to 16 to 1. Judge Bonello dissented to both the substantive findings. Judge Mijović, of Bosnia and Herzegovina, joined by Judge Hajiyev, gave an opinion that dissented from the finding in relation to Article 14 (in conjunction with Article 3, Protocol 1). We shall examine this dissent first, before turning to the truly remarkable dissent of Judge Bonello.

Judges Mijović and Hajiyev agreed with the findings in relation to Article 1, Protocol 12 ECHR, but were 'disappointed' with the terse reasoning supplied by the majority. The dissent in relation to Article 14, invoked in respect of access to the House of Peoples, was founded on a detailed summary of the historical background and state structure of Bosnia and Herzegovina. They began by arguing that the application should not even have been admissible, since there are no elections at all to House of Peoples and therefore there was no sense in which a right to stand for 'election' to it could be engaged. It would seem therefore that Judges Mijović and Hajiyev objected to the implicitly evolutive interpretation of Article 3, Protocol 1, to include not just 'free elections' but issues relating to the legislature more broadly. They also doubted the majority's findings that the applicants were being denied the possibility to participate in the legislature, since there were no ethnic restrictions on becoming a member of the House of Representatives.

As to the merits, Judges Mijović and Hajiyev doubted not only whether sufficient time had passed since the Dayton Accords were signed, but also whether it was the role of the European Court to make such a decision. 'It has been fourteen years since the armed conflict ended, but is there real and significant progress as argued by the Grand Chamber?', they asked. Citing *Ždanoka*, they also questioned whether it was 'absolutely certain' that the special constitutional arrangements of Bosnia and Herzegovina could not still be justified. Interestingly, they raised the issue of whether a measure could be 'justified' but not in pursuit of a legitimate aim. That is to say, it might be possible for a measure to be 'justified' in the normal rather than Convention sense, presumably in the name of securing peace, but be contrary to the European Convention. This was one of the central themes identified in the Introduction, where human rights and transitional justice were described as 'the odd couple' because of their problematic relationship.

81 Ibid., [55].
82 Ibid., [56].

They continued: 'Is it up to the European Court of Human Rights to determine when the time for change has arrived?' They expressed reluctance to give a firm answer to these questions, but classified them as going to the issue of proportionality, which they argued the majority had not tested all. The language and tone of Judges Mijović and Hajiyev was measured, despite the elements of dissent. The dissent by Judge Bonello, which put almost complete emphasis on the question of the passage of time since the end of the conflict, however, is probably the strongest and most eloquent that the European Court has ever heard.

Like Judges Mijović and Hajiyev, Judge Bonello was concerned about the majority's treatment of history. Indeed, he argued that the majority had 'divorced Bosnia and Herzegovina from the realities of its own recent past', including the 'extravagantly violent' events of 1992. He cautioned that although the case, being about clear discrimination against Jews and the Roma, might appear simple, it might be simultaneously one of the 'perverse situations in which the enforcement of human rights could be the trigger for war rather than the conveyor of peace'. He described the majority as having 'disgraced' the Dayton Constitution and he denied that it was the role of the European Court 'by a process of divination' to establish whether the transitional period was over. The tenor of the opinion can be fairly represented by these quotations:

> [T]he judgment seems to me an exercise in star-struck mirage-building which neglects to factor in the rivers of blood that fertilised the Dayton Constitution
> [. . .]
> I cannot endorse a Court that sows ideals and harvests massacre.

The dissenting opinions put the terseness of the majority into context. This had clearly been a divisive case dealing not only with *democratic* transition, but the transition to *peace*. The judgment of the majority simply declined to enter into this territory, perhaps wary that its every word would be scrutinised. The divisions, exemplified by the opinion of Judge Bonello, were so deep because the case presented rather different issues from those seen in the 'simply' post-communist cases: again, this was a transition to peace, not just to democracy. Nevertheless the majority of the European Court declined to recognise any transitional relativism.

The divisions within the European Court in *Sejdić and Finci* were not mirrored by the Grand Chamber in its unanimous judgment in the case of *Tănase v Moldova*.[83] The European Court found a violation of Article 3, Protocol 1, in respect of a restriction on dual nationals sitting as members of

83 *Tănase v Moldova*, App no 7/08 (ECtHR, 27 April 2010).

parliament. The European Court cannot be accused of ignoring the historical context in this case, since in its historical background the European Court began by observing that: 'The Principality of Moldavia first emerged as an independent State in 1359.'[84]

The European Court accepted that for historical reasons there was a particularly high proportion of dual nationals (especially people with dual Russian nationality) in Moldova,[85] but 'left open' the question of whether the restriction was in pursuit of the legitimate aim of securing loyalty to the state.[86] In respect of proportionality, the European Court 'did not exclude' the fact that the restriction could have been justified in the immediate aftermath of independence in 1991,[87] but observed that it was only introduced in 2008.[88] The Court cited *Ādamsons* as authority for the proposition that with the passage of time general restrictions on electoral rights become more difficult to justify.[89] It also observed that the restriction appeared to operate to the disadvantage of the opposition and had been introduced shortly before elections[90] (there are parallels, therefore, with *Paksas v Lithuania*). Even taking into account *Ždanoka* and the special historical context, the European Court found a violation of Article 3, Protocol 1.

The European Court seemed to return to its more assertive stance with regard to its own role in determining the significance of the passage of time in this case. However, there are some important caveats to this observation. The first is that the case did not so much concern the continued justification of a transitional measure, such as in *Sejdić and Finci*, but rather the introduction of a 'transitional' measure well after the end of the communist regime. Moreover, the authenticity of the transitional measure was doubted and like several of the cases discussed elsewhere, there was an underlying interference with political rights of the resident Russian minority (recall how this had vexed the dissent in *Ždanoka*).

8.4 Conclusion

The *Ždanoka* case examined in this chapter is potentially the high point for the recognition of transitional relativism in the jurisprudence of the European Court and we shall return to its wider implications in the Conclusion.

In it, the Chamber and Grand Chamber of the European Court took very different approaches as to the question of whether it was in their power to

84 Ibid., [11].
85 Ibid., [173].
86 Ibid., [170].
87 Ibid., [173].
88 Ibid., [174].
89 Ibid., [175].
90 Ibid., [179].

pronounce that a transition was 'complete'. When the outcome in the Grand Chamber is compared to the judgment in *Refah Partisi*, it would seem that the notion of self-defending democracy must have been extended, via a form of transitional relativism, into self-consolidating democracy.

It is notable therefore that in the other cases discussed here, and in which it seems that the Respondent States were encouraged to claim special, transitionally relative, treatment, they were largely unsuccessful. Indeed, the Court seems to have moved away from the 'self-consolidating' democracy approach, which requires a decision on the status of the transition, to one in which the question of timing is supplemental rather than decisive: *Ādamsons, Paksas* and *Tănase*. Likewise, the hugely significant majority judgment in *Sejdić and Finci* did not really apply the tests of self-consolidating democracy and conclude that they had been failed: its reasoning was actually very narrowly focused on discrimination.

The cases show that the new Contracting Parties have faced some real challenges, but that the European Court has been relatively firm with them – except at the Grand Chamber in *Ždanoka*. The significance of this exception is discussed in the next, concluding, chapter.

Part III

Conclusions

9 Universality in transition

In this chapter, we shall reappraise the jurisprudence presented in Chapters 2 to 8 in the light of the concepts introduced in Chapter 1. The first section examines whether and to what extent the European Court of Human Rights 'does' transitional justice, in the sense of recognising a level of transitional relativism within which transitional states are allowed to find locally relevant solutions to the distinctive circumstances of transition. The second section gauges the impact of the European Court's approach on the universality of human rights, and acts as a conclusion to the book.

9.1 Does the European Court of Human Rights 'do' transitional justice?

Looking back at the content of Chapters 2 to 8 it would be quite difficult to deny that the European Court has engaged with transitional justice fairly regularly. However, and as Buyse and Hamilton have pointed out, the existence of this body of law does not in and of itself prove the existence of a coherent, *sui generis*, approach by the European Court.[1]

In order to determine whether such an approach exists, it was argued in Chapter 1 that we would have to observe the European Court's interaction with transitional justice at two levels: first, its approval or disapproval of particular domestic transitional policies and second, the extent to which it had changed its own reasoning on transitional grounds.

9.1.1 The first level of interaction

Brems has gone a long way towards charting the first of these interactions.[2] She examined the jurisprudence of the Court and argued that it is possible to

1 A. Buyse and M. Hamilton, 'Conclusions', in A. Buyse and M. Hamilton, *Transitional Jurisprudence and the ECHR* (Cambridge: CUP 2011), 293.

2 E. Brems, 'Transitional justice in the case law of the European Court of Human Rights' (2010) 5 *International Journal of Transitional Justice* 282.

identify transitional policies that are required, prohibited or which the Court has said that states 'can do' without requiring them. Within the category of what states must do, Brems would not include the applications that were declared inadmissible *ratione temporis* or *ratione materiae* (such as most claims for reparations) but *would* include positive obligations to investigate death and torture, emanating from Articles 2 and 3 ECHR. Brems also stressed the importance of leaving room for historical debate and ensuring access to documents. She has argued that states are not allowed to impose amnesties or defective restitution policies, but that the Court has given conditional approval to lustration and other restrictions on political freedoms. Brems also argued that, without requiring it, states can if they choose prosecute individuals for acts not considered criminal in domestic law when committed, including crimes in the distant past.

Brems' analysis is thorough and certainly brings some order to the chaos of the European Court's voluminous jurisprudence. However, the approach taken in this book was rather different and, therefore, reveals a different picture. In Chapters 2 to 8, we examined not only cases concerning explicitly transitional policies, but also cases in which distinctively transitional dilemmas were presented in the exercise and limitation of democratic rights. An attempt to examine the jurisprudence of the Court that did not examine *both* these groups of cases would be only partial (to be fair, Buyse and Hamilton's collection and Brems' work deal with both of these categories, albeit without dividing them in quite the same way).

It is striking, therefore, that there is next to no cross-fertilisation between the cases discussed in Chapters 2 to 5, on the one hand, and in Chapters 6 to 8, on the other, except in relation to lustration (Chapter 5) and free elections (Chapter 8). These are very closely connected in any event, even though the Council of Europe guidance made it clear that 'pure' lustration should not apply to elected positions.[3] Nevertheless, it is possible to identify some thematic interactions between the two categories, by looking at our second level (transitional reasoning *by the Court*) – and which go some way to demonstrate what a workable, coherent, transitional jurisprudence might resemble.

9.1.2 The second level of interaction

It is possible to identify certain nascent, but recurrent, themes in the European Court's reasoning.

3 The Explanatory Memorandum to PACE Resolution 1096 (1996), Council of Europe Doc. 7568, Report of the Committee on Legal Affairs and Human Rights, 'Guidelines to ensure that lustration laws and similar administrative measures comply with the requirements of a state based on the rule of law', state that lustration shall not apply to elected office, [16(e)] and [46(e)].

9.1.2.1 *Collaborators and communists*

In his dissent to the Grand Chamber judgment in *Ždanoka v Latvia*, Judge Zupančič hinted at the existence of a cross-cutting theme between some of the cases. Judge Zupančič was discussing the awkward spectacle of former members of totalitarian regimes now relying on the European Convention (in that case a former communist, who may have participated in an attempted coup). In Chapter 8, we noted his statement that: 'They barefacedly claim the very human rights which they spent their life denying to others, nay, often cold-bloodedly violating them in the most brutal fashion.'[4]

In the course his opinion, Judge Zupančič cross-referred to *Streletz, Kessler and Krenz v Germany*, in which we saw the unlikely spectacle of the architects of the Berlin Wall claiming that their human rights had been violated. In *Streletz, Kessler and Krenz*, the Grand Chamber confirmed that: '[I]t is legitimate for a State governed by the rule of law to bring criminal proceedings against persons who have committed crimes under a former regime.'[5] However, in *Ždanoka*, neither Judge Zupančič nor the majority pursued deeper links to cases about people who had participated in, or benefited from, the previous regime.

This category might have included, for example, *Velikovi and Others v Bulgaria*, in which it can be recalled that in relation to the punitive elements of the 1992 Bulgarian Law on the Restitution of Ownership of Nationalised Real Property, the Court stated that:

> Persons who have taken advantage of their privileged position or have otherwise acted unlawfully to acquire property in a totalitarian regime, as well as their heirs, cannot expect to keep their gain in a society governed democratically through the rule of law. The underlying public interest in such cases is to restore justice and respect for the rule of law.[6]

With this in mind, it is also worth reiterating that we saw in Chapter 5 that the European Court has consistently upheld the legitimacy of lustration processes. Surely there are points of principle that can be brought to the surface here about confronting the past.

9.1.2.2 *The use and abuse of legitimate aims*

The cases discussed in Chapters 2 to 8 show that the European Court has been relatively open to the argument that transitional measures may pursue a 'legitimate aim' in the Convention sense. We have just noted the 'legitimacy'

4 *Ždanoka v Latvia* (GC) [2006] ECHR 231.
5 *Streletz, Kessler and Krenz v Germany* (2001) 33 EHRR 31, [80].
6 *Velikovi and Others v Bulgaria* (2009) 48 EHRR 27.

of successor trials, restitution and openness. We also noted in relation to self-defending (or consolidating) democracy cases on Article 3, Protocol 1, such as *Ždanoka* and *Ādamsons*, that the Court found that, in the transitional context, the restrictive measures were in pursuit of aims compatible with the principle of the rule of law and the general objectives of the Convention.[7]

It was more questionable, doctrinally, when, in cases such as *Rekvényi v Hungary*, the European Court appeared to extend the legitimate aims due to the historical context.[8] Likewise, in both *Metropolitan Church of Bessarabia v Moldova* and *Holy Synod of the Bulgarian Orthodox Church (Metropolitan Inokentiy) and Others v Bulgaria*, the European Court again accepted that the transitional context was relevant both to the 'legitimacy' of the aim and to the 'necessity' of the measure. In relation to the latter cases, it failed even to distinguish exactly which legitimate aim or aims were at stake or to separate their identification from answering the questions of necessity and proportionality.[9]

In earlier cases, the European Court had stated that exceptions to freedom of association 'must be narrowly interpreted, such that the enumeration of them is strictly exhaustive and the definition of them necessarily restrictive'.[10] It would seem, therefore, that one feature of the emergent transitional jurisprudence is a certain flexibility with regard to 'legitimate' aims, even though there is little cross-citation of the cases mentioned.

9.2.1.3 *Precision of the restrictive measure/proximity to the transition*

In both *Streletz, Kessler and Krenz* and *K.-H. W.*, discussed in Chapter 2, we saw how the Court found that, from the perspective of foreseeability, the defensibility of judicial interpretation in the criminal law 'remains wholly valid' even in cases such as these, in which one state had succeeded the other.[11] The transitional context did not explicitly reduce the need for foreseeability, but it is fairly difficult to deny that the applicants never foresaw their prosecution.

In *Sidabras and Džiautas v Lithuania*, discussed in Chapter 5, the European Court stated that the timing of the introduction of the impugned lustration measure was relevant to its proportionality in Convention terms. We noted that this implied that a broader lustration measure might have been Convention-compliant had it been introduced earlier.

7 *Ždanoka v Latvia* (GC) [2006] ECHR 231, [118]; *Ādamsons v Latvia*, App no 3669/03, (ECtHR, 24 June 2008) (available only in French), [114].

8 *Rekvényi v Hungary* (1997) 23 EHRR CD63, [41].

9 *Holy Synod of the Bulgarian Orthodox Church (Metropolitan Inokentiy) and Others v Bulgaria* [2010] ECHR 1293, [159].

10 *Sidiropoulos and Others v Greece* (1999) 27 EHRR 633, [38].

11 *Streletz, Kessler and Krenz, op. cit. supra* n 3, [82]; *K.-H. W v Germany* (2003) 36 EHRR 59, [85]; c.f. Murphy, who is not convinced by this reasoning: C Murphy, 'The principle of legality in criminal law under the European Convention on Human Rights' (2010) *European Human Rights Law Review* 192, 201.

In *Ādamsons v Latvia*, the European Court found a violation of the Convention in respect of an overbroad restriction on standing for election. It stated that:

> In the eyes of the Court, the need for [. . .] individualization is becoming increasingly important with the passage of time, since the distance from the time when the actions at issue are alleged to have occurred.[12]

Although the cases do not cross-refer, they present evidence for the existence of a subtle development in the European Court's jurisprudence, where its basic rule of law standards might appear affected by the temporal proximity of a measure's introduction or application to the start of the transitional period.

9.1.2.4 *Self-consolidating democracy*

The centrality of self-defending, or more accurately, self-consolidating democracy to the reasoning in two of the cases where the European Court was most transitionally relative (*Ždanoka* and *Rekvényi*) show that it has played a key role within the emergent transitional jurisprudence.

In *Jahn v Germany*,[13] Judge Ress came perhaps the closest to founding a legal argument that spanned the division between cases on property rights and cases on democratic rights. In *Jahn*, the European Court treated the applicant as having received a windfall by the improper application of the so-called Modrow Law to his property. When the loophole was closed, and the applicant's agricultural land was seized without compensation, the European Court upheld the lack of compensation. In his dissent, Judge Ress contrasted the *Jahn* case and *Rekvényi v Hungary*, finding that they had 'nothing in common'. *Rekvényi* had involved the restriction of the applicant's democratic rights for the wider democratic good, whereas there was no countervailing democratic or rights based value in *Jahn*.

We shall return to the notion of self-consolidating democracy shortly, but for now it is merely important to observe that it was only in a dissenting opinion, and not in a judgment, that the conceptual link permitting these cases to be contrasted was made.

The fact that there is so little cross-fertilisation in the cases that have raised these common themes suggests that Buyse and Hamilton were undoubtedly correct to conclude that there is no coherent *sui generis* approach in the European Court's transitional jurisprudence.[14] But that does not mean that it is impossible to conceive of one, on the basis of what the European Court has already done. In the next section, we shall examine how it might be possible

12 *Ādamsons v Latvia*, App no 3669/03 (ECtHR, 24 June 2008) (available only in French).
13 *Jahn v Germany* [2006] 42 EHRR 49.
14 A. Buyse and M. Hamilton, *op. cit. supra* n 1, 293.

to construct a transitional jurisprudence to deal with the situation in which transitional measures come into conflict with human rights norms.

9.1.3 *Fashioning a transitional jurisprudence*

There are potentially three reactions to the suggestion of fashioning a transitional jurisprudence. It could be argued that not only would the attempt to fashion a transitional jurisprudence be fruitless, it would also be unwise. The argument would have to be that transitional situations themselves simply do not present substantively different issues and, therefore, the Respondent State's arguments about the special circumstances of the transitional context should be dismissed as normatively unfounded: the impugned measure or decision could be neither legitimate nor necessary. This approach can be rejected. Convincing work has demonstrated that transitional justice may operate, usefully, in a different way to ordinary justice. The real question for the European Court is about what it, as both an international and a judicial body, should do about national transitional policies.

This is where the second reaction begins. It might be argued that the Court should alter its own conception of justice in cases from transitional states, since transitional justice measures always outweigh considerations of ordinary justice in transitional democracies. This would recognise that the new Contracting Parties are not only undergoing a transition to democracy, but also a transition to full compliance with the European Convention. It would recommend recognition of self-consolidating democracy as a form of acceptable justification for rights-restrictive measures. The European Court would become an embodiment of an international form of transitional justice: the human rights counterpart to international criminal responses.[15] The cases in which the transitional context goes to the 'legitimacy' of a rights-restrictive measure might suggest that the Court is already doing precisely this. The implication is that via the application of a transitional form of justice, certain otherwise 'illegitimate' actions could be deemed 'legitimate'.

The bestowal of 'legitimacy' on a restrictive measure is significant, legally and politically, even where the measure is found not to be 'necessary'. It is particularly questionable when the stated aim is not one that even the most ardent advocate of transitional justice would recognise as a common transitional policy. As suggested earlier, allowing a margin of appreciation on the legitimacy of the restrictive aim is inconsistent with a normal doctrinal understanding of the stage at which the margin of appreciation figures in the Court's reasoning. Moreover, as demonstrated in the work of Arai-Takahashi, in order

15 In 'Transitional justice genealogy', Teitel notes the displacement of national justice by international justice as a defining feature of post-World War II transitional justice, with the Nuremberg trials as its most recognised symbol: R. Teitel, 'Transitional justice genealogy' (2003) 16 *Harvard Human Rights Journal* 69, 70, 72.

for the margin of appreciation to operate properly it must be seen alongside the question of proportionality, which is clearly more relevant to the question of 'necessity' than 'legitimacy'.[16] Furthermore, and finally, altering the conception of justice and thus legitimacy to be applied to transitional democracies, and condoning less than full compliance with the European Convention, would call into question the European Court's commitment to the universality of human rights.

Likewise the recognition of self-consolidating democracy is rather problematic. Self-*defending* democracy was validated within the Convention system due to the acknowledgement of its:

> special importance in Germany because of that country's experience under the Weimar Republic, which, when the Federal Republic was founded after the nightmare of Nazism, led to its constitution being based on the principle of a 'democracy capable of defending itself' (*wehrhafte Demokratie*).[17]

The point is that, historically, *wehrhafte Demokratie* did take on special significance: *in Germany*. No other state in Europe can claim to have had as violent and tragic a twentieth century as Germany or claim to have come out of World War II with such a strong commitment to democracy, or subsequently to be playing such a central role in the economic development and integration of Europe via the European Union. The assumption that the notion of *wehrhafte Demokratie* might be defensible as a matter of European human rights law in cases emanating from Turkey or the transitional states is far from self-evident.

In the introduction to Part 2, we noted Mahoney's observation that the European Convention offers protection from human rights abuses at two levels.[18] It protects, first, against 'naked, bad faith abuse of power'[19] and also against restrictions imposed in the name of the general, democratic majoritarian, interest and which, while impacting disproportionately on the individual, are imposed in good faith. According to Mahoney:

> It is only in this second context, once the first degree of protection has been assured, that the doctrine of the margin of appreciation comes into play, that is to say, only if the preliminary conditions of normal democratic governance have been shown to exist.[20]

16 Y. Arai-Takahashi, *The Margin of Appreciation Doctrine and the Principle of Proportionality in the Jurisprudence of the ECHR* (Oxford: Intersentia 2002).

17 *Vogt v Germany* (1996) 21 EHRR 205, [51].

18 See P. Mahoney, 'Marvellous richness of diversity or invidious cultural relativism' (1998) 19(1) *Human Rights Law Journal* 1, 2 and 3.

19 Ibid., [4].

20 Ibid.

For the use of the margin of appreciation doctrine to be defensible, this is precisely how it ought to operate. With this in mind, it seems particularly worrying that the European Court has entertained the possibility of defending interferences with human rights on the basis of self-*consolidating* democracy, since it would seem that (and without filing a derogation) the Respondent State is more or less arguing that the conditions of normal democratic governance do *not* exist.

There is yet another, third, reaction to the suggestion that a transitional jurisprudence could be fashioned. It could be argued that although national policies founded on transitional justice have a normative pedigree, the European Court should not change its own conception of justice. It must apply its existing standards in such a way as to respond meaningfully to the factual matrix presented by cases emanating from transitional democracies without altering its general approach. The Court can be transitionally relative without compromising its commitment to the universality of human rights. The Court may check whether a transitional measure is compliant with the rule of law, including the due process rights contained in Article 6 ECHR; that, in regard to its legitimacy, the transitional measure pursues one of the legitimate aims specified in the Convention; and, if it does, it may proceed to consider the necessity and proportionality of the measure in the transitional context via a detailed and coherent application of the margin of appreciation doctrine.

In this model, the transitional context is far more relevant to the basis and width of the margin of appreciation than to the conceptual 'legitimacy' of the measure. This approach is preferred since, while the margin of appreciation in respect of necessity allows for some modulation in the Court's jurisprudence in recognition of the transitional context and between different transitional contexts, it does not (need to) disturb the universality of human rights.

The ability of the European Court to recognise differences between transitions is hugely significant. As Oomen has argued, transitional measures gain legitimacy from their 'endogeneity': the extent to which they are rooted in local values of right and wrong, as well as local laws.[21] On this basis as well as in order to respect the principle of subsidiarity, the European Court would do (and, in fact, has done) well to accommodate a variety of solutions.

It is tempting to think of this as a 'transitional margin of appreciation' or similar, but this would be misleading because it would imply that the transitional margin is different, conceptually, to the regular margin of appreciation. It is not. Neither is the margin of appreciation the only vehicle by which flexibility is accommodated in the European jurisprudence. Instead, the European Court should apply (and sometimes has applied) its regular, even formulaic, approach to the transitional justice cases encountered in Chapters 2 to 8 of

21 B. Oomen, 'Transitional justice and its legitimacy: the case for a local perspective' (2007) 25(1) *Netherlands Quarterly of Human Rights* 141, 146.

this book while remaining fully cognisant of the conceptual relationship between domestic transitional justice policies and the international supervision of human rights protection.

9.1.4 Applying the transitional jurisprudence

The first stage in any of the transitional cases is to ensure compliance with the formal rule of law. Whether a rights-restrictive measure interferes with Convention rights in pursuit of a goal that is related to the transition to democracy, the Respondent State must demonstrate that it is acting through law. Thus, in *Mkrtchyan v Armenia* (freedom of assembly), introduced in Chapter 7, the European Court found that the legal regime on which his being charged with an administrative offence was based did not meet the Convention's requirement of lawfulness.[22] Although *Mkrtchyan* showed that there might be a limited discretion here in relation to getting legislation in order,[23] it should not be extensive. If a rights-restrictive transitional measure is to survive scrutiny from the European Court it must, at the very least, be 'prescribed by law'.

Likewise, the European Court should uphold high standards of procedural justice, as we have seen it do so in relation to restitution, lustration and democratic rights. Moreover, the substantive Convention rights may generate positive obligations to complete transitional measures, such as we saw in relation to stalled efforts at investigations into deaths during the transition[24] and reparatory justice.[25]

The second stage is legitimacy. This could be (and often is) a short step. For Articles 8 to 11, the legitimate aims are listed exhaustively in the Convention itself. For others that might be relevant in religion cases, such as Article 14 or Article 3 of Protocol 1, the Court has fashioned a slightly different approach, albeit one that still carries with it an assessment of whether the aim of the measure is legitimate. (As an aside, it might be noted that the Court could perhaps be a little less taciturn in its assimilation of myriad national policies to the Convention's 'legitimate aims'.) For the approach advocated here, it is vital not to give the impression that the *only* reason a measure is held to be 'legitimate' is that it was imposed in the transitional context. Otherwise, the impression could be created that an alternative, exclusively transitional, form of justice is being applied by the European Court. Instead, the national transitional policy should be shown to correspond clearly to a Convention 'legitimate aim', leaving the impact of the transitional context as a factor to be

22 *Mkrtchyan v Armenia* (2009) 49 EHRR 16.

23 Ibid., 43; see also *Maria Atanasiu and Others v Romania* [2010] ECHR 1502.

24 *Association 21 December 1989 & Others v Romania*, App nos 33810/07 and 18817/08 (ECtHR, 24 May 2011).

25 *Păduraru v Romania*, App no 63252/00 (ECtHR, 1 December 2005).

considered when assessing the means chosen to achieve the aim. Of course, if the transitional policy did not correspond to a Convention legitimate aim then, whether or not it might have some stabilising effect in a fragile democracy, it would be in conflict with the Convention. By joining the Council of Europe, and signing and ratifying the ECHR, it may be that states have thereby disbarred themselves from employing some transitional policies, in favour of a 'human rights-based approach' to transition.

The third and most important stage is *necessity*.[26] It is here where the Court can engage with the question of whether a purportedly transitional measure is widely recognised as pursuing a necessary task in the transitional process. If not, then there is no reason to treat it differently to any other rights-restrictive measure when it comes to the basis or width of the margin of appreciation. Of course, it is equally important for the Court to be alert to the possibility that the transitional context would augment the applicant's claim, such as where there are 'echoes' of totalitarianism, and the Court should consider this both at the merits stage and in relation to 'substantial disadvantage' in Article 35(3)(b) ECHR.

Where a rights-restrictive practice, which is purportedly justified by reference to the transitional context, is to be examined then the Court should, in the first place, enforce the Convention in such a way as to protect against 'naked, bad faith abuse of power'.[27] However much a state stressed a special relationship between religion and democratic transition in the context of a case brought against it, a measure that amounted to an unmitigated abuse of power could never be justified. There would be no question of it falling within the state's margin of appreciation since the margin only allows variations in *how*, and not *whether*, to comply with the Convention. This is the first, but not the only, level of protection offered by the Convention. As noted already, it is only at the second level, when a rights-restrictive transitional measure is imposed in 'good faith', that the margin of appreciation should be considered.[28]

The key here is that only a rights-restrictive transitional measure that contributed towards *democratic* consolidation could benefit from a margin of appreciation.[29] To suggest otherwise would be to radically expand the scope of the margin of appreciation doctrine, provide inadequate supervision of the new Contracting Parties' democratic transition and undermine the rule of law.

This aligns neatly with the approach taken in PACE Resolution 1096 where, in an effort to avoid complaints reaching the Strasbourg institutions, PACE cautioned that:

26 Buyse and Hamilton, *op. cit. supra* n 1, 29.
27 Mahoney, *op. cit. supra* n 18, 4.
28 Ibid.
29 On democracy in the ECHR, see *United Communist Party of Turkey v Turkey* (1998) 26 EHRR 121, [45].

> [A] democratic state based on the rule of law must, in dismantling the heritage of former communist totalitarian systems, apply the procedural means of such a state. It cannot apply any other means, since it would then be no better than the totalitarian regime which is to be dismantled. A democratic state based on the rule of law has sufficient means at its disposal to ensure that the cause of justice is served and the guilty are punished. [. . .] A state based on the rule of law can also defend itself against a resurgence of the communist totalitarian threat, since it has ample means at its disposal *which do not conflict with human rights and the rule of law.*[30]

There is reason to suppose that the European Court itself is sympathetic to this approach. A point of principle can be extracted from the judgment in *Holy Synod of the Bulgarian Orthodox Church (Metropolitan Inokentiy) and Others v Bulgaria*: that transitional societies' common need to remedy unlawful acts of the past cannot, in a democratic society, justify disproportionate state action and further unlawful acts.[31] Likewise, in relation to restitution, the European Court has stressed that although such policies may be legitimate, states should ensure that they do not create 'disproportionate new wrongs'.[32]

As the Court examines the question of necessity in the transitional cases, it should encourage and scrutinise arguments about the basis and, separately, the width of the margin of appreciation. The basis of the margin may relate to the robustness of the domestic mechanisms for verifying the material facts of the case or to the policy expertise and legitimacy of elected legislatures. The width of the margin in particular cases will be tied to some combination of various factors, including the right at stake, the way that it is invoked, and the legitimate aim the restriction pursues.[33] It is conceded that for some commentators the width of the margin of appreciation is determined too haphazardly to play the role suggested in this chapter. Nevertheless, the various factors

30 PACE Resolution 1096 (1996), [4] (emphasis added).

31 *Holy Synod of the Bulgarian Orthodox Church, op. cit. supra* n 9, [142].

32 *Velikovi and Others v Bulgaria, op. cit. supra* n 6.

33 On the width of the margin of appreciation, including those with a critical perspective on the doctrine itself, such as Jones and Hutchinson, see Arai-Takahashi, *The Margin of Appreciation Doctrine and the Principle of Proportionality in the Jurisprudence of the ECHR* (Oxford: Intersentia 2002) 206 *et seq.*; E. Brems, 'The margin of appreciation doctrine in the case-law of the European Court of Human Rights' (1996) 56 *Zeitschrift für Ausländisches öffentliches Recht und Völkerrecht* 240, 256–293; M. Hutchinson, 'The margin of appreciation doctrine in the European Court of Human Rights' (1999) 48 *ICLQ* 638, 640; T. Jones, 'The devaluation of human rights under the European Convention (1995) *Public Law* 430, 438 *et seq.*; Mahoney, *op. cit. supra* n 18, 5 *et seq.*; J. Schokkenbroek, 'The basis, nature and application of the margin of appreciation doctrine in the case law of the European Court of Human Rights' (1998) 19(1) *Human Rights Law Journal* 30, 34 *et seq.*; J.A. Sweeney, 'A "margin of Appreciation" in the internal market: lessons from the European Court of Human Rights' (2007) 34(1) *Legal Issues of Economic Integration* 27, 45.

that are identified as commonly playing a role in determining its width can, it is submitted, provide a useful framework on which to hang discussion of whether a rights-restrictive measure in a transitional case ultimately discloses a violation of the Convention.

If relevant and sufficient reasons were provided that such a rights-restrictive measure had support from the national legislature, as an appropriate response to that state's distinctive experience of transition, this would seem to be a reasonable place to recognise a margin of appreciation within which *different* transitional states might defensibly come to *different* conclusions. Naturally, however, there would still be 'a European supervision' 'hand in hand' with this.[34] The point is not that the margin would allow states to diverge from the standards of the Convention, but that each national response to democratic transition is not expected to be identical.

Thus, the approach advocated here does not demand that transitional measures *per se* should benefit from a wide margin of appreciation, but that the transitional context provides further data relevant to the identification of the existing rationales for the margin's basis and width on a case-by-case basis.

The approach advocated here calls for international human rights enforcement bodies, including the European Court, to engage far more robustly with the difficult question of when, and in what circumstances, national transitional policies that might secure peace or democratic consolidation are trumped by international human rights concerns: when, and in what circumstances to be transitionally relativist. Judge Bonello identified the existence of this dilemma in his Dissenting Opinion in *Sejdić and Fincic v Bosnia and Herzegovina*, when he argued that the Court had 'canonised' the relevant Convention rights while 'discounting' the values of peace and reconciliation. These values were, he argued, 'at least' equally invaluable.[35] Whether his view that, in the particular context, discrimination against Jews and the Roma did not violate the Convention is accepted, at least he identified the crux of the issue.

The main difference between the approach advocated here and 'business as usual' is that it not only recognises, but also strongly recommends, a space for meaningful engagement with the relationship between *national* transitional justice policies and *international* human rights (including those enshrined in the European Convention). Although this space, or margin, would allow a more detailed engagement with the realities of transitional democracies, it remains important not to cast the European Court in the role of having changed its conception of justice. It can accommodate transitional relativism without making such a change. It was suggested earlier that if the Court were to hold that the transitional context could render certain otherwise 'illegitimate'

34 *Handyside v UK* (1976) 1 EHRR 737, [49].

35 *Sejdić and Finci v Bosnia and Herzegovina* [2009] ECHR 2122, Dissenting Opinion of Judge Bonello.

measures 'legitimate' it would be altering its conception of justice and, consequently, would undermine the universality of human rights.

The subtlety of this approach hinges on the difference between acknowledging the transitional context and actually altering the form of justice to be applied in a case because of it. To ignore the context completely would be to engage in what has been described as the 'dynamics of condescension' from western states towards the newer Contracting Parties from the east.[36] However, since transitional justice is always 'non-ideal' the European Court should not seek to become engaged in departing from its conception of justice on this ground, not least of all because the European system itself is not the subject of democratic transition. Moreover, such a departure would put the European Court in the invidious position of avowedly dispensing non-ideal justice in relation to some states but protecting and promoting universal human rights in relation to others.

One might argue that the approach for the European Court recommended here, which allows for discussion of the transitional context via necessity and the margin of appreciation rather than on the question of the legitimacy of the aim, is no better a guarantee against undermining the universality of human rights. Nevertheless, the hypothesis on which the approach here is based is that the accommodation of an element of transitional relativism, particularly via the margin of appreciation doctrine, does not undermine the conceptual universality of human rights. The next section will further substantiate this argument.

9.2 Universality in transition: the implications of transitional relativism

Mahoney has observed that to recognise 'legitimate cultural diversity' via the margin of appreciation is not the same as cultural relativism.[37] Eva Brems has suggested that the doctrine gives a merely corrective role to local values; it is a 'limited counterbalance to the general universalist rule'.[38] It is argued here that the same can be said for the accommodation of some degree of transitional relativism (excluding self-consolidating democracy).

The problem for Contracting Parties is squaring their *particular* transitional ground for restriction with their *general* and overarching commitment to membership of the Council of Europe. It is here where the margin of appreciation is relevant, with an assumption not only that public interests – including

36 Marie-Benedicte Dembour and Magda Krzyzanowska-Mierzewska, 'Ten years on: the voluminous and interesting Polish case law' (2004) 5 *EHRLR* 517, 517.

37 Mahoney, *op. cit. supra* n 18.

38 E. Brems, 'The margin of appreciation doctrine in the case-law of the European Court of Human Rights' (1996) 56 *Zeitschrift für Ausländisches öffentliches Recht und Völkerrecht* 240, 310.

transitional ones – have different weights (and content) from place to place and from time to time, but also that these differences should be respected.

The relationship between 'national' and 'European' values facilitated by the margin of appreciation doctrine reflects that the Council of Europe is comprised of several interlocking normative spheres.[39] The sphere of member states' normatively 'thin' commitment to democracy, including the protection of human rights and fundamental freedoms, exists in conjunction with the sphere of their normatively 'thick' and multitudinous national public policies, including transitional ones. Lest the relationship between thin and thick be mistaken, Walzer's argument that 'thinness and intensity go together, whereas with thickness comes qualification, compromise, complexity and disagreement' is helpful.[40]

Values begin 'thickly', located in particular societies.[41] They become refined and expressed thinly in times of stress. The adoption of the European Convention was the expression of thin aspects of morality stated in the aftermath of World War II, but which actually existed as elements of differing particular thick moralities well before this.[42] It is because thickly constituted values are the *starting place* for European human rights that the European Court rightly allows a margin within which their continued presence is accommodated. The challenge is to see the relationship between interlocking normative spheres not as a crisis, but as part of the everyday life of a Council of Europe whose values are essentially contested and thus in a constant state of flux.[43] The limited variance permitted by the margin of appreciation doctrine, properly applied, is a product of this and is perfectly able to accommodate transitional concerns.

39 This argument has been made also in relation to the EU: Z. Bańkowski and E. Christodoulidis, 'The European Union as an essentially contested project', in Z. Bańkowski and A. Scott (eds), *The European Union and its Order* (Oxford: Blackwell 2000), 17.

40 M. Walzer, *Thick and Thin: moral argument at home and abroad* (Notre Dame, OH: University of Notre Dame Press 1994), 6.

41 Ibid., 4; on applying Walzer's work to human rights and the margin of appreciation doctrine, see J. Chan, 'Thick and thin accounts of human rights: lessons from the Asia values debate', in M. Jacobsen and J. Bruun (eds), *Human Rights and Asian Values* (Richmond: Curzon 2000); E. Brems, *Human Rights: universality and diversity* (The Hague: Kluwer 2001); R. Mullender, 'Human rights: universalism and relativism' (2003) 6 *Critical Review of International and Social Political Philosophy* 70; J.A. Sweeney, 'Human rights, cultural dialogue and the margin of appreciation' *Human Rights Law Review Student Supplement 2000–2001* (University of Nottingham Human Rights Law Centre 2001); J. Sweeney, *Human Rights, Cultural Relativity and the European Court of Human Rights* (PhD thesis on file at the University of Hull, 2003).

42 Walzer also notes that even an agreed minimal morality will often be forced into the idiom of a maximal morality (Walzer, *op. cit. supra* n 40, 9), which may explain why some cultures find the objective of human rights familiar but their expression as 'rights' alien.

43 Z. Bańkowski and E. Christodoulidis, *op. cit. supra* n 39, 18.

The approach to transitional jurisprudence argued here, which incorporates discussion of the complex interrelated factors that might justify an element of transitional relativism, is capable of capturing the essentially contested essence of both the Council of Europe and the notions of democracy and transitional justice. Indeed, the notion of transition *to democracy* is a fairly blunt tool to describe the various options available to states and, likewise, it is important to recognise the essentially contested nature of democracy for all states in the Council of Europe.

The form of transitional jurisprudence recommended here allows the impulses of human rights universality and transitional relativism visibly to interact but never fully to defeat each other. Moreover, demonstrating a commitment to local values and conditionally devolving the balancing of these overlapping values to national institutions via the margin of appreciation doctrine reiterates a commitment to subsidiarity. The notion of subsidiarity, introduced in Chapter 1, suggests some degree of loyalty to or (at least) a relationship with a central norm. The internalisation and normalisation of questions about the universality of human rights and transitional relativism becomes a reflection of the Council of Europe's nature. According to this view, there is no longer a series of individual and bipolar conflicts between the European Court and the Respondent States, but a continual series of structured interactions along the subsidiarity continuum within a healthy and diverse Council of Europe.

It is against this normative background, which values diversity, subsidiarity and a dynamic approach to European identity and national public policies, that the approach to transitional jurisprudence noted here could be deployed. To the extent that it is grounded on analysis of an extensive range of cases brought before the Strasbourg institutions, it provides a starting point to inquire into whether any of the lessons learned in Europe have relevance outside of it.

But that is a matter for a different book.

Index